JUDGING STANDARDS AND EFFECTIVENESS IN EDUCATION

*edited by Bob Moon
with John Isaac and Janet Powney
at The Open University*

HODDER AND STOUGHTON
LONDON   SYDNEY   AUCKLAND   TORONTO
in association with The Open University

This reader forms part of the Open University course E271 *Curriculum and Learning*. For further information on the course, write to School of Education (E271), The Open University, Walton Hall, Milton Keynes MK7 6AA.

This reader is one part of an Open University integrated teaching system and the selection is therefore related to other material available to students. It is designed to evoke the critical understanding of students. Opinions expressed in it are not necessarily those of the course team or of the University.

The E271 course team is against the use of sexist language and gender stereotyping. We have tried to avoid the use of sexist language in this reader but some examples may remain from the original articles, and for this we apologise.

British Library Cataloguing in Publication Data

Judging standards and effectiveness in education.—
  (Curriculum and learning)
  1. Education. Evaluation research
  I. Moon, Bob   II. Isaac, John   III. Powney, Janet   IV.
  Series
379.154

  ISBN 0 340 54009 5

First published 1990

© 1990 The Open University

Typeset by Butler & Tanner Ltd, Frome and London
Printed for the educational publishing division of Hodder and Stoughton Ltd, Mill Road, Dunton Green, Sevenoaks, Kent by Clays Ltd., St Ives plc

CONTENTS

Acknowledgments   v
Introduction
Bob Moon   vi

PART 1: STANDARDS: THE ONGOING DEBATE

1.1   An Open Letter to Members of Parliament
      C. B. Cox and A. E. Dyson   3
1.2   Causality: A Riposte to the Black Papers
      Nigel Wright   18
1.3   The Debate Over Standards and the Uses of Testing
      Caroline Gipps   32
1.4   Mathematical Attainments: Comparisons of Japanese and English
      Schooling
      S. J. Prais   47
1.5   The Second International Mathematics Study in England and
      Wales: Comparisons Between 1981 and 1964
      M. Cresswell and J. Gubb   51
1.6   Standards in Mathematics: The Perspective of the Working
      Party on Mathematics 5–16 for the National Curriculum
      National Curriculum Working Party   56

PART 2: STRATEGIES FOR EDUCATIONAL EVALUATION
Prepared by Janet Powney

      Introduction to Part 2
      Janet Powney   63

2.1   Methods: Issues and Problems
      Rob Walker   65
2.2   The Art Department
      Philip Clift   78
2.3   Outdoor Play
      Linda McGill   92
2.4   Inside the Lego House
      Elizabeth Burn   95
2.5   TVEI in Caister High: A Case Study in Educational Change
      Ian Stronach   99
2.6   Inspection and its Contribution to Practical Evaluation
      Brian Wilcox   116
2.7   Developments in the Appraisal of Teachers
      Department of Education and Science   124
2.8   Evaluation of Teacher and Pupil Performance
      Joan Sallis   133

PART 3: EFFECTIVE SCHOOLING: OLD AND NEW ISSUES
Prepared by John Isaac

      Introduction
      John Isaac   139
3.1   Effective Schools and Pupils' Needs
      Tim Brighouse   140
3.2   School Effectiveness and School Improvement: A Review of the
      British Literature
      David Reynolds   152
3.3   Studying Schools and their Effects
      D.J. Smith and Sally Tomlinson   170

Index   183

ACKNOWLEDGMENTS

The Publishers would like to thank the following for permission to reproduce material in this volume:

Basil Blackwell for 'The debate over standards and the uses of testing' by Caroline Gipps from the *British Journal of Educational Studies*, 36:1, 1988; Carfax Publishing Company/Professor S. J. Prais for 'Mathematics attainments: Comparisons of Japanese and English Schooling' by S. J. Prais from *Compare*, Vol. 16, No. 2; Professor C. B. Cox for 'An open letter to members of Parliament' by C. B. Cox and A. E. Dyson from *Black Paper 2*; Croom Helm for 'Causality: a riposte to the Black Papers' by Nigel Wright from *Progress in Education* by Nigel Wright; Falmer Press Ltd for 'The Art Department' by Philip Clift from P. Clift, D. Nuttall and R. McCormick (eds) *Studies in School Evaluation* (1987); HMSO for the extracts from *Developments in the Appraisal of Teachers*, *Standards in Mathematics*, *The Perspective of the Working Party on Mathematics 5–16 for the National Curriculum* and *The School Effect: A Study of Multiracial Comprehensives*; London Residuary Body for 'Outdoor Play' by Linda McGill from *Primary Matters 1986*; Methuen and Co for 'Methods: issues and problems' from *Doing Research* by Rob Walker (1985); NFER Nelson for 'The second international mathematics study in England and Wales: comparisons between 1901 and 1964' by M. Cresswell and J. Gubb from *IEA Second International Mathematics Study in England and Wales* and 'Inspection and its contribution to practical evaluation' by Brian Wilcox from *Educational Research* Vol. 31, No. 3, 1989; Open University Press for 'Inside the Lego House' by Elizabeth Burn from C. Skelton (ed) *Whatever Happens to Little Women?* (1989); Routledge for 'Evaluation of teacher and pupil performance' by Joan Sallis from *Schools, Parents and Governors: a new approach to accountability* (1988) and 'Effective schools and pupil needs' by Tim Brighouse from M. James and T. Southgate (eds) *The Management of Special Needs in Ordinary Schools* (1989); University of East Anglia for TVEI in Caister High: a case study in educational change' by Ian Stronach from *CARE*; University of Wales for 'School effectiveness and school improvement: a review of the British literature' by D. Reynolds from *School Effectiveness and Improvement Proceedings of the First International Congress, London 1988* by D. Reynolds, B. P. M. Creemers and T. Peters (1988).

Every effort has been made to trace and acknowledge ownership of copyright. The publishers will be glad to make suitable arrangements with any copyright holders whom it has not been possible to contact.

INTRODUCTION

BOB MOON

Judging Standards and Effectiveness in Education is one of a series of Readers*
prepared to accompany an Open University course called 'Curriculum and
Learning'. The aim of the book, like the course, is to explore a number of
issues that are to the forefront of educational debate in the 1990s. Aspects of
the ongoing debate about 'standards' are explored and alternative strategies
for providing evaluation information are considered. The widespread interest
in the quality and effectiveness of schools and other educational institutions
provides a focus for three extracts from contemporary comment and reseach
in this area.

Part 1 looks at three perspectives on the standards debate. The Black
Papers, published at the end of the 1960s, have become a part of educational
folklore. Written in polemical, academic and quasi academic style, they set
out to provoke a polarised debate about what they saw as declining standards,
a problem they laid firmly at the door of the prevailing orthodoxy of progressivism and egalitarianism. They were spectacularly successful. The media
loved them. The stances adopted (or those assumed to have been adopted)
provided a position point to which, at the political level, the next two
generations of educational discourse were drawn. A Labour Prime Minister
(James Callaghan) was to echo many of the sentiments in his famous Ruskin
College speech of 1970. And his Conservative successor (Margaret Thatcher)
chose in the mid 1980s not only to deploy an almost identical brand of rhetoric
but, also, to bring in as advisors a number of those who originally contributed
to one or more of the Black Papers. It is unclear today how many people who
quote these publications actually read them. They are long out of print. Some

---

* Other titles in the series are:
   New Curriculum – National Curriculum edited by Bob Moon
   Children's Learning in School edited by Victor Lee
   Assessment Debates edited by Tim Horton

of the style and tone is conveyed by the introduction to the second Black Paper that took the form of an Open Letter to Members of Parliament and this is reproduced here. Readers can judge for themselves the adequacy of argument and evidence. Although dated in some particulars, it has a resonance for the debate that has surrounded the passing of the Education Act in 1988. This is followed by Nigel Wright's painstaking but eloquent analysis of the foundations upon which the Black Paper position was established.

Caroline Gipps pursues similar themes and focuses on a number of developments directly relevant to the standards debate in the 1990s. She begins by pointing out that, as long ago as the 1840s, standardised examinations were being used in the USA to try to maintain standards. There are numerous other examples going back even further in time. They are frequently quoted. And as Caroline Gipps observes, 'the interesting thing, of course, is the way standards are nearly always thought to be falling'. If the decline that has been heralded by some Jeremiahs from the nineteenth century onward had really taken place, our schools would be in a sorry state!

Changes in standards over time represent one dimension of this controversial topic. When linked, however, to a comparative perspective, the issues became even more complex. In the 1980s, Sig Prais acquired much attention and some notoriety as a pundit arguing for a traditional approach to mathematics teaching. He pointed to other countries, Germany and Japan for example, as economic competitors where levels of mathematics attainment were significantly greater than in Britain. Mathematics has often been central to the discussion of standards and provides the focus for this extract from an Anglo-Japanese comparative study. Following the mathematics theme further, an extract is then included from the national report on mathematics that evolved from the surveys of the International Association for the Evaluation of Educational Achievements (IEA). This organisation has been looking at academic outcomes across a range of countries since the early 1960s. The reliability of such results is often the subject of considerable debate and this extract points to the caveats that must surround any simplistic interpretations of rising or falling standards. Finally, the working group that was set up to establish a framework for mathematics in the National Curriculum also looked at standards and in particular the apparent changes in mathematics achievement discussed in the National Foundation for Educational Research in England and Wales (NFER) report of the IEA results just mentioned. They too point to the complexity of the issue. In one paragraph (3.7) they attribute to themselves an observation that had been clearly articulated in the Cresswell and Gubb study, but they do go on to elicit further qualifications that any interpretations should take account of. Their final point, however, provides the grounds upon which the debate in the 1990s is likely to focus. Namely, if you cannot establish that there has been an overall decline in standards of attainment (and the evidence suggests that you cannot), and you have to acknowledge the cultural complexities of international comparison (and again all the evidence suggests that you must), then there still remains the issue as to whether standards at any moment in time and within one context are sufficiently high. Here the working party report is unequivocal in saying that English and Welsh children could achieve a great deal more than the evidence of attainment at the end of the 1980s suggested.

See also separate introductions to Parts 2 and 3.

part one
STANDARDS: THE ONGOING DEBATE
PREPARED BY BOB MOON

AN OPEN LETTER TO
1.1 MEMBERS OF PARLIAMENT

C. B. COX AND A. E. DYSON

This second Black Paper owes its existence to the controversy arising from the previous one, and to the continuing crisis in education. In it, Professor Sir Cyril Burt tells us that today standards in basic education are lower than they were 55 years ago, just before the 1914–18 war. Mr S. H. Froome, a headmaster, examines mathematical questions worked by children of 12 plus in 1929, and indicates that now, 40 years later, there has been a marked decline in standards.

As Professor Burt points out, this alarming situation has been obscured because since 1948 there has been an improvement in reading standards of eleven and fifteen year olds, and the Plowden Report used this as a triumphant vindication of 'progressive' methods (para. 585). But because of evacuation and call-up of teachers during the war, standards in 1948 were particularly low. Statistics based on that year are bound to give a false impression. In *Crisis in the Classroom* (1968), Keith Gardner, a leading British expert on reading, explained how the Plowden figures had obscured the disturbing real situation, and commented: 'Our costly present system apparently achieves little more, in terms of reading ability, than the years of economic depression' ... (p. 21).

The facts about the low standards in 1948 have been well known for some time. They were mentioned in a *Times* leader of 28 May 1969, where it was argued that the improvement since 1948 'is not too great to be accounted for, perhaps, by better nutrition and social conditions rather than by better teaching'. And yet in July Mr Short was reported in the *Times* as quoting the Plowden figures without any reference to how misleading they are. On 18 July, in a letter to the *Times*, Sir Alec Clegg quoted the Plowden figures

Source: Cox, C. B. and Dyson, A. E. (1969) 'An open letter to Members of Parliament', from Cox, C. B. and Dyson, A. E. (eds) *Black Paper 2*, Critical Quarterly Society, London, pp. 2–15.

without mentioning their fallibility. Why are these distinguished leaders in British education so ill-informed?

STANDARDS IN READING

Meanwhile, our leading experts in reading produce frightening statistics. In March this year, Dr Joyce Morris, perhaps the most well-known British authority on reading, reported to a Cambridge conference on the professional preparation of teachers for the teaching of reading that 'only 35 per cent of students following infant courses had satisfactory training in the teaching of reading. Over 22 per cent of the students', she went on, 'were given no specific information at all on the subject' (*Teachers' World*, 4 April 1969). Similar findings were reported by Keith Gardner in *Crisis in the Classroom*. Mr Gardner also told of recent research that proved that in the last few years reading standards among young children had gone down: 'From 1961 to 1967 I studied trends in early reading standards in the junior schools of one area. I estimated that in 1961, 25 per cent of 2,000 first-year primary school pupils had not made a start in learning to read. In every subsequent year of my study this number increased. By 1967 it had reached 40 per cent' (p. 23). In July this year [1969] Mrs Betty Root, who is in charge of the reading centre at Reading University's Institute of Education, reported 'that there are now more backward readers than ever, in spite of the large number of teaching methods now available'. She said 'lack of available statistics before 1945 made comparisons difficult, but it was clear from the postwar pattern "that children, through no fault of their own, are not learning to read in the early stages as they used to"' (*Times*, 5 July 1969).

In the June issue of *Reading*, Nancy W. Green, an experienced American educationist, now living in Britain, wrote: 'I have done some tutoring in England and can verify that despite the good intentions of infant teachers to recognise pupils' needs and teach children individually, it is possible for an intelligent child to spend three years in an infant school and emerge with a sight vocabulary of about 20 words and no word attack skills' (p. 20). She explained how anxiety about such low standards in America in the 1950s led to a reaction against 'progressive' teaching methods, and how in Boston, Mass., today a visitor to a classroom would see 'a subject-divided curriculum where the teaching of reading is given the greatest number of hours in the day'. Up-to-date research, particularly that of Professor Jerome Bruner of the Harvard Centre for Cognitive Studies, has persuaded young teachers to put into practice formal, structured reading programmes. While this advanced work proceeds in America, we in Britain invest our capital in out-of-date play-way and open-plan types of junior school.

THE TABLES CONTROVERSY

'Progressives' all agree that their methods demand more effort and higher intelligence from the teacher. This is one major reason for the chaos in so many schools. These methods are not suited to the average teacher, who may well have only one or two years' experience, and who is facing a class of 35 or more. In *Trends in Education* (April 1969), R. C. Lyness, HM Staff Inspector for Mathematics, discussing the new maths, pointed out that many teachers do not themselves understand the new concepts they are supposed to be teaching. The result is seen when teachers write to the *Times Educational Supplement* to complain that intelligent children of twelve plus and older no longer know their tables. In March, a Physics master in Devon complained that his second year could no longer manage simple division:

> Are HMIs still frowning on the old practice of learning the multiplication tables in junior schools? I know maths workshops are the latest gimmicks, but let's keep our feet on the ground. May I suggest that table learning be called 'Programming the human computer'...

A maths teacher followed this:

> 'I have been advised by two separate inspectors that the learning of tables by children is unnecessary ... Significantly I find that the children of any new intake knowing tables and capable of sensibly manipulating numbers are from primary schools that boast no maths workshop or "discovery" methods, but use the formal approach.'

Sensible teachers try to combine the ideas of the 'new maths' with firm grounding in basic rules.

Such letters provide evidence for our first Black Paper's contention that standards are low at secondary as well as junior level. In May 1969 a headmistress in Slough wrote to her divisional education executive to complain about the extremely low standards in her school's eleven plus intake: 'children being sent to her school had been so badly taught at primary level that her teachers were having to spend most of the time teaching them the basic principles of reading and writing' (*Daily Telegraph*, 10 May 1969). No wonder that earlier this year the National Conference of Head Teachers passed an almost unanimous resolution calling for an enquiry into colleges of education, and deploring the low standard of teachers. Both the editors of the Black Papers are experienced external examiners at colleges of education, and can testify that while the best students are excellent, and must be an inspiration to their pupils, a disturbing percentage at the bottom is semi-literate. It is rare for a student to fail because of semi-literacy. Of course, there are many excellent schools, particularly where a sensible head teacher uses the best of formal and informal methods, but this Black Paper shows that the general situation is extremely disturbing.

The increased number of students passing 'O' and 'A' levels is often cited as proof of an improvement in academic standards. In this Black Paper, Professor Pollard, a chief examiner for many years, explains the fallacy of these arguments. Put briefly, the point is that marks are usually scaled each year not to an unchanging standard, but to a pass/fail percentage, so that the increased number of passes means not that more means better, but simply that more means more. It is, of course, true that the best public, grammar and direct grant schools are by and large better now than they were before the war, particularly when they draw on their own preparatory schools. These are among the best schools in the world. High standards of discipline and work are balanced by new flexibility, new methods, and the educational achievements are impressive. These are the schools that the Labour Party wishes to destroy. But the general picture all over the country is quite different. Examiners are appalled at the low standard of English among candidates, the supposed intellectual cream of their generation.

Comprehensive disaster

It has been easy for the Labour Party to argue that the eleven plus is unjust, and this has an obvious appeal to the 80 per cent or so of candidates who fail. There is certainly a need for reform, and Professor Lynn puts forward a possible scheme. It seems likely that thirteen would be a more appropriate age for selection than eleven, and it is certain that machinery for picking out and transferring late developers should have the highest priority and be continually reviewed. What needs to be remembered, however, is that late developers may stand at least as good a chance under the bipartite system as they do in a comprehensive school. The boy of intellectual ability who emerges late tends to be given personal attention in good secondary modern schools and carefully nurtured; in a comprehensive, there is less incentive for teachers to look for such people in a crowd. And the fact remains that possible injustices are inescapable wherever there is competition and grading, wherever there is excellence; and that to solve this problem by removing competition and grading and by denying excellence is to solve it by denying education itself. Our educational system must certainly be humane, and must seek out injustices and remedy them, but it cannot take its standards from the unlucky, the ungifted, the indolent, or the otherwise lame. At the same time, it seems undeniable that while bipartite education recognises the different capabilities and needs of children, comprehensive education, in unstreamed schools particularly, blurs the lines. The chief sufferers will always be the bright children forced to proceed at a pace too slow for them, but *all* the children will suffer to some degree.

A first problem for the comprehensive school is its building; or its lack of building, as is more often the case. To build a real comprehensive involves costs approaching £1,000,000; and there is by no means the money to go round. When you have buildings originally devised for grammar or secondary modern schools, it is often virtually impossible to adapt them in a suitable way. Mr Bell describes how at Cheltenham the difficulties of this enforced change have so far proved insuperable, and no viable scheme has emerged. The only possible plan seems to be to knock down their expensive new grammar school and start again. Mr Ralph Harris describes the disastrous happenings at Enfield when a foolish scheme was forced through too quickly, and in the face of determined opposition from parents and teachers alive to its flaws. This kind of mess is being repeated in many parts of the country, and the harmful effects will limit our cultural and economic life for decades to come.

A major irony is that the Labour Party 'reforms' particularly harm the intelligent working class child. This is argued with great force by Tibor Szamuely, who draws on his own experiences in Russia and Hungary. Both editors of the Black Paper were born in working class areas, and they feel bitter and angry that the fine opportunities given to them in grammar schools in the 1940s are from now on to be denied to children with similar backgrounds. Mr Short has said that 'if he believed that the more able child would suffer in the comprehensive school, he would oppose reorganisation' (*Times*, 6 May 1969), but this suggests that he has not read the latest research. Advocates of the comprehensive school often refer to J. W. B. Douglas's *The Home and the School* (1964), but in the follow-up, *All Our Future* (1968) Dr Douglas, who is a researcher of integrity, has new doubts. He tells us 'it is however by no means certain that the able manual working class pupils are more favourably placed in comprehensive schools' (p. 60), and reports: 'pupils of high ability leave comprehensive schools at an earlier age than those of similar ability in other maintained schools ... It is the boys and girls them-selves who differ in their aspirations and they do so dramatically. Only 29 per cent of the comprehensive school pupils of high ability wish to continue with full-time higher education after leaving school, compared with 60 per cent of the pupils at other maintained schools' (pp. 62–3). Comments, Mr Short?

Dr Douglas finds some possible virtues in comprehensive schools, and it would be wrong to suggest his conclusions are all against them. He ends with sensible advice which ought to be accepted by politicians of all parties: 'An opportunity for experiment is needed in which comprehensive education is fostered in some areas and selective education in others, the areas chosen being equivalent in social composition and educational opportunity'. He stresses 'the dangers of changing to a comprehensive system before adequate information exists to show how the new schools should be planned. The fact that inequalities existed within the old selective system does not mean that they will disappear when selective examinations are abolished ...'

We print a fascinating account by Dr Rhodes Boyson, the headmaster of one of the most successful of the London comprehensives, on how in a new building a comprehensive can be made to work. In a local paper it was reported that because of the success of Dr Boyson's Highbury Grove School, too many parents are applying: 'Next term Highbury Grove has room for a seven-form entry – about 210 boys. But 331 parents have put the school down as their first choice. That leaves 121 disappointments.' How in these circumstances is selection to be carried out? In the past it has been done by competitive exams made as fair as possible. Will it now be done by bureaucrats? Problems at Haringey have drawn attention to this issue.

Dr Boyson regards the success of Highbury Grove as depending on a number of factors. The first is its intake – more weighted towards the academic than any typical comprehensive in a poor neighbourhood could ever hope to be. The second is its building, which replaced the grammar school at a cost of over £650,000, but inherited the name and site of the grammar school, and so some of its prestige. The third is the staff, a very good one, but attracted in part by the intake and by the buildings. The fourth is the disciplined though friendly atmosphere and the resolute rejection of that Achilles Heel of comprehensives, 'progressive nonsense'. But Dr Boyson believes too that the competition provided by other kinds of school is necessary. If the public and grammar schools did not continue to offer their own achievements, a comprehensive might have to fight hard to keep academic standards fully alive.

It is clear enough that the achievement of Highbury Grove cannot be a blueprint for all comprehensives, and that most of the conditions peculiar to it will not combine elsewhere. One usual method now is to allow only certain neighbourhoods to send children to a specific comprehensive school – a plan which removes parental choice, limits the size and intake of a school in a manner often fatal to real comprehensiveness, and produces other adverse results of the kind analysed by Ralph Harris and Tibor Szamuely. It is also, of course, grossly non-egalitarian, since parents who want their children well-educated in the state system might now have to move to another district where the comprehensive achieves a high standard, and how many working-class parents will have the money, the opportunity or the inclination to do this? Some areas are bound to fall into decline, and it is here that clever working class boys will be victimised in the way we have described.

This pattern has produced well-known adverse effects in America and Russia, from whose mistakes we seem unable to learn. A key factor is that there are not enough good teachers to go round, especially in mathematics and science. The result is that poor neighbourhoods suffer from a shortage of teachers, to which no easy answer can be seen. In the House of Commons on 24 April, Mr Short was asked: what consideration had he given to the misgivings of American educationalists who have an almost universal comprehensive system? He replied: 'I know nothing about American misgivings'. Those of us who are not so ill-informed and who have taught in America know about the low standards of American high schools. The Americans spend enormous sums in providing a four year university course specially designed to overcome the weaknesses of their schools, and in developing their excellent graduate schools. Such money is not available in Britain. In America it is often pointed out that the good grammar and public schools in Britain attract teachers of high calibre and with good honours degrees to do advanced sixth form work with intelligent students. This is a special kind of teaching career, with its own attractions, and its own important contribution to society. Such teachers are rarely found in American high schools and if we steam ahead with comprehensivisation they will soon rarely be found here. In May this year 28 teachers at Christ's College, Finchley, a London boys' grammar school, threatened to resign if their school went comprehensive (*Daily Telegraph*, 10 May). The pattern is occurring all over the country. In *Crisis in the Classroom*, Dr Boyson has written: 'I believe that the success of the large comprehensives will be decided in the end on purely academic grounds and this should be fully appreciated. If they succeed then the academic tradition and achievement of the country will have been strengthened. *If they fail then the local authorites must step in rapidly to save the remaining grammar schools*' (p. 65).

Possibly the most serious defect of the comprehensive is the failure of their sixth forms. The underlying cause of this was analysed in our last Black Paper by Mr R. R. Pedley, who first warned of this danger several years ago. In a neighbourhood school of mixed and unselected ability, you need a far larger number of students than such schools are likely to have to run a fully viable academic sixth form. As a result, we are now seeing the development in many areas of 'tertiary' education – a system whereby pupils leave the comprehensive school at around 16 and proceed to a sixth form college or a technical college. Earlier this year, Mr Short gave his blessing to this pattern, and the ILEA, among other authorities, is taking it very seriously. A scheme of this kind is to be operated at Exeter. For the comprehensive school the result can only be disastrous. It will lose most of its best teachers, who will surely choose to teach in the sixth form college if they can, and so be lost to the secondary school. It will lose all its senior pupils – all those who most help to develop the traditions of a school, and define its identity. Decapitated in this manner, it can only become an uneasy transit camp between the primary school, perhaps extended to 12 or 13, and the tertiary school at 16. In these circumstances, it is not unrealistic to fear that in a few years' time standards will very dramatically decline. There will be many children who spend their junior years in a 'progressive' primary school, and who then pass to an unstreamed, unexamined comprehensive with no sixth form. At sixteen, many of them may still be semi-literate, at a stage when such basic defects are almost impossible to correct. The possibility of this situation was amply demonstrated in the 1950s in America. But why are we risking it in Britain? Why are we undermining a primary system which has proved its ability to produce numeracy and literacy? Why are we destroying the finest secondary schools in the world?

MOVING PROGRESSIVELY BACKWARDS

It is now necessary to return more specifically to 'progressive' education, which despite the extravagant claims of its advocates is quite old-fashioned. In his Introduction to Maya Pines's *Revolution in Learning* (1969), Willem Van Der Eyken writes:

> 'Discovery' and 'self-learning' have become clichés that the colleges of education trot out to their students as Tablets recently brought down from Sinai, instead of admitting that Caldwell Cook wrote about them more than fifty years ago. Few teachers have mastered modern maths teaching and fewer still are able to carry out the kind of science teaching that the Malting House School staff pioneered in Cambridge in the twenties. We are still with permissiveness, and our nursery schools – those few we have – are based on nothing more recent than the thinking of Froebel and Maria Montessori (p. xiv).

Maya Pines's book is a popular account of recent American research. She interviewed Professor Bruner, who believes that children's learning processes can be accelerated by carefully structured learning programmes. In 'The Growth of the Mind' (*American Psychologist*, Dec. 1965), Bruner explains the difference between the learning processes among juvenile baboons, primitive tribes and a civilised society. In the complex society, 'there is knowledge and skill in the culture far in excess of what any one individual knows. And so, increasingly, there develops an economical technique of instructing the young based heavily on *telling* out of context rather than *showing* in context' (p. 5).

This *telling* may take various forms. It may consist of letting children find out for themselves in a carefully structured environment. It may involve straightforward explanation, of a mathematical process for example, by a teacher standing in front of a class. Good teaching demands a flexible use of all methods of telling, adapted to the particular needs of the situation. In *Perspectives on Plowden* (1969), Professor Peters points out the *naïveté* of the Plowden picture of the teacher – 'its suggestion that there is one ideal method of teaching, which is usually contrasted with the old formal teaching and "rote-learning"' (p. 18).

The Plowden Report ends by informing us: ' "Finding out" has proved to be better for children than "being told".' In reply Professor Peters quotes a contributor to a recent symposium:

> Many strong claims for learning by discovery are made in educational psychology. But almost none of these claims has been empirically substantiated or even clearly tested in an experiment (p. 12).

In this Black Paper, Professor Bantock tells us: 'It must indeed be said quite categorically that the superiority of discovery methods cannot at present be justified on grounds of empirical research'. We are not denying the value of informal methods, as Professor Bantock makes clear; indeed, we frequently use these methods in our own teaching. But we prove that the Plowden assumptions have ossified into dogma, and are being applied unthinkingly in many schools throughout the country. The result is the decline in standards already alluded to, which the latest research alarmingly bears out. In *Perspectives on Plowden*, Professor Brian Foss tells us:

> Ausubel (1961) concludes that there is no good evidence that children learn better through discovery methods. In one study of older children learning arithmetical principles (Kersh, 1962) the experimenter was obviously dismayed to find rote learning was superior to directed discovery (p. 48).

In the same book, Lionel Elvin, Director of the University of London Institute of Education, asks how it was that the Plowden Committee got itself into this position of adumbrating a theory that does not fit what good teachers do:

> The fight against the old authoritarianism led us to neglect the degree to which the teacher's function must be positive, and has left us in a poor mental state to deal with the different problem of our own time. Our problem is not too much guidance of the young, but too little. This point is crucial. And all the fears we may have of being labelled 'authoritarian' must not prevent our saying it (p. 87).

Many people seem unaware of the *laissez-faire*, permissive attitude now condoned by many education lecturers and applied in schools. In *Crisis in the Classroom*, Keith Gardner writes: 'In the post-war infant school it has been considered slightly old-fashioned to teach reading at all. The belief is that children will learn to read in their own way and in their own good time. Anxious parents have been fobbed off with such pious statements as "He will learn to read when he is ready". Inspectors have actually criticised schools that try to teach reading. In the modern craze for child-centred education, *reading has become something that is acquired* – not taught' (p. 25). He says that 'there are just no grounds for believing that a delay in learning to read does not matter, *yet this is the daily advice given to teachers.*' In her Introduction to Donald Moyle's *The Teaching of Reading* (1968), Dr Joyce Morris writes:

> Another notable feature of this book is that, whilst drawing attention to all that is best in modern practice, it underlines the dangers of too great a reliance on discovery methods and incidental learning. We are reminded that reading is a product of civilisation not, like physical growth, a natural phenomenon. Hence, children generally will neither begin to learn to read nor proceed to acquire the necessary reading skills if left to their own devices no matter how rich the reading environment provided by their

teachers. They must be given systematic instruction based on an accurate diagnosis of their individual needs throughout their school lives.

By making this the central theme of his book, Mr Moyle has shown courage at a time when an educationist who even uses the word 'instruction' is liable to be classed as a reactionary. He has done so in accordance with the findings of recent research, my own included, and in the interests of children (p. 9).

In contrast, 'progressivists' are trying to force their child-centred methods into the comprehensive school which is particularly vulnerable to these sentimental theorists. In *Who Are The Progressives Now?* (1969), Maurice Ash, a leading progressivist, tells us how in primary schools the battle for progressivism, if far from won, is at best fully engaged. Progressivists, he says, must now fight for power in the secondary schools, must 'push back the frontiers of society's intrusion upon the person'. It is made clear that society's 'intrusion' consists not only in rules and discipline, which are seen as a simple denial of freedom, but in learning and instruction themselves. Ash and his fellow contributors condemn streaming, selection, marks, examinations, anything which could ensure that children learn actual subjects or that they are competitively tested at any stage. One of the contributors, Dr Douglas Pidgeon, Deputy Director of the National Foundation for Educational Research, describes the new progressive comprehensive school. On entry the pupil will join a group of all ages from 11 to 18, not selected on ability:

> About a third to a half of his time would be spent in the subject wings of the school, either doing individual experimental work in the practical rooms or participating in small group discussions. Again, about a third to a half of his time would be spent in his home room in individual study, and for the remaining time he would be engaged in large group activities, such as games, music and drama (p. 192).

There will be no formal teaching. In other words, one of the major kinds of *telling* devised by civilised man will not be used.

Such schools already exist in Britain, particularly at junior level, and more are being built every year. On 12 March 1969, the *Times* carried a report about a new kind of school which 'might lead to the abolition of the GCE examination':

> This is the new £286,361 Manor High School at Oadby, Leicestershire, where learning is stimulated by the pupils' own interests rather than by formal teaching and where each child will be free to follow through any individual project he wishes. The first 240 boys and girls, aged 11–14, arrived last term, and there will be 400 within a year. By the 1970s figures will have doubled again.

Manor High School is the brain child of Leicestershire's Director of Education, Mr Stewart Mason, who instigated a pioneering plan to abolish the 11 plus examination over ten years ago. Many counties followed his lead. Mr Mason sees this secondary school as an extension of the free and progressive system now working very successfully in many primary schools and he would eventually like to see it extended to pupils of all ages. This he regards as a possibility only if external examinations are abolished.

But when external examinations are abolished, or replaced by teachers' assessments, who will know whether standards are being maintained? Such a school is not likely to achieve the advanced skills in maths and science on which our economic survival depends. Lord Bowden, Principal of the University of Manchester Institute of Science and Technology, has written:

As far as we are concerned, the rigour of the scientific disciplines has been unimpaired by 'progressive education'. If a man wants to learn how to design a suspension bridge or to remove an appendix, he has to accept traditional discipline and submit himself to formal examination, before he can be let loose on the world. I think for this reason that institutions such as my own and the medical schools, which prepare people for professional life, are fortunate at this particular time.

This is reassuring for scientists in the university world; it is less reassuring for teachers of literature, history and the other humanities. They too have complex subjects to teach, and professional responsibilities, but their subjects are particularly vulnerable to 'progressive' attack.

FALSE RESEARCH

Large sums of money are now being spent on useless research. An amusing instance was provided by the *Radio Times* on 22 May. Readers were invited to fill in a questionnaire about 'progressive education'. We were told that this had been prepared by a research team at Birmingham University School of Education, and that 'this important project is financed by the Schools Council'. On page 97 of this Black Paper Mr Crawford, a headmaster, comments on the foolishness of the questions on the three Rs. But even more remarkable is the article printed beside the questionnaire, which argues the 'progressivist' case. One of the questions was: 'Do you agree with progressive methods in primary education?' Presumably readers will be influenced towards a favourable reply by the accompanying article. Will this mean that ten per cent more will reply 'yes'? Or twenty per cent? Who can tell? The research is meaningless, but we expect that soon the results will be quoted as showing that parents favour progressive education. And why should tax-payers' money be wasted in this way?

Another example is provided in *Who Are The Progressives Now?* After testing groups of children in different schools, Isabel Cabot tells us her results must be approached with caution, because of the small numbers involved, the shortness of the tests (they lasted only a year), the doubtful validity of tests devised to isolate convergent and divergent thinking, and the impossibility of measuring parental influence. She tries to show that pupils at 'progressive' schools may be more flexible (which is possible), but obviously there are too many imponderables for the point to be proved. In the same book, Dr Liam Hudson says sensibly that in much recent educational psychology 'the beliefs support the facts rather than *vice versa*'.

Apparently such folly is not confined to this country. In an astonishing article in *Education*, Stuart Maclure reported on recent developments in Sweden. It seems that Sweden's move towards comprehensive schools and non-streaming was influenced by a Stockholm study under Professor Husen and Dr Nils Svenson, which showed that bright children suffered no harm while the less able benefited from non-streaming. Mr Maclure tells us (*Education*, 2 May 1969):

> Since then, as always happens, someone else has gone over the ground again – Urban Dahlof, a former colleague of Svenson's, and now a professor at the University of Gothenburg. He examined the Stockholm study and in particular, the tests used to assess the relative progress of the pupils in the different types of schools. He discovered that these were fairly elementary, and that while the survey showed little difference in the efficiency of selective and unselective, unstreamed schools in achieving similar elementary standards the picture looked very different if the rate of learning was also measured. In the unstreamed, unselective schools the rate of learning was three times slower than in the selective schools, and no allowance has been made in the study for this.
>
> Dahlof's model is like this. He reckons that the teacher must divide his material into units and cannot move on from one unit of instruction to the next till 75 per cent of the children have mastered the work in hand. In a selective group consisting of – say, the top 25 per cent – the teacher will clearly reach this point long before a teacher with a group consisting of the whole range of ability. If Dahlof is right then, water does not flow uphill: quicker children can learn faster than slower children and to proceed at a pace acceptable to the majority must hold back the abler pupils.

There are many possible comments. We wonder why the original research of Professor Husen and Dr Nils Svenson was so naive?

PRIVATE EDUCATION

As increases in taxation make it difficult for middle-class people to send their children to private schools, so the very rich become more privileged. Yet all parents need educational choice at the present time. As the state moves towards a system of uniform, neighbourhood comprehensives, the need for some alternatives, some freedom of movement, must grow. And it is profoundly important that parents should have the right to opt out of the pseudo-religion of progressivism, if they judge this a denial of their own beliefs, values, standards or way of life.

Are freedoms of this kind to be taken from us? As the possibilities of *1984* come perceptibly close, private education is going to be an essential feature of any society that wishes to maintain its liberties. There are already too many dangers of coercion and control by central government, too many restrictions on what we can do with our money or choose for our lives. It is also clear that the abolition of private schools would entail sanctions of a kind still barely contemplated, and wholly at odds with freedom of choice. Would it be forbidden for a parent to send his child to a private school in Ireland or Switzerland, for instance, or for him to pay a tutor to give private lessons at home? One of our correspondents envisaged an England where teachers would be smuggled into the houses of the rich by underground tunnels, and concealed from informers and state spies in teacher-holes. It seems certain that the suppression of private schooling would lead to some form of penal sanctions, and that parents who gave up luxuries to pay for their children's private education would have to bear some criminal taint.

Private schools are a necessary aspect of our liberties, but their positive importance to education is our chief concern. This importance is not confined to the pupils who attend them, but extends to everyone who benefits from the competition they provide. The great public and direct grant grammar schools set a standard of achievement which is internationally recognised, and without which the standards of other institutions might imperceptibly start to slide. They stand in relation to other secondary schools as Oxford and Cambridge stand to the newer universities, a continual reminder of what excellence is. In our view, the need for the times is to extend the possibility of private education to more and more people, by making loans and grants available to those who qualify for entrance but cannot afford fees.

EQUALITY OF OPPORTUNITY

'You can have equality *or* equality of opportunity. You can't have both.' As Angus Maude demonstrated in our first Black Paper, equality of opportunity is totally different from the present cult of egalitarianism, which is indeed its chief enemy at the present time. The frightening aspect of egalitarianism is that while it costs far more to bring into effect than equality of opportunity, it disintegrates the standards and structures on which education depends. It is a levelling down process, actively unjust to brighter children, who become a new under-privileged, and for this same reason dangerous for the nation as a whole. We *need* first-class surgeons, engineers, scientists, mathematicians, lawyers, scholars, and these can only show up through a system of elitist training and competitive exams. This has been called a 'fascist' viewpoint; but we should like to hear a progressivist arguing this one with a patient in need of complicated surgery, or with the Chancellor of the Exchequer in his more realistic moods.

THE END OF CONSENSUS

The Black Paper has been called a 'backlash', which is a misuse of language. It has been enlightening to watch the dogmatism and totalitarianism of our opponents, some of whom imply that we have no right to hold views differing from their own. Our arguments on student revolt have gone unanswered, but are now generally accepted by the leader writers of most newspapers. The moderate, sensible views of Imre Lakatos and Geoffrey Hudson are already held by a large number of university dons. We print here further balanced arguments from the Vice-Chancellor of Edinburgh University on why it is against the students' own interests for them to be involved in major decision making. Our notion that 'progressive education' might be in some part to blame for lack of knowledge or for naive and destructive political attitudes in its victims has been seen as common sense by many people, though the progressivists themselves have professed to be amazed. In this Black Paper, we again suggest that if informed, civilised, mature and well-balanced citizens are wanted for the future, we must scrutinise most carefully those educationalists who teach hatred of authority and contempt of tradition; who nurture ignorance and self-indulgence as a point of principle; and who disregard the claims or indeed the realities of the social world.

New Society reported that the Black Paper had broken the consensus on education. No longer can it be accepted that progressivism and comprehensive schemes are necessarily right, or that the future inevitably lies with them. The Black Paper has encouraged parents, teachers, MPs to speak out on the present day abuses in education. There are many signs that the trend is now back to more balanced and tried views, the best of old methods and new. We believe that everyone who agrees with this has a duty to fight for education, and that Parliament has particular responsibilities in the coming year.

1.2 CAUSALITY: A RIPOSTE TO THE BLACK PAPERS

NIGEL WRIGHT

The intention of this [chapter] was to examine the following proposition: 'a decline in educational standards has taken place *because* schooling has been harmed by the progressives and by comprehensives reorganisation.' This view is often stated in some newspapers[1] and is a central tenet of the Black Papers. The proposition suggests a simple cause-and-effect relationship between modern developments in education and falling standards. But I find myself in some difficulty. There seems to be very little positive evidence that standards are falling in general[2]; and some evidence suggests that standards are rising.[3,4] Nor have I found much evidence that 'progressive' ideas have had a significant influence on the majority of schools. In fact, given the rapidity of social change in general over the past twenty years, schools on the whole have proved quite resistant to change. There are, of course, notable exceptions: but it would be unwise to base any general proposition upon notable exceptions. It is clearly true that *some* schools have 'gone progressive' in a big way; and it is probably true that standards of attainment have declined in *some* schools. But there is no evidence that it is those schools which have 'gone progressive' which have suffered the decline in standards.[5] Broadly, we seem to face two facts which need an explanation:

1 Schools, in general, have not changed very profoundly in the past 25 years. Many of the changes that have taken place are purely superficial.[6]
2 There has, on balance, been no very significant rise *or* fall in standards in recent years. The notable exception is the number of pupils achieving public examination success at the age of sixteen–plus; I shall discuss this in the final section of this chapter.

Source: Wright, N. (1977) *Progress in Education*, Croom Helm, London, chapter 10.

To a middle-of-the-roader seeking a simple cause-and-effect relationship, we seem to have it here: not much change in the schools, therefore not much change in standards. This, however, is not good enough for the Black Papers, and indeed it is not good enough for me. We must look at the matter more closely.

Take the Black Paper case first. They are convinced that 'standards are falling everywhere'.[7] Yet in the four Black Papers there are not more than a few scraps of reasonable evidence to support this view. Moreover, contrary to popular belief, it is not a view that many parents appear to hold. The National Child Development Study has been one of the biggest investigations into education ever conducted in this country and, indeed, in the world. The study followed all the children born in a single week of 1958, and therefore includes a representative sample of that generation.[8] When these children were sixteen, in 1974, their parents were asked about their dissatisfactions with their children's schooling. 11,650 parents replied. Sixty-six per cent said they had been satisfied; 26% said they had been satisfied in some ways but not in others; and 8% said they were dissatisfied. When asked about their reasons for dissatisfaction, 3% of the parents complained of 'low standards', 6% complained of disciplinary problems, and 5% felt that their child had 'not been stretched'.[9] While this evidence is more reliable than the normal opinion polls reported in newspapers, we must treat it with considerable reservations. Nonetheless, it really does not support any suggestion that in 1974 there was widespread concern among parents about school standards. By that time the Black Paper view had been 'on the market' for five years, although there has been much more publicity in the last three years which may have made more parents conscious of schools' defects. It should be added that the NCDS found much greater dissatisfaction with schools among the pupils themselves, but little of this seemed to be related to the kind of problems pin-pointed by the Black Papers.

Another difficulty in the Black Paper case is that they do not say when the decline was supposed to have begun; or rather they offer a host of dates which vary according to the complaint being made and the writer making it. Let us suppose that standards are falling everywhere. What might be said of the causes of this? The question of cause and effect is a tricky one. It is well known, for instance, that the parents of children who are doing well at school visit the school more frequently than the parents of children who are doing badly. But it is not easy to decide whether children do well because their parents take an interest or whether parents take an interest because their children are doing well. And it need not be a simple question of cause-and-effect: probably the relationship between the two facts – parental interest and child's achievement – is a complex one. Examples of this difficulty abound: in economics, it has been observed that there is a connection between the quantity of money and the rate of price rises. But economists are unable to agree whether the increased money supply causes the price rises or whether the price rises call forth an increased money supply or whether either of these explanations will do. So instead of saying that 'progressive' education causes falling standards, we could just as easily suggest that falling standards give rise to 'progressive' reforms. It is quite easy to find evidence which might support this second view. The general theory would go like this: educators find that something is wrong in education and therefore take steps to remedy the problem. Such steps may consist of 'progressive' changes. To test this theory would involve a major historical study which I cannot undertake. But it is possible to cite a number of examples which would appear to support it.

One approach would be to see what teachers have to say about why they change their styles. Consider this reminiscence of a teacher working in 1930:

> The astonishing thing about [the children] is that they are alert and keen as needles for the knowledge that's not imposed, but the earplugs are in as soon as you force any knowledge upon them. I am trying to find methods of unorganised education, informal lessons, with lots of facts dropped casually, so that they do not realise they are being taught. But, if they once suspect that you want them to learn, they resist.[10]

Of course this teacher – Janetta Bowie – did not *have* to search for new ways of doing things. The teacher in the next classroom was apparently quite satisfied:

> Sara ... is a bird of well-kent feather – the Great Blackboard Tapper, first cousin to the Lesser Woodpecker. The tapping nearly drives me crazy. The chanting goes on through arithmetic tables to spelling (where it increases in frequency) and then to geography. Through the partition the chorus finally resolves itself into 'Gourock is a holiday place' (repeated twelve times); 'Glasgow is the biggest city in Scotland' (twelve times); 'Edinburgh is the Capital of Scotland' (twelve times).[11]

But often teachers *do* change their style because the inadequacies of the old style are all too clear.[12] The chain of causality seems to be: poor results, *therefore* change and not the other way round. Of course the new way may be no better or even worse than the old, in which case the search for improvement must go on. But this search for improvement must be seen as a consequence of the failure of the old ways.

Organisational changes too seem to arise from dissatisfaction with existing results. Consider streaming. Many schools went for un-streaming *because* all was not well: while one section of the pupils (those in the high streams) were getting on all right, those in the lower streams were a constant source of worry. A moment comes when a school is no longer satisfied with minority success and mass mediocrity. Un-streaming was seen, rightly or wrongly,[13] as a way of dealing with this problem. Here again we have the pattern: a perceived problem, a 'progressive' reform. It may be that the 'progressive' reform failed to produce the desired improvement, but it would not be true to say that the reform was the cause of problems which had not hitherto existed. Curriculum reform provides other examples. The 'new mathematics' originated in the late 1950s because of widespread discontent with the teaching of mathematics.[14] The curriculum of 1955 was little different from that of the 1930s and it was not meeting the needs of the modern age. The country did not have enough mathematicians, and they were not of the right calibre. Most people regarded mathematics as a mystery beyond comprehension. Changes came, and they were worked out with enormous care by large numbers of capable people expending a great deal of time. Stuart Froome's article in *Black Paper Two*[15] which claims that the new maths was a fad wafted in by over-enthusiastic ignoramuses is just about as far from the truth as it is possible to get. The introduction of the new maths was as good a piece of curriculum reform as we are ever likely to see. To be sure, there were faults, some of which remain to be corrected. But the basic story is very simple: here was a 'progressive' development which took place specifically to remedy a palpable deficiency. The causality is precisely the opposite of that suggested by Froome and several other Black Paper writers.

Perhaps the best documented example is comprehensive reorganisation. We have already seen [...] how the failure of the bi-partite system became increasingly obvious. The government's Newsom Report of 1963, while it did not come out for or against comprehensive schools, argued that technological change was making increasing demands on the nation's 'average' and 'below average' children. A far better education was needed for them. Comprehensive schools were seen in many quarters (Conservative not excepted) as the answer. It could be that high hopes have not been fulfilled, but it is a travesty of history to claim that everything was fine until interfering busybodies spoiled it all by pushing through comprehensive reorganisation. The constant search for new ways of teaching reading to that small minority who have always failed[16] provides us with yet another example. And so we could go on. Time and again we can find the same pattern: *failure therefore change*. I believe that the historical evidence would support this theory rather than the contrary one that modern developments have been the cause of failure. But I certainly do not have enough evidence to claim that the case is proven. In any case, I do not believe it can be more than partially correct, because there are bigger causes at work.

It is a mistake to see the education system as an isolated world of its own. If changes take place in education, it does not follow that the *cause* of those changes are to be found in the education system. Consider, for instance, the figures [overleaf].

The figures show that as the 1930s progressed more and more grammar school pupils were leaving before they had completed a full secondary education. The change was a dramatic reversal of earlier trends and must have caused considerable concern at the time. Had Cox and Boyson been old enough, they would probably have produced a Black Paper blaming the teachers and the growth of permissiveness. But the real cause of the change, as the Gurney-Dixon report pointed out,[17] was the acute economic crisis the country was going through. Comparisons of the present day with the 1930s are not entirely out of place and everyone with a television set knows that we

Age of Leaving School		Grammar-School Pupils, 1931–7[18]	
		(Cumulative Percentages)	
Year of Intake	Under 16	Under 17	Under 18
1927	27.3	64.2	84.3
1928	29.4	67.9	86.7
1929	30.3	70.4	87.7
1930	32.7	72.5	89.4

Table 1 *Leaving age of grammar-school pupils*

are now going through a period of severe economic and social crisis. We can be quite sure that this crisis will be affecting what goes on in schools. Some effects are easy to observe (like the cuts in educational spending) or predict (like loss of confidence in educational credentials as a sure-fire guarantee of a good job) while others will be much more subtle. How social, economic and political developments in the 'outside world' affect schools is a massive subject, but some points are relevant to the present discussion. First, we might suppose that the decline of certainty and confidence in society would be reflected in the schools, with a consequent loss of cohesion, satisfaction, and commitment. As in the 1930s, increasing numbers of people see authoritarianism as the simple answer to it all. The Black Papers represent this view in the field of education. But it is not made clear how it would solve the real problems we face. The past twenty-five years have seen a steady decline in respect people hold for the traditional sources of authority: the Church, the Law, politicians (who in happier days could expect to be called statesmen), employers, the family. All have found their authority diminishing, not in every case without reason. It would be extraordinary in these circumstances if teachers had not similarly experienced a decline in their authority. In fact, it is quite surprising how much authority they have retained. In plain terms, these are difficult times and it is not a matter for wonder that schools are having difficulties. To attribute these difficulties to incompetent teachers or the wrong method of teaching reading or the wrong way of classifying pupils is about as close to the whole truth as saying the *Titanic* sank because it had too much food on board. Second, a number of important changes in the last quarter-century have placed a heavy strain on schools, particularly when they have made no attempt to adapt to them. Consider, for example, the increased number of working mothers, the rising standards of living and the growing spending power of youth, the change in the status of unskilled work and, perhaps above all, the stupendous problem of urban decay. To seek the causes of schools' problems without giving prominent attention to such factors would be blindness. Third, the belief of children, and parents, in education as something that will get you somewhere has taken a knocking. Quite simply, the economic crisis has destroyed the old myth which kept competitive education going: the myth that if we all ran hard enough towards the finishing line, we could all expect a prize. As Christopher Jencks has put it: 'Schools cannot convince all their students that they will "get ahead" because teachers cannot believe this and neither can the students. Students can, however, believe that they are going to get ahead if they can see that someone else is going to get left behind.'[19] At a time when even those who might have thought they would 'get ahead' are led to doubt it, the schools have few carrots to offer the pupils. In the absence of rewards we could turn to punishments to motivate the pupils: but not all of us want to, nor is it clear that it would work. Perhaps things might have been easier if schools had not been so heavily committed to a utilitarian, competitive ethos.

Related to this is the ubiquitous question of 'relevance'. If one thing remains in my mind after seven years' teaching it is a line of children asking, 'Sir, what's the point of learning this?' Complaints about the irrelevance of the school curriculum, while nothing new, are coming not only from progressives and radicals, but equally loudly from associations of industrialists.[20] If educators and employers doubt the value of the curriculum we have now – and let us be clear that schools overwhelmingly maintain a traditional curriculum[21] – it may be too much to expect pupils to engage with maximum enthusiasm in the learning tasks we set them. These things have been brought to a head by the economic crisis. But in my view schooling was in any case losing much of the *meaning* it may once have had[22] and there has been a consequent loss of commitment on the part of teachers as well as parents and pupils. This analysis would probably be shared by some of the Black Paper contributors. But while they would look to the values and practices of the past for some solution, I believe we must look to the future.

I have been arguing that even if it could be shown that school standards are falling, the cause of it would have to be sought largely, though not entirely, *outside* of school and in the conditions of society as a whole. And because there is manifestly a crisis in society, one might reasonably expect there to be a crisis in the schools. But what evidence have we that there *is* a general crisis in schools? The very fact that 'the Crisis in Education' has become such a cliche would seem almost to be sufficient reason for accepting that there is such a crisis. When we all get in a panic like lemmings then *that* is something to panic about even if, after we've all disappeared over the cliff and the dust has settled, it transpires that there was nothing worth panicking about in the first place. I myself wrote an article in 1968 called 'The Crisis in Education', but I find it hard to see now quite why I chose that title; the problems I was writing about were perennial ones. Of course I was not alone: in the same year, for example, Rhodes Boyson contributed to a book called *The Crisis in the Classroom*.[23] How much of the crisis exists only in our imaginations; how far has anxiety been deliberately whipped up? Is it too cynical to suggest that some people have built a career on stirring up ill-founded fears? Can the meteoric rise of Rhodes Boyson – to Front-Bench spokesman within little more than two years of his first election to parliament – be attributed entirely to his brilliance as a thinker, orator and statesman? Or is it that he has 'manufactured' a 'problem' and then presented himself as the only person who can deal with it?[24] Personally I doubt whether public anxiety can be whipped up if there is not *some* foundation in truth for it.[25] But the media have not played a responsible role, and there is a good deal of public misinformation and confusion. It is this confusion which allows demagogues to emerge. There *is* a crisis and, in part it *is* connected with standards. The Black Papers are on to a half-truth when they raise a hullabaloo about standards. To get nearer to the whole truth we need a historical perspective.

Fears of falling standards have been a constant feature of the education scene since the middle of the nineteenth century.[26] The state had been making grants to schools since 1833 yet the Newcastle Commission, which reported in 1861, found that basic standards had remained unacceptably low. Something had to be done, and 'objective criteria' were sought to help enforce improvement. The upshot was the 'Revised Code' of 1862 which introduced 'Payment by Results'. This was a system whereby the financial grant to a school depended in part upon the number of its pupils who passed a test in the 'three Rs'. Inspectors administered the tests and their visits were invariably dreaded: if sufficient children did not pass the test the grant would be cut and teachers would have to take a pay cut or lose their job. In fact only about twenty-five per cent of pupils passed the tests – a percentage which had not improved significantly by the 1880s. The other major measure intended to raise standards was the Act of 1870 which gave local boards the power to set up schools where voluntary agencies were not already doing so. The outcome of these measures seems familiar. In the 1880s the Cross Commission heard witness after witness complain bitterly about falling standards. A few felt that state education was to blame, but more saw Payment by Results as the real evil. It became increasingly obvious that Payment by Results was indeed having the opposite of the effect intended,[27] and in the 1890s it was gradually phased out. The lesson was clear to virtually everyone: there is no simple mechanism by which the State (or any other authority) can *enforce* standards.[28] Payment by Results was not just a flop: it was an educational disaster for millions of children, and its abolition made way for great advances in public education. But, *plus ça change*, fears about falling standards were not allayed.[29] Employers, in particular, were unhappy: indeed, during the first decade of the century they had to bring thousands of clerks over from Germany to get their paperwork done. Nothing changed the conviction of many that things were getting worse and worse. Concern rose to a peak at the end of the First World War and the 1918 Education Act was, in part, a response to it.

The 1920s, far from being an era of roaring excellence as some present-day writers would have us believe, saw ever more expressions of alarm. The Newbolt Report on the Teaching of English reported that the supply of young people who could speak and write well was 'almost non-existent'.[30] A survey by HMIs revealed that many twelve-year-olds hadn't mastered even the 'mechanical difficulties' of reading.[31] A respected inspector administered tests used in the 1890s and found that the children of 1925 were 'palpably and consistently worse'.[32] And an alarmed Board of Education set up a major enquiry into arithmetic standards. Concern did not diminish in the 1930s, as queues of witnesses to the Spens Committee and, later, the Norwood Committee, testified.[33] And these witnesses were grumbling about the 'cream' – the top fifteen per cent or so who succeeded in getting into grammar school. The public – amply assisted by the popular press – were scandalised in 1941 by reports about the poor educational standards of recruits to the army.[34] And in 1945, Cyril Burt suggested that '15 to 20 per cent' of the 20–25 age group were 'semi-literate'.[35]

The period 1947–53 produced yet again an extended public outcry about falling standards. It was at the end of this period that an excellent little book, *The Importance of Illiteracy*[36] by M. M. Lewis, was published. It charts the history of 'falling standards' and puts forward a theory to explain the incessant public anxiety and the periodical national alarums. Anxiety persists, Lewis argued, not because standards are falling (although there are always some people who feel certain they are), but because people want them to be higher. The point was taken up by the Newsom Report in 1963: 'One of the reasons why there is quite proper anxiety over general standards of literacy today is not that fewer and fewer people can read and write, but that more and more people need to do so with greater competence.'[37] The advancing technological society has a voracious appetite for ever more competent manpower. It is at times when this appetite is not being satisfied that alarm about poor standards (all too easily converted into allegations that standards are *falling*) reaches a peak. Often this is at times of economic uncertainty when people are searching for scapegoats for problems which might more properly be attributed to the economic structure. But it is not easy to analyse the economic structure; it is easy to point fingers at teachers and schools. As far as the technological society is concerned, these national alarms are all to the good. For they have the effect of urging teachers and their pupils to set their sights higher. In the jargon of economists: aspiration levels are up-graded. A new wave of energy and expectation is released, and general standards may in due course be dragged up a notch. Unfortunately, what the technological society needs is not necessarily the same thing as educators seek to produce. [...]

There is another dimension we need to be aware of. Going back to the nineteenth century, we all know (especially if we've read Dickens) that a large part of the population was brutishly ignorant and illiterate. The higher classes viewed this as an inevitable fact of nature. Little could be expected of the masses and low educational attainment was rarely remarked upon because few people believed it could – or should – be otherwise. In this century our views have by stages been modified. Particularly since 1945 the class nature of our society has been openly recognised and widely challenged. It is no longer tolerable to keep a large sector of society in poverty and ignorance. If children, whatever their origin, have low educational attainment or behave abominably, it is no longer dismissed as an unfortunate inevitability. Comprehensive schools mark the institutional recognition of this: never again can part of the populace be hidden away in back-street sink schools where few 'decent' people need worry about them.[38] Everyman's child now sits in the same classroom as the vicar's daughter and the doctor's son. We are now moving into an era when high standards are expected of – and by – everyone.[39] It is because these high standards are by no means always achieved that there is so much discontent with schooling. Maybe it is right of critics to endorse, and 'stir up' this discontent. But it is quite wrong of them to assert that things now are worse than they used to be. On the contrary, it is because things are so much *better* that their criticisms receive so much attention. Fifty years ago an ill-clothed, uncouth and ignorant child would have turned few heads. Today the same child would call forth a chorus of condemnation of our education system. A remarkable change in our view of society has taken place.

Unfortunately, views change more easily than reality. If we look back at the evidence, one fact is particularly striking: that the biggest differences in educational attainments are related to social class. If there is one factor which reliably predicts educational failure, early leaving, low assessment by teachers, allocation to low streams, truancy – or dozens of other measures – it is social class. The conclusion would seem to be obvious: if we *really* want to eliminate educational failure, illiteracy, or disaffected behaviour, we must first eliminate social class differences. Those who wish to maintain class divisions will have to learn to live with the educational consequences. I want to make it quite clear that I am *not* saying there is a simple cause-and-effect relationship between class and educational attainment. I would not align myself with Sir Cyril Burt – or Sir Keith Joseph – who see the lower classes as a mass of congenitally incompetent people for whom nothing can be done.[40] The relationship between class and educational behaviour is enormously complex and deserves the intense study it is receiving.[41] The point I am seeking to establish is a simple one: that our educational expectations are higher than they have ever been, but our expectations will be frustrated so long as we continue to maintain a society divided by social class. So my conclusions about standards are these: yes, standards are far too low. Every person in the country should be able to get 30 out of 30 on the Watts-Vernon reading test, not because it is worth reading or because it is a good test, but because it really is quite easy. Every one in the country should be capable of writing a book if they want to, like those published by the Centerprise Publishing Project in London.[42] No one should be thrown into confusion by simple figures, numbers or graphs. Of course standards could and should be enormously higher. *But this is not the same thing as saying that standards are falling.*

The crisis which the Black Papers have pointed to amounts to this: standards have not kept up with the rise in expectations. (Note the causality: it is not a fall in standards, but the rise in expectations which has caused the crisis.) Now one might reasonably ask: why have standards *not* risen when so much effort and expenditure have been put into education? We must be careful here: all we can say from the evidence reviewed is that standards in the basic skills do not appear to have risen in the last fifteen years or so, although the point is not proven. But there are areas in which there have been significant changes, most notably in the number of people getting further or higher education, and in the number of pupils passing public examinations in school. It is an open question how far this can be taken to indicate educational advance. Not everyone sees exam passes as a good measure of education[43] nor does everyone think that examinations are important. And in the immediate post-war period the fact that secondary modern pupils were not intended to take public examinations was seen as a virtue.[44] Be that as it may, the attraction of 'examination success' proved irresistible, and secondary modern schools slowly became aware that they *could* take pupils to O- and even A-Levels. And the grammar schools, noting the examination success of secondary modern pupils, readjusted their ambitions for their less promising pupils. Comprehensive schools have consolidated these tendencies: some now enter *all* their pupils for O-Levels or CSE even though these exams were not originally intended for all pupils. The boom in examination passes took place simply because more and more youngsters stayed on at school and entered the examinations[45] and their teachers became aware that this kind of success was open to them. This is a good illustration of the rising expectations I have talked about. We have beyond doubt made great strides towards equal opportunity *to pass exams* in the last thirty years. But can we expect this growth to continue *ad infinitum*? Economists are familiar with the 'law of diminishing returns', which states that as you put more effort into something you can expect increasing benefits. But eventually you reach a point where further benefits become harder and harder to get from further efforts. And in the end, no amount of extra effort will produce any further benefits. Not, that is, unless the fundamental conditions are changed. This may apply to schooling. The improvements in reading standards which took place in the 1950s and early 60s seemed to tail off by the 70s. In the case of O-Level and A-Level passes we may now be facing a similar tailing off – though it is far too early to be sure, and other factors like the economic situation complicate the picture. In general, however, there is no reason to suppose that *any* educational advance can carry on indefinitely at an undiminished rate; some slowing off must be expected at some stage. And when this happens, only a fundamental change in the basic conditions can be expected to trigger off a new wave of advance. In this country legislation has often revised the basic conditions and made a new surge of progress possible. Such were the Acts of 1870, 1902, 1918 (somewhat thwarted) and 1944. But perhaps more important than the legislation was the change in social conditions and attitudes which brought forth the legislation and the subsequent advances. It may be that our current crisis marks the end of another era. New demands, new forces, new attitudes are growing up; only if we recognise and use these imaginatively can we hope for a new wave of progress. This progress may not be a mere quantitative advance on what has gone before: we must also explore the possibility of a qualitatively different education. Perhaps the stagnation of the present, which is causing so much frustration, will only be ended if education can take on new meanings, and new forms, and recapture the confidence of the generality of people.

NOTES

1 Notably the *Daily Mail, Daily Telegraph* and the *Sun*.
2 Of course, there are *particular areas* where there is strong evidence of falling standards. Inner London is a case in point. But even here there are signs that the downward trend has been halted; and in any case, there may be particular explanations for London schools' problems which have little to do with 'progressivism'.
3 See *The Times Educational Supplement*, 29 October 1976 and the *Report from Research and Statistics Branch* (ILEA Document 915) presented to the Schools Sub-Committee of the ILEA on 2 March 1977.
4 London, like other major cities, faces all the problems of 'urban decay'. It has a population whose composition is rapidly changing, and many of the traditional communities have been broken up. Until last year it was particularly badly hit by high teacher turnover rates and a very severe dearth of experienced teachers. At the same time, London youngsters are possibly the most sophisticated in the country and may have been particularly restive at the failure of schools to adapt to changed conditions.
5 Even in the case of the highly publicised 'School of Shame', William Tyndale Junior School in Islington, North London, the actual evidence (ignored by the media) was that standards of reading had not fallen during the controversial headship of Terry Ellis. Indeed the mean reading scores of ten-year-olds increased slightly (though not significantly) during Ellis's eighteen months as headmaster, and this despite the fact that some of the most advantaged children had left the school. Furthermore, the mean reading score of William Tyndale pupils was not significantly worse than that for other Inner London schools. Details can be found in Document 113a (which was agreed by all parties) of the Auld Inquiry.
6 See [Wright, N. (1977) *Progress in Education*] chapter 11, pp. 195–7.
7 Cox and Dyson, *Black Paper Two* (Critical Quarterly Society 1969), p. 155.
8 Except insofar as children born in March are different from those born at other times of the year. I know that the fact that they were all born under Pisces will seem of enormous significance to some people. I must confess that I am sceptical. But there may be other reasons why people born in March are different.
9 Ken Fogelman (ed.) *Britain's Sixteen-Year-Olds* (National Children's Bureau 1976), p. 50. A public opinion poll in February 1977 found that eighty per cent of parents were 'very satisfied' or 'fairly satisfied' with the education their children were getting: see *The Times Educational Supplement*, 18 February 1977, p. 12.
10 Janetta Bowie, *Penny Buff* (Constable, 1975), p. 64.
11 Ibid., p. 49.
12 Other kinds of evidence might support this theory. For instance, the finding of J. G. Anderson in America (*Bureaucracy in Education*, Baltimore, Maryland: Johns Hopkins, 1968, pp. 148–149) that teachers in lower socio-economic neighbourhoods had a greater interest in new techniques and curricula. H. C. Dent, *1870–1970 Century of Growth in English Education* (Longman, 1970) also sheds some interesting light on this matter.
13 See [Wright, op cit.] chapter 3.
14 F. R. Watson, *Developments in Mathematics Teaching* (Open Books, 1976), Part 1; *Mathematics in Primary School*: Schools Council Curriculum Bulletin No. 1 (HMSO, 1965).
15 Cox and Dyson, *Black Paper Two*, pp. 104–7.

16 E.g. Frank Smith, *Psycholinguistics and Reading* (Holt, Rinehart and Winston, 1973).

17 Figures taken from *Early Leaving* (The Gurney-Dixon Report), (Ministry of Education, 1954), p. 5).

18 Ibid.

19 Jencks, *Inequality* (Penguin, 1975), p. 158.

20 See, for instance, the report of the Rubber and Plastics Industry Training Board, summarised in *The Times Educational Supplement*, 3 December 1976, p. 12. The criticisms made by radicals are of course of a very different nature from those of the industrialists.

21 Douglas Holly, *Beyond Curriculum* (Hart-Davis, MacGibbon, 1973). It is sobering also to see what the Spens Report had to say about the curriculum in 1938 (*Secondary Education with Special Reference to Grammar Schools and Technical High Schools*, Board of Education, 1938).

22 Though I would not want to overstate the case: I suspect that for a very large section of the population schooling never had much meaning. But it may be that in the past they were more prepared to be cajoled or coerced into going through the motions than they are now. I do not know how much good it did them.

23 N. Smart (ed.) *Crisis in the Classroom*, (IPC, 1968).

24 One does not get the impression that Rhodes Boyson is over-concerned with 'pursuing truth wherever it may lead'. In a Capital Radio broadcast on 20 May 1976, Boyson made the rather odd remark: 'I do not claim all truth on my side like [sic] is claimed on the other side.' Boyson's book, *The Crisis in Education* (Woburn Press, 1975) contains over 300 errors of *fact* in 160 pages. The most charitable interpretation one can put on this is that Dr Boyson is a careless man. He does seem an odd choice for chairman of the 'non-political' National Council for Educational Standards.

25 It is worth noting this stanza of Tennyson:

> And the parson made it his text that week, and he said likewise,
> That a lie which is half a truth is ever the blackest of lies,
> That a lie which is all a lie may be met and fought with outright
> But a lie which is part a truth is a harder matter to fight.
>
> (*The Grandmother*).

26 This is very well documented in M. M. Lewis, *The Importance of Illiteracy* (Harrap, 1953).

27 The iniquitous effects of Payment by Results are described in every history of education which covers the second half of the nineteenth century.

28 A lesson sadly not yet learned by the editors of *Black Paper 1975* who call for State 'enforcement' of standards.

29 See [Wright, op cit.] chapter 11 below, note 2.

30 See [Wright, op cit.] chapter 1 above, p. 24.

31 Ibid, p. 22.

32 P. B. Ballard, quoted in Lewis, *The Importance of Illiteracy*, p. 28.

33 See [Wright, op cit.] chapter 1.

34 A summary of the Press reaction was provided by a correspondent of *The Times Educational Supplement*, on 23 August 1941: 'Some prominence has recently been given in certain sections of the Press to the results of testing recruits to the services, and attention drawn, rather gleefully, to the number of adults of a given age who ... have forgotten the elements of vulgar fractions ... or the recognised conventionalities of English spelling. Much capital is made of the so-called failure of the schools, and

hints are not wanting as to the incompetence of civilian teachers.' An editorial in *The Times Educational Supplement* of 6 September 1941 had this to say: 'However far-reaching reforms may be effected in the education system after the war, it will still remain a primary aim of any curriculum that is evolved to enable all pupils to use and understand their native language with ease and accuracy. That we are as yet far from realizing that aim is all too painfully evident ... large numbers of children leave school incapable of the simplest oral narrative – much less of sustaining an oral argument – and without the least idea of how to comprehend – much less to assess the value of – any reading matter which demands anything in the way of mental effort.'

35 'The Education of Illiterate Adults' in the *British Journal of Educational Psychology* vol. 15, 1945, p. 21.

36 See Lewis, *The Importance of Illiteracy*. Note also the quotation from Professor J. W. Tibble in [Wright, op cit.] chapter 6, p. 114 above.

37 *Half Our Future*, (The Newsom Report), (Ministry of Education, 1963) p. 5.

38 The attitude of many middle-class people in the 1950s to secondary modern pupils is nicely captured in James Barlow, *Term of Trial* (Hamish Hamilton, 1961).

39 This question of expectations is a complex one. While the 'public in general' may have high expectations of the schooling system, the achievement of pupils is significantly limited by what teachers expect of them. See Roy Nash *Teacher Expectations and Pupil Learning* (Routledge and Kegan Paul, 1976).

40 This view is not supported by the empirical evidence. See Bill Jordan, *Poor Parents: Social Policy and the 'Cycle of Deprivation'* (Routledge and Kegan Paul, 1974), and Michael Rutter and Nicola Madge, *Cycles of Disadvantage* (Heinemann, 1976).

41 The historical progress of this area of study is described in Harold Silver (ed.) *Equal Opportunity in Education* (Methuen, 1973). In recent years the focus has moved on from simply observing and measuring the relationship between class and school performance, to investigating possible explanations for the relationships. Three areas have received particular attention: language, culture, and the nature of school knowledge. All have produced ample controversy. See [Wright, op cit.] chapter 4, notes 47, 48, 49. See also Nell Keddie, (ed.) *Tinker Tailor: The Myth of Cultural Deprivation* (Penguin, 1973).

42 Centerprise have led the way in encouraging ordinary people to write poetry and prose, particularly autobiography, for publication. Good examples are Ron Barnes, *Licence to Live* (Centerprise, 1974) and Leslie Mildiner and Bill House, *The Gates* (Centerprise, 1975).

43 It needs to be pointed out that criticism of examinations is not something new dreamt up by ultra-progressives. In the first half of this century it tended to be conservatives who opposed exams. In 1911 *The Times*, 5 September) carried a leader which debated whether examinations should be abolished. The view of many at the time was put by P. J. Hartog, who wrote: 'Examinations tend to dig up the plant we wish to grow.' (*The Times*, 9 January 1912). The 1930s saw another rash of opposition to exams. Thus Dr James Steel told the North of England Education conference (8 January 1931): 'I am a rebel to examinations dominating the curricula. The only fitness that examination tests provide is fitness to pass examinations. They do not even test the teacher's work ... their most serious indictment is that they always assume a prescribed norm ...'. The objection to examinations was twofold: first that they were unreliable (P. J. Hartog and E. C. Rhodes *An Examination of Examinations* Macmillan, 1935) and second, that they had a crippling effect on education: 'Standards, right values, the science of good and evil – to implant these is an essential part of education. Many forces thwart this work, but two of the most serious hindrances to it are examinations and specialisation

... The examination system is both an opiate and a poison.' (Sir Richard Livingstone, *Education for a World Adrift* Cambridge University Press, 1943, p. 119). The boot nowadays seems to be on the other foot, and it tends to be only radicals who dare to question the examination system: see, for instance, Tristan Allsop 'Examinations' in Bob Cudihy, Douglas Gowan and Colin Lindsay, (eds.) *The Red Paper* (Islander Publications, 1970). Exams, meanwhile, remain unreliable: see Alan Willmott and Desmond Nuttall, *The Reliability of Examinations at 16-plus* (Macmillan, 1975).

44 William Taylor *The Secondary Modern School* (Faber 1963), pp. 104–105.

45 The Crowther Report (*15 to 18*, Ministry of Education, 1959) put it with magnificent bluntness when it opened with these words (vol. 1, p. 3): 'This report is about the Education of English boys and girls aged from 15 to 18. Most of them are not being educated.' The Crowther Report did much to encourage the already growing trend towards staying on and entering examinations. It recommended that 'rather less than half' of the pupils of modern schools should stay on till sixteen to do either O-Levels or a new public examination designed to cater for that group of pupils who were not quite up to O-Level. This recommendation led ultimately to the CSE (Certificate of Secondary Education) in 1965. This exam was, as Crowther had recommended, controlled at local level (vol. 1, pp. 450–451).

The Debate Over Standards and the Uses of Testing

1.3

Caroline Gipps

Introduction

In this paper I want to concentrate on the notion of standards in education, to look at how testing is used in the school system and whether, or how, testing can raise standards.

The first thing to say is that concern over standards is not the prerogative of the third quarter of the twentieth century. Both the Bullock Report and the Cockroft Report quoted complaints about standards in reading and maths from 60 and 100 years ago respectively.[1] In the USA standardised examinations were being used to *maintain* standards in the 1840s.[2] The interesting thing, of course, is the way standards are nearly always thought to be falling. Public concern over standards comes in waves and is often triggered off by activities outside the world of the classroom. When a cause for poor economic or technological performance is sought, the school system is an easy target.

What Do We Mean By Standards?

'Standards' is a term which is probably more loosely used than any other in education. When we talk about standards we may be referring to levels of attainment in basic skills such as reading and maths, or levels of attainment

Source: Gipps, C. (1988) 'The debate over standards and the uses of testing', *British Journal of Education Studies*; Vol. 26, No. 1, pp. 104–118.

in a much wider range of school activities; we may be talking about standards of provision, e.g., the number of teachers and books per child, or we may be talking about levels of behaviour, dress and other social phenomena. Thus, in the narrowest sense, standards can mean levels of performance on a test, and in the widest sense can encompass notions of social and moral behaviour and discipline as well as educational attainment. It is when defined most widely, moving into the area of general values, that it is most prone to subjective and anecdotal use. The link between the narrow and wide uses of the term is tenuous, but one that is often made. In the minds of the general public, a decline in standards of dress and 'moral' behaviour, which may well be due to changing social and cultural conventions, is likely to be linked with a perceived decline in educational standards. The fact that many members of the public seem to feel that educational standards are falling (despite evidence to the contrary from, e.g. the DES School Leavers Survey)[3] is one to which educationists must face up. In the current climate, when consumerism is the dominating educational ideology,[4] parents', employers' and politicians' opinions about standards are vitally important.

History should have warned us that the view that standards are declining would provide politicians with the impetus and rationale for the setting of approved standards (in the form of levels of test performance) in order to ensure quality control. First there was Sir Keith Joseph's objective for GCSE: to bring 80–90 per cent of all 16 year old pupils *at least* (his emphasis) up to the level now associated with that grade of CSE which is currently achieved by average pupils. Now we have Kenneth Baker's benchmarks accompanied by testing (and a national curriculum).

The Director of Education for Croydon has a lot to say on standards:

The establishment of standards, which must be consistent with inter-national expectations, is a necessary condition of the restoration of the commitment to excellence missing from many parts of the education service. In the absence of external standards, pupils and teachers have no alternative but to establish their own. Understandably, these standards are all too often too low ...

Standards will make the education service truly accountable to parents ...

They will also provide the public with a means of measuring the effectiveness of the education system ...

Standards will enable administrators to target their budgets where improvements are needed, instead of, as now, in ways unrelated to any sense or expectation of educational performance: there is little point in comparing levels of expenditure – unit costs, pupil-teacher ratios or class sizes – if no one knows how effectively the money is used ...

The introduction of a national curriculum and universal standards would guarantee equality of opportunity to the pupil, accountability to parents and the public, intellectual rigour to the programme of learning, and enable the education service to be managed in ways which relate financial output to educational output ...[5]

Not only do his comments make the 'establishment of standards' seem immensely sensible, they bring up the difficult issue of how to get a measure of value for money within the educational system. Anathema though such a concept may be to many professionals, it is another issue which we cannot afford to ignore in the 1980s and 1990s. The thorny question is: How do we know that we are getting value for money unless we have some assessment of standards of performance?

As this preamble has indicated, 'standards' always come back in some way to pupil performance, which is in turn assessed by exams or tests. The current debate assumes that testing will somehow raise standards but this is an assumption which needs some discussion. The current talk about benchmarks and national testing programmes makes it sound as though, public examinations apart, there is little testing within the system and certainly that testing children at seven and eleven would be a new development. We have, however, evidence to show that this is simply not true; there is a considerable amount of testing going on in schools at seven, nine *and* eleven and one of the major purposes of this testing has been to monitor standards. We have carried out two surveys which relate directly to this issue and I shall outline the findings in the next section.

THE EXTENT OF TESTING IN LEAs

In 1981 we carried out a survey of all LEAs asking about any testing programmes they had, that is, standardised tests of reading, maths, etc., given routinely to all or part of an age group.[6] We discovered that testing was widespread, with at least 79 per cent of LEAs doing some kind of testing. The breakdown of LEAs which test is given in Table 2.

	London	Metropolitan Boroughs	County Councils	Total No.	%
Testing	18	29	35	82	78.8
Not testing	3	3	7	13	12.5
No information	0	4	5	9	8.7
Total	21	36	47	104	100%

Table 2 *Number of LEAs with testing programmes in 1981*

Table 3 gives a picture of what subjects are being tested and at what ages. We can see from Table 3 that testing at seven to eight is, or was, fairly common. Testing at eleven-plus is even more common than at either seven or eight, and it is at this age that verbal reasoning tests are most used. There was little testing of this sort at 14, though no doubt school exams featured in the lives of this age group. The testing at 13 was often for the purpose of aiding option choice.

	Infant				Junior			Secondary			No. LEAs testing each subject
	5	6	7	8	9	10	11	12	13	14	15	
Reading		1	30	41	15	12	36	2	10	5	2	71
Maths			3	14	7	11	21	3	4	2	3	36
IQ[1]			3	12	5	5	34	1	3			40
English				3	4	5	8	1				10
Test Batteries[2]				2	1	1	2	2	1			4
Spelling							2					2
Infant Checklists	4	5	2									10

Notes
[1] IQ tests include verbal and non-verbal reasoning tests.
[2] Batteries include the Richmond Tests and the Cognitive Abilities Test.

Table 3 *Number of LEAs testing at different ages in 1981*

Towards the end of 1983 we sent another questionnaire to all LEAs, this time asking specifically about screening programmes, that is, tests or checklists given routinely to all or part of an age group with the purpose of identifying children with special educational needs.[7] Again, testing was widespread with 71 per cent of all LEAs having at least one such programme (see Table 4).

	London	Metropolitan Boroughs	County Councils	Total No.	%
Screening	16	24	34	74	71.1
Not screening	4	5	7	16	15.4
No information	1	7	6	14	13.5
Total	21	36	47	104	100%

Table 4 *Number of LEAs with testing programmes in 1983*

Although this might look like a relative decline in the level of testing since 1981 we cannot make this assumption, since in the two surveys we were asking different things: in the second survey we were asking specifically about screening programmes. These tend to be used at younger ages (see Table 5) and to involve reading tests more exclusively.

	Infant			Junior				Secondary			
	5	6	7	8	9	10	11	12	13	14	15
Number of LEAs	18	22	37	36	11	13	28	4	5	0	0

Table 5 *Number of LEAs screening at different ages in 1983*

Yet again, the evidence shows that there is a great deal of testing particularly in the seven and eight year old groups.

THE USES OF TESTING

In our earlier study we asked LEAs why they had these testing programmes and to what uses they were put. The reasons LEAs gave us for introducing testing programmes can be grouped broadly into three categories – political, organisational and professional. *Political* reasons included the atmosphere in the mid to late 1970s at the time of the Great Debate, the Black Papers and the William Tyndale affair, resulting in pressure from members of Education Committees and a desire by some Chief Education Officers to be fore-armed in the event of questions over standards. *Organisational* factors included the ending of the eleven plus, school reorganisation and LEA reorganisation, all leading to a demand for information particularly relating to primary/secondary transfer. Lastly, *professional* reasons included concern over the numbers of children being referred for remedial help – both too large and too small – and concern over, for example, reading standards following publication of the Bullock Report and identification of children with special needs following Warnock. Clearly, apart from the identification of slow learners, 'standards' are and were a prime mover.

These three categories result in testing programmes for three purposes: monitoring, transfer and screening. In this paper I shall concentrate on monitoring programmes, since these relate specifically to the standards theme.

Monitoring is the business of examining *group* scores, where the groups may be classes, school age-cohorts or authority-wide age-cohorts, with a view to making comparisons. A total of 50 LEAs out of 82 from which we obtained information gave monitoring as the sole, or one, reason for one or more of their testing programmes.

Purpose	No. of LEAs	No. testing schemes
Screening only	7	23
Monitoring only	5	22
Transfer only	2	11
Record keeping only	1	10
Allocation of resources only	0	4
Screening + Monitoring + / − other	43	81
Screening + other	16	23
Monitoring + other	2	16
Other	3	13
Total	79	203
No information	3	5

Table 6 *The purpose of LEA testing*

There are predominately *two kinds of monitoring*: monitoring of LEA authority-wide results, which involves comparison with national norms 'to get a general picture of standards', and monitoring of school results which involves comparing schools.

Monitoring does not necessarily imply any particular testing plan and it is not necessary to test all children; comparisons can be made using samples. Indeed most people, with the APU in mind, probably think of monitoring strictly in terms of sampling, or *light sampling* as it is called. In practice, however, most LEAs which claim to be monitoring engage in blanket testing, partly, or perhaps mostly, because they wish to screen at the same time, and also because light sampling of the order of 10 per cent is not thought to provide enough information on which to base inter-school comparisons. This latter feeling is not confined to LEA officers. The head-teachers in schools being tested often prefer to have *all* the relevant age group tested.

The way in which the test results of individual schools are used tends to be private and informal. Commonly each school will receive its own test scores together with those of the LEA as a whole or divisions within the LEA. There may be a visit from the adviser/inspector to discuss the school's results, or there may be discussion at a Heads' meeting. However, our research in schools showed the use of formal meetings to be infrequent.

So we know that LEAs use tests quite extensively to monitor standards in schools, but tend to use the results 'professionally', which means privately.

PUBLIC EXAM RESULTS

By contrast, public exam results are now analysed rather more publicly, particularly in the wake of the 1980 Education Act which requires schools to produce their results for the benefit of parents. The DES analyses these exam results. The English School Leavers Survey – essentially a statistical analysis of exam results – says: 'Taken over the six years (1977/8 to 1983/4) the qualifications of school leavers have shown modest but steady improvement.'[8] But of course this is not proof that 'standards' are rising. Statistics of this kind are virtually meaningless because GCE grading is largely norm-referenced (when grades are awarded on the basis of how a student fares in comparison with other candidates) rather than criterion-referenced (where there is an attempt to compare a student's performance with some 'absolute' standard). If this is the case, the number of passes will increase automatically as the number of candidates rises (to keep the proportion of passes stable) even if the overall performance of candidates does not rise. Nevertheless, the accusation that, for example, A Levels are wholly norm-referenced is vehemently denied by the senior examiners who play the key role of carriers of standards from year to year.

Another problem is that the content of exams is different from year to year and this reflects changes in the syllabus. A Schools Council study of the feasibility of comparing standards of grades awarded in 1963 and 1973 in A Level English literature, mathematics and chemistry (basically by getting 1973 examiners to mark 1963 scripts) concluded that changes in syllabuses and methods of examining over the period made it impossible to draw conclusions about changes in standards.[9] These conclusions effectively disqualify public examination results from being used to make statements about general levels of educational performance.[10] So public exam results are analysed publicly, but cannot be used to comment on standards accurately.

Will the GCSE be any better at telling us whether 'standards' are going up or down? It can only do that, of course, if it becomes a true criterion-referenced examination. Since the development of grade related criteria is causing many problems at the moment, it seems a long way off.

THE ASSESSMENT OF PERFORMANCE UNIT (APU)[11]

We do, of course, have a national assessment programme which was set up with a brief to monitor standards. The APU is a unit within the DES which supervises the national assessment of performance in maths, language, science, modern languages and design for technology. Although the APU was set up at a time of concern over the education of minority children and has as one of its tasks to identify 'under-achievement', in reality its main task, as far as the DES was concerned, was to operate as an indicator of educational standards and to give ministers information on whether, and by how much, these were rising or falling.[12]

The APU has made little progress on its task of providing information on standards and how these are changing, because there is a major technical problem in measuring changes in performance on tests over time. That is, changes large enough to be meaningful will only be detected over a number of years, at least four or five, and any serious monitoring of performance would go on over a longer period than that. For example, the NFER national reading surveys ran from 1948–72.

The problem is that the same test used over that sort of period becomes dated. The curriculum changes, teaching changes, and society changes, thus affecting, for example, our use of language. Thus the test becomes harder and standards will seem to fall. To make the test 'fair' it is necessary to update it, but then you cannot compare the results on the modified version of the test with the results on the original form because it is not a true comparison.

> The problem here is that various statistical techniques are needed to calculate comparable difficulty levels and there is no consensus on which of them is satisfactory. It seems that 'absolute' measures of change over time are difficult if not impossible to obtain and, at most, we can only hope to measure 'relative' – between group – changes.[13]

In the early 1980s the APU had to drop the controversial Rasch technique of analysing difficulty levels of test items and admit that it could not comment on trends over time, i.e., 'standards'. What it does do, however, is use a pool of common items which it deems not to have dated and looks at performance on those over the four years of the original surveys. This gives some guide to what is happening to levels of performance, but the pool will, however, decrease over time.

What the maths work has shown is that, on these items, there has been a small but significant increase in the percentage of children passing at both 11 and 15 between 1978 and 1982. More interestingly, perhaps, what they have also shown is that some sex differences in mathematics performance which are thought to appear at adolescence are, in fact, present at 11. At 11, boys are ahead of girls on measures but behind on computation, while, at 15, boys are ahead on both. The 11 year old finding has not shown up before because standard maths tests usually combine the two elements and report a single score.[14] The reporting of a single score is something the APU teams have by and large avoided on the grounds that there is far more useful information to be gained in looking at performance in different sets of skills or areas of the curriculum. Of course, the problem is that this sort of detailed information is much more difficult to digest and to handle; what many politicians and members of the public would like is a single figure, like the old reading quotient.

We can see that what the APU is doing, therefore, rather than making comments about overall levels of performance or standards, is comparing the performance of sub-groups at points in time, for example, boys and girls, regions of the country and children with different levels of provision of science equipment, laboratory accommodation, etc. This has been one of the main activities of the APU over the last 4–5 years, and could be described as looking at 'relatively low performance', which is the unit's working definition of under-achievement.

Although the APU can only make the most tentative comments about changes in levels of performance in the way that the general public, if you like, would expect, its results can be used to give hard facts about what children of 11 and 15 can do in certain subjects. For example, when the Chairman and Chief Executive of Jaguar Cars claimed that of the young people applying for apprenticeship a third 'couldn't even add up six plus nine', the Deputy Director of Education for Coventry responded by pointing out the disparity between this comment and the findings of the APU. After all the APU had reported that 94 per cent of 15 year olds could add two *four-digit* figures.[15] The same article reported the Minister for Information Technology as saying 'Schools are turning out dangerously high quotas of illiterate, innumerate, delinquent unemployables'. The appraisal of the findings of the APU Language Team reported, however, that 'No evidence of widespread illiteracy was discovered. On the contrary the evidence is that most pupils have achieved a working literacy by the age of 11' and 'No collapse of standards was discovered. Over the five years of the surveys, improvements in the performance of primary pupils was evidenced, while secondary performance remained "fairly static".'[16] There is, of course, always room for politicians to ignore the data if it does not suit them, and for educationists to argue over its meaning.

To try and sum up this section, we must conclude that, although there is a great deal of testing and examining in the school system, it can only provide us with limited information on standards of performance. This is for a number of reasons: at LEA testing level because of the limited number of subjects covered, and private/professional use of results; at public exam level because of the norm-referenced approach which does not permit measure of 'absolute' standards; at national level because of the difficulties in analysing tests which have to change in content over extended periods of time. However, the current emphasis of the Government seems to be to use tests to *set* (and raise) standards rather than to measure them.[17]

USING TESTS TO SET STANDARDS

The idea that tests can measure standards in education is one thing. The idea that testing can raise standards is quite another, yet this has received even less critical attention. The implicit belief among some of those who are concerned about standards is that introducing a testing programme will raise standards. The publication of exam results was seen as being one way of maintaining standards, an argument foreshadowed in a leaflet produced by the National Council of Educational Standards.[18] This essay suggests 17 ways of 'improving standards in our schools' including monitoring through tests, exams, and HMI full inspections, the results of which should all be made public. The connection between testing and improved performance is, however, rarely made explicit. The stimulus (testing) is applied and the outcome (improved test performance) hoped for, but the process linking the two remains largely undiscussed; it is the 'black box' metaphor.

There are, however, various hypotheses about how the introduction of testing might result in improved test performance. At a general level there is the possibility that accurate estimates of performance levels will stir reaction (and reform) that will in turn lead to higher levels of performance.[19] This reaction may take several forms:

1 It may result in teaching to the test, which is quite likely to result in improved performance on the test, as an American newspaper quote illustrates below, but if test results rise as a consequence of teaching to the test rather than as a consequence of some other change in the classroom process, what is such a rise worth?

2 It can focus attention on the subject area being tested. At the primary level we do know that in some cases heads have insisted on reading being timetabled for the fourth year classes, because LEA tests have been introduced for this age. We also know that, in an authority which tests maths at 11 using items from a bank, some teachers are quite open about spending more time on maths than they would otherwise choose to and/or of making certain that they cover the specified areas. But the latter could also be true, of course, of LEAs which have maths guidelines – it is not necessarily a consequence of testing programmes.

3 Curriculum backwash may occur: that is, test content may have an impact on teacher practice. We know that advisers choose certain tests because they want teachers to move their teaching in a certain direction. For example, the Edinburgh Reading Tests have been chosen by some LEA advisers, not only because of their diagnostic element, but also because they promote a wider view of reading which advisers would like to see their teachers embrace. Also, some advisers we have spoken to are frankly delighted with the content of the APU maths and science tests and wish them to affect the curriculum of their teachers, as did some of the head-

teachers in our sample. This is an example of what we would call 'positive backwash'. The received notion has been that backwash is bad, mostly on the grounds that tests concentrate on only a small part of the curriculum and the danger is that too much time can be spent in preparing for them. But the message we have also received from advisers and heads is that, sometimes, tests can be used as an engine of covert curriculum reform in order to enrich the curriculum, and certainly some of the APU test developments seem to have had this effect.[20]

4 Knowledge of results can have an impact. We know that it is common practice where results are analysed centrally for heads to receive their school's mean score each year together with the authority or division mean score. If their mean score on a test is very different from that of the authority as a whole or from their own score last year, the head may well encourage staff to direct more attention to that subject, and we do know that this happens.

Two quotes from both sides of the Atlantic illustrate some of the problems which can be associated with testing. The first is from a local paper in California, the second from the Cockroft Report.

'Teaching to Test' Credited with Improvements in Basic Skills. Students in San Diego County public schools scored better this year on every phase of the state's annual battery of basic skills tests, especially in districts gearing their curriculum to fit the exams ... The lesson many school districts have drawn ... is that if a school system wants to score high it should 'teach to the test'. 'That doesn't mean they're cheating', said Pierson (pupil services director) 'But they are moulding their curriculum to fit what the CAP tests'.[21]

The availability of tests, however well-constructed, would not of itself lead to the increase of mathematical understanding ... we seek. We are well aware of the dangers of subjecting pupils to more, and more frequent, testing and we accept that the combination of certain kinds of testing and teaching could produce results which are the opposite of those we desire.[22]

Thus the introduction of testing, whether LEA programmes such as those that already exist or new programmes to assess benchmarks, will not of itself bring about raised levels of performance, short of teaching to the test. It needs to be coupled with other moves to encourage enhanced performance, for example changes in teaching methods or content, or the provision of extra resources.

CURRENT DEVELOPMENTS

At the local level the London Borough of Croydon is a particularly interesting example. Children there are tested on maths and reading at seven, nine and eleven, with non-verbal reasoning tests at nine as well. This testing programme was introduced in 1985 with much opposition from the teaching unions. The LEA's parents' guide 'Primary Education in Croydon' sets out aims and objectives for primary schools. The guide states that the children are given the tests so that 'their performance can be measured against set standards'.[23] Ultimately the LEA plans to introduce tests in other subject areas, linked closely with curriculum guidelines, in order to produce a profile of each child in all areas of the curriculum at seven, nine, eleven and fourteen.

However, for the moment schools are judged on this limited range of performance and each school's results reported to the Education Committee. Each (named) school is given a profile including the number and percentage of pupils scoring above or below the Croydon mean. On this basis year-by-year comparisons are made within a school and between schools. Any school which has interesting scores – that is particularly high or low, or which vary considerably from those of neighbouring schools – is visited by the inspectorate.

This then is the new form of LEA testing programme and it differs in a number of significant respects from those we observed five years ago. First, although the tests are the same – short, standardised and only covering the basic skills – they are linked to defined (albeit loosely) objectives for different ages. Secondly, there is the intention to link the assessment with detailed curriculum guidelines, rather than to let them 'float free'. Finally, named school results are presented to the Education Committee and selected schools are followed up by formal visits from inspectors.

There are those who see in this a reductionist approach to education which limits the teacher's professional role and imposes an unacceptable burden of testing on young children; while there are others who see it simply as good sense, good management and the best way of providing accountability to parents.

The effect of this assessment and curriculum package on schools and children will be keenly observed, not least by the parents and teachers in Croydon. It is too soon yet to know how it will turn out or how many other LEAs will adopt a similar approach. Interestingly, the London Borough of Brent announced in 1986 that they were going to set attainment targets in the basic skills for their primary children because of concern about under-achievement. The LEA will then draw up guidelines setting out what should be achieved in teaching basic skills.[24] Thus we have two London boroughs, Croydon and Brent, which are politically very different, but making similar moves.

However, many LEAs may be holding back from developing new assessment programmes until it is clear what the DES intends to do about bench-marks and their assessment.

In October 1986 Mr Baker, Secretary of State for Education, said that he wished to see attainment targets for children of different ages developed on the grounds that they would help pupils to achieve the best performance they were capable of.[25]

Mr Baker's comments can be foreshadowed in Eric Bolton's (Senior Chief HMI) comments in November 1985:

> Much of the work on assessment and evaluation to date is biased towards the secondary phase. We lack broad agreement about how to describe and scrutinise the primary curriculum. The absence of clarity and agreement about what children should be capable of at various stages of their primary education leads to a distinct lack of information about standards of pupil achievement in individual primary schools and a consequent difficulty of establishing any standards of achievement as a basis for an assessment of performance.[26]

The blue-print for a national curriculum now includes attainment targets which take account of the need to differentiate between pupils of diverse abilities and aptitudes.[27] As Lawton points out:

> an essential feature of the Baker plan is to have age-related benchmark testing. This has all sorts of bureaucratic advantages in terms of pres-entation of statistics and making comparisons between teachers and schools. But age-related testing makes it very difficult to avoid normative procedures, norm-related criteria, and judgements based on the expec-tations of how a statistically-normal child should perform.[28]

There has been a considerable amount of concern voiced over the effect of testing children and labelling some as failures. Mr Baker does not seem concerned about this, however:

> In his conference speech he poured scorn on the non-competitive schooling advocated by Left-led Labour authorities . . . 'It has become rather unfash-ionable to give tests to children today because there is the belief that that segregates the winners from the losers,' he said. Parents knew such an approach was bogus.[29]

It is not at all clear what form the assessment of attainment targets – or as they are now more commonly called benchmarks – will take, particularly since some HMI now seem concerned about whether benchmarks would be helpful, and about the dangers of introducing a national testing programme. To add to the confusion the former chief HMI for primary education, who thinks that widely accepted benchmarks would be helpful, has said that they do not need to be followed by mechanical testing.[30]

Murphy has considered the implications of assessing a national curriculum[31] and I have already covered much of the ground in this paper. However, in addition to the concerns over teaching to the test and narrowing the curriculum to what is testable, I believe one of the most worrying aspects of the attainment targets plan is the suggestion that they be differentiated. No doubt this is meant to reduce the amount of failure young children will be exposed to. But the implication is that children will be categorised (and streamed?) from the age of seven and this will have profound implications, not only for the children, but for the nature of primary education.

CONCLUSION

To summarise, attainment targets, benchmarks and their assessment, are in the melting pot at the moment. It is hard to predict their eventual form, or what LEAs will do to set up their own testing programmes, but clearly testing is firmly on the agenda to set and raise standards. What I hope to have made clear in this paper is that to use testing to set, raise, or measure standards is not as straightforward a task as some would have us believe.

ACKNOWLEDGMENTS

I should like to thank Harvey Goldstein and Richard Pring for their helpful comments on a draft of this Chapter.

NOTES

1 *Education*, 2 July 1982.
2 D. P. Resnick (1980), 'Educational policy and the applied historian: testing, competency and standards', *Journal of Social History*, June.
3 *Times Educational Supplement*, 27 June 1986.
4 D. Lawton (1987), 'The role of legislation in educational standards', *NUT Education Review*, 1, 1.
5 *Sunday Times*, 12 April 1987.
6 C. Gipps, S. Steadman, T. Blackstone, and B. Stierer (1983), *Testing children: standardised testing in Local Education Authorities and schools*, London, Heinemann Educational.

7 C. Gipps, H. Gross and H. Goldstein (1987), *Warnock's 18%: Children with special needs in the primary school*, Lewes, Falmer Press.
8 *Times Educational Supplement*, 27 June 1986.
9 T. Christie and G. M. Forrest (1980), *Standards at GCE A-level: 1963 and 1973*, London, Macmillan Educational Books.
10 H. Goldstein (1986), 'Models for equating test scores and for studying the comparability of public examinations', in D. Nuttall (ed.), *Assessing Educational Achievement*, Lewes, Falmer Press.
11 Some of this section is taken from the author's paper 'The APU: monitoring children?', *NUT Education Review*, 1, Spring.
12 C. Gipps and H. Goldstein (1983), *Monitoring children: An evaluation of the Assessment of Performance Unit*, London, Heinemann Educational Books.
13 H. Goldstein (1983), 'Measuring changes in educational attainment over time: problems and possibilities', *Journal of Educational Measurement*, 20, 4, Winter.
14 Cambridge Institute of Education (1985), 'New perspectives on the mathematics curriculum: an independent appraisal of the outcomes of APU mathematics testing 1978–82', London, HMSO.
15 *Times Educational Supplement*, 16 May 1986.
16 G. Thornton (1986), 'APU language testing 1979–1983: an independent appraisal of the findings', London, HMSO, pp. 71 and 78.
17 *Times Educational Supplement*, 10 April 1987.
18 V. Bogdanor (1979), *Standards in Schools*, National Council for Educational Standards.
19 H. Acland (1981), 'Beliefs about testing: the case of the NAEP', University of Southern California, unpublished paper.
20 C. Gipps (1987), 'The APU: from Trojan Horse to Angel of Light', *Curriculum*, 8, 1.
21 San Diego Union, California (1982), 'County Students Improve CAP Scores', 2 December, p. B-1.
22 W. H. Cockroft (ed.) (1982), *Mathematics counts: Report of the committee of inquiry into the teaching of mathematics in schools*, London, HMSO, para. 552.
23 Croydon LEA (1985), 'Primary Education in Croydon', Croydon LEA, p. 9.
24 *Times Educational Supplement*, 1 August 1986.
25 *Times Educational Supplement*, 3 October 1986.
26 *Times Educational Supplement*, 22 November 1985.
27 SCDC (1987), 'Towards a national curriculum: a response to initiatives on the need for a national curriculum', SCDC, March.
28 *Times Educational Supplement*, 1 May 1987.
29 *Daily Telegraph*, 9 February 1987.
30 *Times Educational Supplement*, 20 February 1987, 8 May 1987, and 21 April 1987.
31 R. Murphy (1987), 'Assessing a national curriculum', *Journal of Educational Policy*, Autumn.

MATHEMATICAL ATTAINMENTS: COMPARISONS OF JAPANESE AND ENGLISH SCHOOLING

1.4

S. J. PRAIS

[...]

THE IEA COMPARISONS AT AGES 13–14

Scientifically-organised international comparisons of mathematical attainments of secondary school pupils were carried out in 1981 among some two dozen countries, and in 1964 among a dozen countries by the International Association for the Evaluation of Educational Achievement (IEA). At both dates Japan appeared well ahead of England (and, indeed, ahead of almost all other countries). Japan was also well ahead of England in tests of school attainments in science carried out by the IEA in 1970. The seriousness of the disparities emerging from these comparisons have been inadequately noticed by economists; the disparities shown by the earlier comparisons continue to be of important practical consequences today, since pupils who were then at school are now in the central ages of the workforce of each country, and affect each country's technical efficiency.

Provisional findings of the 1981 survey have been published, but for detailed comparisons at present it is necessary to go back to certain of the 1964 tests. These were based on a set of some 70 internationally agreed mathematical questions which were put to representative samples of 3200 pupils in England and 2050 pupils in Japan, with an average age of $13\frac{1}{2}$ in both countries; the English pupils obtained an average correct score of 19.3, and Japanese pupils an average of 31.2.[1] The tests were carried out at that

Source: Prais, S. J. (1986) Educating for productivity: comparisons of Japanese and English schooling and vocational preparation, *Compare* Vol. 6, No. 2, pp. 121–147.

age because it was the oldest age at which virtually all pupils in most countries were still at school.

How many years of additional schooling might it have taken to bring the average English pupil to the Japanese level? An approximate answer can be obtained by referring to a parallel sample of pupils, tested in England as part of that study, who were ten months older on average than the sample mentioned above; they obtained an average score of 23.8, that is 4.5 points higher.[2] At that rate of progress, if it could be maintained, it would take English pupils about two years' extra schooling – that is, till they were nearly 16 years old – before they reached the average score of $13\frac{1}{2}$ year-old Japanese pupils.

As in the ancient race between the tortoise and the hare, the Japanese will not have stood still in that interval. Any more complex calculation must bring into account that the Japanese start compulsory schooling over a year later than the English;[3] hence, what Japanese pupils learn of mathematics in their first *seven* years of schooling (between the ages of five and thirteen) would have required nearly 11 years in England (between the ages of five and sixteen). In other words, the Japanese seem to learn their mathematics 50% faster per annum of schooling; by the time they reach the age of sixteen it is thus to be expected that they might be even further ahead.

These are of course only hypothetical calculations, intended to yield a more easily understood indication of the order of magnitude of the gap between the two countries. In reality, low-attaining pupils in English comprehensive schools have often become so discouraged by the age of 14–16, that further schooling along existing lines is no longer a realistic way forward.

Another important feature of the success of the Japanese schooling system is that it managed to reach relatively more equal attainments than the English system: the coefficients of variation of the scores were 78% in England, 54% in Japan (similar to Germany's 46%). As a consequence there were fewer very low achievers in Japan; for example, only about 8% of Japanese pupils attained scores below those attained by the lowest 25% of English pupils. England had the largest percentage of pupils with a score of five points or less (out of a maximum 70) of the ten countries compared in that study.[4] Amongst pupils who did best in those tests (with a score of 61 points or over) England did not do too badly, coming second behind Japan (1.4% of pupils in Japan, 0.7% in England). There is thus apparently a greater relative backwardness amongst low-attainers in England – a conclusion also reached in our previous comparisons with Germany.[5]

Information so far available from the more recent IEA mathematical comparisons indicates little change in the relative position of Japan and England. Japanese pupils in 1981 attained an average score of 62% correct answers at an average age of 13 years and 4 months compared with England's average of 47% at an average age of 14 years and 1 month.[6]

Some simple examples from the 1981 comparisons help to convey the nature of the gap between the countries. Adding two simple fractions, $\frac{2}{5}+\frac{3}{8}$

was correctly answered by 89% of Japanese pupils, but by only 42% of English pupils. Multiplying two negative integers,

$$(-2) \times (-3),$$

was correctly carried out by 85% of Japanese pupils, but by only 45% of English pupils. A simple algebraic question, find x if

$$5x + 4 = 4x - 31,$$

was answered correctly by 58% in Japan and 22% in England.

The greater variability of scores in England in 1981 was as evident as in the previous survey; the coefficient of variation was 46% in England, and 28% in Japan. Marks as low as those obtained by the lowest quarter in Britain were obtained by only approximately the lowest 7% in Japan.[7]

The Japanese tested their pupils both towards the beginning and end of their first year in Junior Secondary Schools (in May 1980 and February 1981) on similar questions; at the end of the year, when the main test was carried out, the number of correct answers had risen by a quarter.[8] At that rate of progress it may be inferred – on the same basis as above – that Japanese pupils would have attained the average English score when they were just over a year younger, that is, at an age of about 12:3. The pupils in the English sample were nine months older at the time of their tests than those in Japan, making a total gap of just under two years. In these terms the relative position of the two countries was hardly changed after an interval of 17 years.

Nonetheless, a closer comparison restricted to those questions that were identical in both 1964 and 1981 mathematical tests shows a slight advance by Japanese pupils – from 62% to 63% of correct answers; but a fall in the attainments of English pupils – from 50% to 44% of correct answers. England was the *only one of the ten countries* for which these comparisons were possible which showed a fall in average scores in *all* three main components – arithmetic, algebra and geometry.[9] It is possible that the shift in the past twenty years away from traditional mathematics has been greater in England than in Japan and Germany: however that may be, it must be a matter of concern that the overall performance of English pupils is not more distinguished, and that the changes in school curricula in mathematics in England in this period have not borne any obvious fruit when judged by international standards [. . .].

NOTES

1 T. Husen (ed.), *International Study of Achievement in Mathematics* (Stockholm, Almquist & Wiksell, 1967), vol. I, p. 270 (average ages); vol. II, p. 22 (scores). The low average percentage of marks reflects, not an inability to carry out the tests quickly enough, but rather (a) the need to make provisions in the design of the tests to elucidate the proportions in each country who did particularly well, and (b) the diversity of national curricula. The samples compared here are those labelled as 'Population 1a' in that study, and related to pupils in their thirteenth year of age. In our previous comparisons between Germany and England we were obliged to rely on 'Population 1b', which related to all pupils in the class in which the *majority* were aged 13, since Germany did not participate on the alternative basis. Certain non-negligible problems arose in the application of these definitions, and were discussed in Appendix B of our previous paper (Schooling Standards in Britain and Germany, by S. J. Prais and Karin Wagner, *National Institute Economic Review*, May 1985). The Japanese samples appear to have been identical for 'Populations 1a and 1b'; this reflects the assumption that Japanese pupils advance from one class to another purely on the basis of their age. I am told that this is not precisely true and that a pupil may be required to repeat a class if absence (due to illness or injury) is a relevant factor.

2 Population 1b (see preceding footnote), and Husen, ibid., vol. I, p. 271 and vol. II, p. 23.

3 Median age of starting school at the time of that survey was 5 years and 2 months in England, 6 years and 6 months in Japan (ibid., vol. I, p. 227).

4 Husen, vol. I, p. 22.

5 This comparison is based on 'Population 1a' of the IEA study relating to samples of pupils who were all 13 years old. The alternative 'Population 1b' related to pupils from classes in which the *majority* of pupils were 13 years old; it consolingly showed England as having the greatest proportion of top scorers: 2.4% had 61 points or more, compared with 1.4% in Japan. The position at the bottom of the range in 'Population 1b' is barely changed, with 19% of English pupils having 5 or fewer points and 7.6% in Japan. The difficulty with a comparison on the basis of 'Population 1b' is that the English sample was about a year older than the Japanese sample (of footnote 1 above). The good results of the top performers in the Dutch sample in 'Population 1a' have been ignored here because the sample was small (429 pupils), and differed markedly from their 'Population 1b'.

6 Based on a weighted average of the five sub-scores of 137 questions as given in the published report of the 1981 survey by R. W. Phillips, 'Cross national research in mathematics education', in T. N. Postlethwaite (ed.), *International Education Research: papers in honor of Torston Husen* (Oxford, Pergamon, 1986), p. 82.

7 Interpolated from the summary in chart 8.3 of the paper by Professor N. Postlethwaite (President of the IEA) on 'The bottom half in lower secondary schooling', in *Education and Economic Performance* (ed. G. D. N. Worswick; Aldershot, Gower, 1985) p. 96. This chart is based on a maximum mark of 40 relating to the core items in these tests; the coefficients of variation are also on this basis.

8 See (Japan) National Institute for Educational Research, *Mathematical Achievements of Secondary School Students* (in Japanese), Tokyo, 1982; pp. 36–38 give the results for the sixty questions, of which I have taken a simple average.

9 R. A. Garden, the second IEA mathematics study, *Comparative Educational Review* (forthcoming), see Table 8. I have here quoted a simple average of the scores in arithmetic, algebra and geometry.

THE SECOND INTERNATIONAL MATHEMATICS STUDY IN ENGLAND AND WALES: COMPARISONS BETWEEN 1.5 1981 AND 1964

M. CRESSWELL AND J.GUBB

COMPARISONS BETWEEN THE 1981 AND THE 1964 SURVEYS

The international committee decided to include in the tests used in the 1981 survey a number of the items that had appeared in the survey carried out in 1964. It was intended that these 'anchor' items, as they were designated, would afford a comparison between standards of performance on the two occasions.

[...] These data are weighted, that is any discrepancies in the samples have been allowed for. (Weighting is carried out after merging data on each pupil obtained from different tests and questionnaires. This sample is therefore smaller than the total number of pupils for whom test results are on file.)

Source: Cresswell, M. and Gubb, J. (1987) *The Second International Mathematics Study in England and Wales*, NFER/Nelson, Slough, pp. 54–68 (abridged).

FACTORS AFFECTING THE COMPARABILITY OF THE RESULTS

Comparison between the success rates in 1964 and 1981 for the 37 anchor items shows that 29 items obtained significantly lower success rates than in 1964 and one item showed the opposite pattern.

In interpreting the results of this comparison there are various factors that need to be considered. During the period between 1964 and 1981 there have been changes in the content of the mathematics curriculum that are likely to have affected the levels of performance on various items in the test. There were changes also in the test items themselves and in the circumstances in which they were administered that have almost certainly influenced the outcome. [...]

One of the most obvious factors affecting the validity of the comparison is the Opportunity-to-learn. Any differences between the amounts of time that pupils on the two occasions had been able to devote to acquiring the knowledge and skill with which particular test items were concerned would clearly have a bearing on the results.

OPPORTUNITY-TO-LEARN: TIME OF TESTING

The international committee's design for the 1981 survey set fairly wide limits within which the participating countries were allowed to choose the time for administering the tests. In 1964 the testing of third-year pupils (the equivalent of Population A in the 1981 survey) was carried out in July. When the UK Steering Group considered the arrangements for the 1981 survey it was agreed that it would be inadvisable to choose June or July for the time of testing on the grounds that large-scale APU tests were planned for the summer term. [...]

Tests in mathematics, languages and science were to be administered to 11-year-olds in May: and the survey of 13-year-olds in science was scheduled for June. It was already becoming apparent that many schools were finding the volume of APU testing somewhat burdensome and the Steering Group agreed that the imposition of the IEA survey within the same term would meet with considerable resistance and would probably therefore result in an unacceptably high refusal rate. A further factor is that testing late in the summer term clashes with public examinations. These took place on a much larger scale in 1981, after the establishment of the Certificate of Secondary Education (CSE), than was the case in 1964 when O-Level examinations were the only ones taking place. These considerations led to the choice of March 1981 as a suitable time for administering the tests.

This difference in the time of testing meant that the pupils in the 1964 sample were, on average, three months older than those in the 1981 survey. The 1964 sample had thus enjoyed an extra term of teaching, as compared with the 1981 sample, and one, moreover, that must be regarded as of vital importance in that during this final term of the school year a good deal of time is commonly devoted to revision and to the consolidation of what has previously been learned, often as a preparation for internal school examinations. [...]

OPPORTUNITY-TO-LEARN: CHANGES IN THE CURRICULUM

Between the two occasions of testing the secondary school mathematics curriculum underwent such considerable changes – including, for example, the introduction of modern mathematics – that a test appropriate for pupils in 1964 was unlikely to be equally suitable in 1981.

Of the 37 'anchor' items, very few reflect the new approach, and those which look at mathematical structure can be successfully answered using traditional arithmetic and understanding of the use of brackets. It is of course impossible to estimate the size of the effect that curricular changes have had on the generality of items. Nevertheless, it is reasonable to suppose that since, for example, only about one-third of schools today teach purely traditional courses,[1] many of the items would yield different responses in 1981 than they did in 1964.

CHANGES IN THE PRESENTATION OF THE ITEMS

The period from 1964 to 1981 also involved changes in the use of units of measurement, the gradual replacement of Imperial measures with metric ones. Several items are affected, the one most noticeably so being Question 10, in which the units in 1964 were 'feet'. In 1981 the lack of an appropriate metric unit, given the numbers involved, necessitated the use of the abstract 'units'. A number of other items also underwent presentational changes, which may well have affected the results. It should also be noted that it was not possible for the position of the items within test, or the context of the surrounding items to be held constant.

FAMILIARITY WITH THE TYPE OF ITEMS USED

Although the general pattern is for fewer pupils in the 1981 sample to select the correct alternative answer than was the case in 1964, this is not reflected in a higher rate of omission. Indeed, the opposite is the case: the average rate of omission was 2.6 per cent lower in 1981 than for the third-year sample in 1964. More of the sample pupils in 1981 attempted 32 of the 37 items, four items had the same omission rate and only one was left out more frequently in the second survey.

For items showing larger differences in success rate between the 1964 and 1981 samples, it is often the case that one of the distractors (incorrect answers) attracted a larger proportion of pupils in the latter year. For example, Item 2 in the table required an answer to the addition of $\frac{2}{5}$ and $\frac{3}{8}$. The first of the incorrect responses $(A = \frac{5}{13})$ was endorsed by 34 per cent of the 1981 sample, compared with only 19 per cent of the 1964 pupils. In the APU surveys of 11- and 15-year-old pupils no fractions item was responded to in this way by more than a quarter of any of the samples used in ten surveys.

All the 'anchor' items are in multiple-choice format, but the APU ones are not. There is some suggestion that the task of selecting an answer may have been approached differently by the 1981 pupils than by their counterparts in 1964. In the more recent survey pupils were less inclined to omit and more inclined to select incorrect answers, possibly by guessing. The relative familiarity of multiple-choice items to 13-year-olds in 1964 and 1981 is difficult to estimate. In 1964 the widespread use of multiple-choice items both in the 11-plus examination and in revision and practice for it ought to have ensured familiarity for most pupils. In 1981 such familiarity would have depended on the prevalence of such items in internal school examinations unless the local education authority concerned made use of multiple-choice items in tests used for, for example, obtaining data when transfer from primary to secondary education was due.

INTERPRETATION OF THE RESULTS

It is clear from the foregoing that qualifications must be attached to the results of the comparisons based on the performance of the two samples in the 'anchor' items. Changes during the period in the content of the curriculum and changes in the format of the items and their position in the test are likely to have had an influence on the outcome.

Another important factor, the effect of which is difficult to quantify, is the difference in timing of the tests on the two occasions in that the pupils in the 1981 sample had enjoyed three months less secondary schooling than their counterparts in 1964.

It is also of interest to compare the results for 13-year-olds outlined here with those from the APU surveys of 11- and 15-year-olds. The APU surveys were carried out yearly from 1978 to 1982. At age 11 over this period scores improved by about $1\frac{1}{2}$ per cent, and by about 2 per cent at age 15. The APU results are based on hundreds of items rather than the 37 used in common between the IEA studies and provide a much broader and deeper picture of performance over a wide range of mathematical activity. Both the IEA and APU studies involve taking a 'snapshot' of the performance of samples representative of the target age group at selected points in time. The two studies differ markedly in the timespan involved and in the breadth and depth of data used to make comparisons over time.

NOTE

2 Department of Education and Science (1980). *Aspects of Secondary Education in England. Supplementary Information in Mathematics.* London: HMSO.

STANDARDS IN MATHEMATICS: THE PERSPECTIVE OF THE WORKING PARTY ON MATHEMATICS 5–16 FOR THE
1.6 NATIONAL CURRICULUM

NATIONAL CURRICULUM WORKING PARTY

BACKGROUND

1 At the time of the publication of the Group's Interim Report there was a spate of articles in the press about the style and content of school mathematics. The media debate reflected widespread concern in the community about standards, in particular concern that too many children may be leaving school without basic arithmetical skills. This concern, which is of long standing, had been given a new focus by the publication last November of a study which appeared to show a significant decline in standards achieved by pupils in England and Wales in 1981 compared with 1964. The press reports also referred to international surveys, which, it was claimed, showed that the standards of mathematical knowledge and skills of pupils in England and Wales compared unfavourably with those of pupils in West Germany, France and Japan.

2 In his response to our Interim Report, the Secretary of State asked us to take these concerns into account. In particular, he asked us to consider the weight to be given to traditional pencil and paper practice of important skills and techniques, the risks as well as the opportunities which calculators in the classroom offer; and the need to ensure that all pupils on leaving school are equipped with at least a basic numerical competence.

3 We tackled this aspect of our remit from the standpoint that we owe it to ourselves and our children to ensure that they are equipped at school with the knowledge and skills in mathematics that they will need in adult and

Source: National Curriculum Working Party (1989) *National Curriculum Working Party Report*, DES, pp. 5–7.

working life. We began by looking at the available evidence about current standards of achievement in England and Wales compared with standards in other countries. We went on to consider the mathematics which pupils can expect to need as adults in the twenty-first century, both at work and at home. Finally, in the light of this examination, we considered very carefully the place which calculators and other new technology should play in school mathematics. This chapter presents the results of our consideration. It has been informed by visits made by a number of members, on the Group's behalf, to Japan, West Germany, France and the Netherlands. We have also discussed the issues with employers.

STANDARDS

4 Last November the NFER[1] published a report[2] which compared the performance of a sample of 13+ year old pupils in England and Wales in 1981 with the performance of a sample of 13+ year olds, on 37 virtually identical 'anchor' questions in 1964. Average test scores in 1981 were nine percentage points lower than in 1964.

5 The England and Wales survey was part of an international survey of the performance of 13 year olds, involving 20 countries. This has not yet been published, but we have had access to unpublished data which show that the performance of pupils in England and Wales on the items tested ranked some way behind Japan (which came out top) and France.

6 The relatively poor showing of England and Wales in this survey and the apparent decline in our performance between 1964 and 1981, is disturbing. We decided therefore to take a closer look at the data, both to assess the validity of the comparisons and to consider any implications for the design of the new mathematics national curriculum.

7 Our closer examination of the data identified a number of reasons for treating the straight comparisons with some caution. These include:
(a) in England and Wales, schools' response rate to the 1981 survey was less than 50 per cent of those approached;
(b) in England and Wales the 1981 tests were administered in March, three months earlier than in 1964 and crucially before the summer term when much consolidation and revision of previous work is done.

8 A further factor, which is possibly of greater significance than those noted above, is that since the 1960s, the content and style of mathematics teaching has changed, making some of the test items used, which test a narrow range of skills, less appropriate. This factor may have affected a number of countries' results, since the data for ten developed countries, including Japan, show some decline in test scores over the period. The quite widespread pattern of decline reinforces the hypothesis that the emphasis of mathematics syllabuses and teaching had changed over the period. Nonetheless, it remains a matter of concern that the decline recorded for England and Wales is greater than that for any other com-

parable country and shows up on a wider range of items within arithmetic, algebra, geometry and measures.

9 Other factors can be adduced to help to account for the relatively poor England and Wales results. For instance, the amount of time devoted to teaching mathematics to 13+ year olds is significantly lower in England and Wales than in some other countries which participated in the survey, notably Japan, even without taking into account the amount of special coaching which most Japanese pupils receive out of school. The status, pay, supply and qualifications of mathematics teachers in England and Wales compare badly with Japan (though they are on a par with the USA which came out of the international comparisons slightly worse than England and Wales). Perhaps most important of all, international comparisons of single subject performance cannot reflect the diverse aims, traditions and structures of the different education systems involved and the societies in which they are set.

10 However, while these and other factors qualify the straight comparisons between England and Wales and other countries, we cannot afford to be complacent: there is a clear message that at the very least there is room for significant improvement. With increasing technological sophistication it is becoming more and more important for economic survival to raise standards of mathematics attainment of pupils across the whole ability range, so that pupils will be adequately equipped to meet the challenges of life in general and the workplace in particular in the twenty-first century. We must ensure that our workforce is at least as well qualified mathematically as those in other developed countries – and ideally better.

11 We have looked at the 37 'anchor' questions used in both the 1964 and and 1981 England and Wales surveys, referred to in Paragraph 4 above. Many of the questions are testing basic arithmetical knowledge and skills, for example of fractions, the decimal system, percentages, ratios and the metric system.

For example:

Questions (an asterisk indicates the correct response)	% of pupils responding (England and Wales)	
a) The arithmetic average of: 1.50, 2.40, 3.75 is equal to	1964	1981
A 2.40	3	10
B 2.55*	51	36
C 3.75	3	4
D 7.65	26	31
E None of these	11	14

b)

On the scale at the foot of the previous page the reading
indicated by the arrow is between

A	51 and 52	2	2
B	57 and 58	20	33
C	60 and 62	3	3
D	62 and 64	16	19
E	64 and 66*	56	43

c) The value of $2^3 \times 3^2$ is

A	30	2	6
B	36	22	27
C	64	4	5
D	72*	44	35
E	None of these	23	25

12 We are disturbed by the high proportion of the 13-year-olds in the England and Wales sample who did not appear to have mastered these basic skills in 1981. We believe that pupils in this country ought to be aiming for far higher standards than the performance in these surveys – both in 1964 and 1981 – implies. In defining our attainment targets, we have therefore sought to ensure that all pupils are given maximum opportunity and encouragement to learn appropriate basic number skills for life in today's world.

13 It is interesting to recall that the late 1970s was a time of growing concern in this country about standards of mathematics attainment in maintained schools. In July 1977 the House of Commons Education Arts and Home Office Committee spoke of the '*large number of questions about the mathematical attainment of children which need much more careful analysis than we have been able to give during our enquiry*'. It was in response to the Committee's recommendation that the Government, in 1978, set up the Cockcroft Committee of Inquiry into the teaching of mathematics in primary and secondary schools. The Cockcroft Committee completed their report in autumn 1981, just after the survey of that year had been taken. The Cockcroft Report served to highlight and disseminate good practice in our schools. Since its publication, local education authorities (LEAs) and teachers have done a great deal generally to raise standards of mathematics teaching. Government initiatives, through the Education Support Grant and through teacher in-service training grants, have also helped. We are glad to note that there is some evidence that standards in England and Wales have picked up since the late seventies. Evidence from the Assessment of Performance Unit points to a 1.5 per cent increase in performance – over a wide range of items – of 11 year olds between 1978 and 1982 and a two per cent increase over the period for 15 year olds. We must sustain this increase – and continue to improve on it. [. . .]

NOTES

1 National Foundation for Educational Research in England and Wales.
2 The Second International Mathematics Study in England and Wales, published by NFER Nelson.

part two
STRATEGIES FOR EDUCATIONAL EVALUATION
PREPARED BY JANET POWNEY

INTRODUCTION TO PART 2

JANET POWNEY

There is no one way to conduct educational evaluation, nor should there be, given its different purposes and scale of operation. The articles in this section of the Reader have been selected to convey the range of methods, audiences, resources and concerns from a few recent evaluation studies. Walker, in the chapter (abridged) from his book, *Doing Research* (1985), also underlines the need for the way in which evaluation is conducted to be appropriate to the expertise and interests of the evaluator. The methods adopted by two teachers, Burn and McGill, working with their own classes, are necessarily different in scale and method from the DES review of teacher appraisal. They share many common features of the studies by professional evaluators Clift and Stronach, not least the careful, documented observations of school life that provided the research base for the evaluations. Although the accounts have been published, the teachers were themselves their prime audience. By reflecting on practices within their own classrooms and within their own control, they could quickly act upon the analysis and conclusions of their own report. As external evaluators, Clift and Stronach were not empowered to enact their own recommendations and Clift is able to review the fate of his recommendations a year after he presented them. Evaluation is an intrigue of power, influence, survival and vulnerability – a very political activity.

Inspection was the earliest means of monitoring and evaluating public education provision. Increasing importance and resources have recently been given to inspectorial functions. A new inspectorate, the Training Standards Advisory Service, was established by the Manpower Services Commission in 1986 to inspect the Youth Training Scheme. The Education Reform Act (1989) has broadened the context in which local authority inspectors complement the work of Her Majesty's Inspectorate. Yet Brian Wilcox argues that its methodologies are still not well understood. Consequently inspectors are not automatically exposed to the critical appraisal of public scrutiny experienced by other researchers.

Evaluation is both a tool and vehicle for change – a tool in the sense that being engaged in an evaluation changes the participants. When we know that some aspect of our professional life is being evaluated, our first reaction is usually to put ourselves forward in our best light. We feel vulnerable, perhaps even threatened. That focuses our own attention on that behaviour or attitude or policy which is being evaluated by outsiders. We become self-reflective and that changes the situation. People are often surprised by how interesting they find an evaluation. It gives them opportunities to discuss areas of concern, of commitment. It may also open up other opportunities – such as enabling the teacher in the art department in Clift's study to meet her head for the first time since she had been appointed.

Evaluations are primarily seen as vehicles for change – to identify whether change is necessary or to monitor the effectiveness of changes already implemented. *Developments in the Appraisal of Teachers* is a timely review of the current state of teacher appraisal. The evidence came from a survey by HMI of six local education authorities' pilot schemes funded by central government and other LEA initiatives. The succinct final commentary focuses on the factors and resources that would encourage feasible, helpful schemes of local and national appraisal. In somewhat provocative terms, Joan Sallis in *Evaluation of Teacher and Pupil Performance* suggests evaluation should extend beyond professionals in education. Parents and governors will not only be increasingly important audiences for evaluation; they will also engage in it.

This section of the Reader relates to inspection, institutional self evaluation and teacher appraisal but it would be somewhat arbitrary to separate the readings under such headings. A school or college being inspected will also engage in some institutional self evaluation; staff performance and competence underpin the school profile; institutional self evaluation inevitably contains teacher appraisal – as is evident in both Clift and Stronach. The gender studies by Burn and McGill could be located as self appraisal but also raise questions about institutional policy on equal opportunities.

Evaluation is always unfinished business. It has been likened to a series of snapshots. Maybe evaluators are closer to artists such as Turner who found that before he had completed a landscape, the light had changed and he had to start another. Education, like the sun, moves on (perhaps full circle?) and evaluators portray images to help our understanding and improvement of ephemeral situations. To examine the strategies used is not merely to be concerned with technicalities. Methodology becomes in Walker's terms 'an intrinsic part of the project' determining what is and is not possible.

2.1 | METHODS: ISSUES AND PROBLEMS

ROB WALKER

SOME PRELIMINARY DEFINITIONS

The terms 'method', 'technique' and even 'methodology' tend to be used interchangeably. In order to clarify what follows it is useful to restrict the use of the term 'methodology' to its strict meaning as denoting 'the logic of methods'. It is in this sense not strictly appropriate to refer to 'qualitative methodology' except when the intention is to refer to the relation between particular methods and their context of use. A 'methodology' should specify methods but only in order to justify their use for defined purposes in specified situations and circumstances. It is in this sense both a higher-level and more abstract term – concerned with issues of meta-method – and a more specific term in that its context of use requires elaboration and justification.

Between 'method' and 'technique' it is more difficult to draw a demarcation. Some people use the term 'method' to specify research recipes and use 'technique' to refer to the detailed practice of these strategies. Hence, observation, interviews and questionnaires would be methods, while check-lists, multiple choice questions and interaction analysis would be techniques. Others use the word 'technique' to describe strategies and 'methods' to refer to a rather more general level of discussion (hence, 'statistical methods' or 'research methods').

The distinction is obviously a difficult one to make and perhaps always arbitrary. Precise definition is not necessary so long as you realise that the terms are used somewhat loosely and that there is considerable variety of usage in different texts and in different discussions. Here I will try to restrict

Source: Walker, R. (1985) *Doing Research*, Methuen, London, chapter 3 (abridged).

myself to using 'methods' more generally, and use 'technique' to describe research recipes.

MAKING APPROPRIATE SELECTIONS

A key decision in any research project involves the selection of methods. It is a decision that is usually made early in the life of a project, and once made not easily reversed, though it may be enhanced by the later addition of supplementary methods.

In most textbook discussions it is assumed that the selection of methods is made on a rational basis. Given the research problem, what is the best way to set about creating relevant research data? In practice decisions are rarely so clearly defined as this implies. As we have seen, 'research problems' do not often present themselves ready-made from educational practice. They have to be worked on, reformulated and worried over before they take on a conformation that makes them amenable to a research approach. Even at this stage where the problem is formulated in research terms and a research design can be created, the 'real' problem may not emerge with any clarity until the data appear and some preliminary interpretation is made. In this sense the strict logical progression which a rational approach suggests, and which often appears in texts on research in one form or another, is inappropriate (see diagram on p. 67).

Emphasising the sequence from problem formulation to empirical testing and then to explanation not only reduces the significance of the 'pre-world' of problem formulation, but as I have suggested does not allow for the fact that, in practice, the choice of particular methods may predate the existence of the research problem. Selection of methods may be an act of faith rather than a rational response to a clearly formulated problem.

The method may even be an intrinsic part of the problem, rather than extrinsic and disconnected from it. Just as recipes are not simply things that are done to food, but become concepts within which method and substance are compounded, so 'method' in research can become an intrinsic part of the project.

The methods we choose to use are, in this sense, there to be tested, just as much as the substantive hypotheses.

This is reinforced by the fact that we tend, as researchers, to favour some methods rather than others. Just as an instrumentalist will not change from playing the clarinet to playing the trumpet because a particular piece demands it, but will instead usually turn to another piece of music, searching for pieces that suit both the instrument and the player, so researchers generally give a lot of time and thought to the formulation of possible and potential research problems, looking for those that appear to fit their interests and preferred methods. Occasionally they will venture into new areas, but more often they

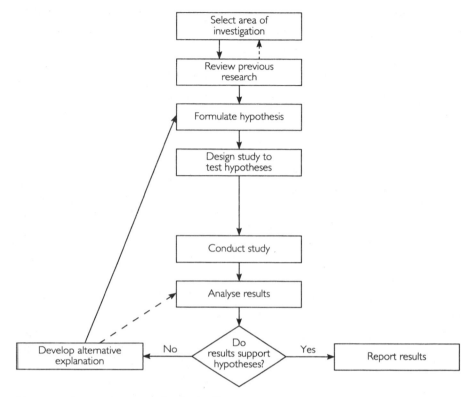

Figure 1 *Research process 'by the book'*

Source: Boehm, 1980, p. 496.

will have a series of methods and approaches up their sleeves, some tried, some untried and awaiting testing. That methods go in search of problems is no surprise: it is after all the basis of most research in science, and it is in methods that most professional researchers vest their experience.

This presents particular problems for the applied researcher or evaluator who attempts to work at and from starting points and concerns presented by others outside the research community. In such cases it may be necessary to work with unfamiliar methods or with one where you lack expertise and are unsure of your judgment as to what can and cannot be done. [...]

The list of available methods needs extending, however, beyond the rather basic and conventional list that the Ford Teaching Project provides. Nick Smith, of the North West Regional Educational Laboratory in Oregon, has recently investigated a much wider range of possible sources for research and evaluation methods. The 'Research on Evaluation Program' has come up with an impressive and surprising range of possibilities. The catalogue of reports available from the project includes thirty-eight distinct and different methods ranging from those involving elaborate statistical techniques through to literary criticism and water–colour painting. A sample of the catalogue is given here as an illustration, including the full contents page and two examples of data collection and analysis strategies.

REVISED CATALOGUE OF METHOD DESCRIPTIONS

Data collection and analysis strategies
  1 Assignment models
  2 Transportation models
  3 Dynamic programming
  4 Queueing theory
  5 Minimum–maximum goal projection
  6 Geocode analysis
  7 Trend surface analysis
  8 Social area analysis/ecological analysis
  9 Concept analysis
 10 Thematic matrix analysis
 11 Document analysis
 12 Legislative history
 13 The key interview
 14 Interviewing: circling, shuffling and filling
 15 Documenting files and summaries
 16 Cost–benefit analysis
 17 Cost–effectiveness analysis
 18 Cost–utility analysis
 19 Cost–feasibility analysis

Sampling strategies
 20 Blanket sampling
 21 Shadow sampling
 22 Time–based sampling
 23 Event–based sampling
 24 Dimensionally based sampling

Reporting strategies
 25 Research briefs
 26 Appeals procedures
 27 Storytelling
 28 Compelling the eye
 29 Representation of reality
 30 Accurate, sharp descriptions
 31 Graphic displays
 32 Stem and leaf displays and box plots
 33 Still photography
 34 Oral briefings

35 Briefing panel presentations
36 Adversary hearings
37 Committee hearings
38 Television presentations of hearings

[...]

MULTIPLE METHODS, TRIANGULATIONS AND TRIADS

It is important to consider ways in which methods and techniques might be mixed and interrelated. Indeed in many projects the most significant findings have emerged from points at which different methods have complemented each other. For example, in a recent study of bilingual education (MacDonald and Kushner, 1983) an attempt was made to study issues inside one school by means of participant observation, and in the arena of city politics and educational administration through a series of interviews. The choice of methods, participant observation within the school and interviewing outside it, was used to search for continuities across a natural divide within the system.

In a rather different field, a fascinating study by Robert Faulkner has looked at the occupation of the freelance composer of musical film scores in Hollywood (Faulkner, 1982). Faulkner began with a series of interviews with composers which provided him with an initial understanding. (Strictly speaking this is inaccurate, since, as a musician himself, Faulkner already had an initial understanding from the inside.) While the interviews provided him with an interesting set of data, this raised a number of questions that needed pursuing further. In particular the composers talked about their relationships with producers and directors, who in terms of the process of film-making come together in the editing rooms at the point where the music is dubbed on to the sound track of the film. Faulkner found he had to switch to an observational mode of research in order to look more closely at the nature of this collaboration, which had come to his notice through the interviews. Later he had to return again to interviewing when he found that a statistical and documentary study of film credits led him to certain interpretations about the 'market' for composers in the film industry. This set of interviews was rather different from the first set, for instead of attempting to see the occupation from a subjective viewpoint, he was trying out interpretations that had arisen from observation and analysis.

The subject of this study might seem obscure to the educational researcher, but the principle of working from a number of different methods and inter-relating them, which Faulkner calls a 'triad', is an important one that is often appropriate in education investigations. Faulkner describes it generally:

A triad mode of data collection involves carrying out a sequential step-by-step testing and discovery of ideas, hunches, hypotheses. The imagery is one of a loosely linked, interdependent set of strategies. It involves, of course, the selection and explicit definition of research problems, concepts, and indices. It involves frequent checking on the distribution of phenomena – an explicit parameter estimation operation. It also involves the development of provisional hypotheses and a controlled but relaxed (and ecumenical) approach to nailing down the relationship among variables. Multiples in data collection – a triad of, for instance, *observation, interviewing, and archives* or records – stimulate (one hopes) complexity and subtlety of insight. A Triad advocates a distinctive stance toward qualitative and quantitative information, namely, that it takes multiples and complexity in the data collection to capture and preserve multiples in the phenomenon of interest (i.e., industries, organizations, careers). A taste for improvisation in the simultaneous use of a Triad may keep one's enthusiasms pitched at moderate to high levels, may overcome defensiveness toward any single mode of data collection, may increase playfulness with respect to the object of study, may boost estimates of error contained in any single source of data, may cross-validate measures of the phenomenon, and may break the singular focus toward a problem that often accompanies monomethod research.

My enthusiasm for multimethod inquiry was acquired during my study of career development in this high performance industry. [Hollywood film score composers.] The strategic strengths and advantages of multimethod inquiry stand on three legs that I have called a Triad. Each leg represents a unique mode of data collection: one from interviews with both informants and respondents; the second from observation of people at work; and the third from documents, records and archives of the organization or industry in question. Each leg presents the researcher with a different vantage point. While it may be useful to focus extensive time and energy on one mode, the advantages of moving sequentially across all three are formidable.

(Faulkner, 1982, pp. 80–1)

A similar example of multiple methods being used, but in educational research, comes from a study I carried out into the work of school inspectors (Walker, 1982). Like Faulkner I began by observing inspectors at work, travelling with them on 'typical days' and writing up descriptive accounts of 'a day in the life' kind. These I gave back to the people concerned and their responses provided the basis for interviews. At a later date they would often ask me to observe them on particular visits because they wanted a third person account. ('I'm going to a school next week that really puzzles me; why don't you come along?' or, 'I am not sure about my relationship with the head of F— School; if you came too you could tell me what you thought.') Such initiatives provided the focus for a visit that might or might not prove to be the focus of part of the research, but it lent a purpose and provided an intention which allowed the research to proceed in a more focused fashion.

Faulkner would perhaps reserve the term 'triad' for cases where there is a degree of separation between the methods used; the term more commonly used for the close intercutting between methods is 'triangulation'. Triangulation was advocated by Webb *et al.* (1966) in their often quoted book *Unobtrusive Measures*. Like Faulkner they saw the use of multiple methods as providing a basis for research in which the whole was stronger than the sum of the parts. By combining methods to a single purpose it was possible to observe the same events from several points of view – to 'triangulate' in order to fix more accurately a position. Triangulation was used by the Ford Teaching Project, mentioned earlier, in the more specific sense of looking at classroom events from the three points of view of the observer, the teacher and the children. The Ford T booklets, *Three Points of View in the Classroom* and *The Tins*, describe and illustrate the approach in more detail.

The 'triangulation' approach developed by Ford T begins to do something rather different from the kind of triangulation advocated by Webb *et al.* Their formulation was based on positivist assumptions and in the accounts they give it is clear that the reality that concerns them is seen as existing outside the observer and the methods. In Ford T you begin to get a more phenomenological perspective, for in the triangulations they present the 'reality' comes to be seen as located in the different perceptions and suppositions of teachers, pupils and observers. The events are still there, but the paradoxes and ambiguities that arise between different points of view are less easily arbitrated or resolved. It is an approach that begins to take on some of the characteristics of the analyses of the families of schizophrenic adolescents 'treated' by R. D. Laing and his colleagues (see, for instance, Esterson, 1970). In these studies, which proceed through multiple interviews with different members of the family in various combinations with each other, the 'schizophrenia' ascribed to the 'patient' is seen as a response to a situation which contains within it essential contradictions. The person who finds herself at the centre of very different perceptions and views, and is faced with organizing them into a reality, can only do so, it is argued, by moving outside what is considered 'normal' behaviour. The triangulation approach is therefore reversed, for instead of looking at one fixed reality from various points in order to describe it more fully, the aim instead is to start from the central event (or person) and to look outwards at the very different perspectives that create its context.

PARTICIPANT OBSERVATION AND ACTION RESEARCH

The power of multiple methods flexibly used should not be underestimated. What might at first sight appear to be not very rigorous methods, such as the open interview and unstructured observation, become much more powerful when used in conjunction with each other. Indeed part of the recent enthusiasm for qualitative methods in educational research stems more from their flexibility than from any other intrinsic merit they possess; for, unlike most quantitative methods, they can be adapted and changed as a project progresses.

It is important to mention participant observation in this respect, for though it is often referred to as a method, it is in fact more accurately described as a *role*. The participant or non-participant observer has access to a number of different methods and techniques which can be flexibly used. You can observe, interview, converse, search documents, collect measures or simply 'hang out'. You can use your research role as an instrument; for example, if in observing a school staff meeting you feel uncomfortable or embarrassed, this in itself may tell you something about the nature of the meeting and what is happening in it. What you feel may relate to how the school feels about your being there, or it may be that your feelings echo what others feel. Either way your feelings, rather than being simply 'noise' in the system, give you a starting point for possible further investigation. Similarly, if, as a woman, you feel ignored, not taken seriously or dismissed by senior staff in the school, this too may tell you something about the character of the school that you can use as a starting point for research. Reinterpreting what may be felt as a personal response into social terms is a process often not acknowledged as a research technique, but it is one that is valuable to learn both for the benefit of research and for self-preservation! The point is that in the reactions you create in a field role, the field reveals something of itself to you; what you have to learn is how to use this information productively. A classic example is given by Barry MacDonald from one of his interviews conducted as part of the Humanities Curriculum Project evaluation:

TEACHER: Don't expect me to tell you anything about the Head.
MACDONALD: You just have.

You might find the suggestion that you use subjectivity in this way in itself unscientific, but there is no reason for not using subjective impressions as starting points for trying to get more conventionally objective data. The point is to select significant questions to pursue, a process which is inevitably one involving judgement, and so equally inevitably a subjective element.

The research project, too, can become its own instrument in a participative study. I described earlier how, in studying the work of school inspectors, I used a process of regular reporting-back to the inspectors in order both to sustain their interest and support for the research and to establish a degree of collaboration in the study. Again there are those who will say that to do this is unscientific since it contaminates the data and may bias the interpretation, so threatening objectivity. There are research problems, and ways of conceiving research, where this is undoubtedly the case; but applied research in education may demand a different conception overall, for in education the distance between those who are the subjects of research and those who execute it is remarkably small. Educational research is, in itself, an educational activity and an educational process. It will often include its subjects in its audience, and so it would seem sensible to design projects and carry them out with learning in mind. This is not to advocate a heavy instructional hand, for to use research as a means of propaganda would be inappropriate, counter-productive and non-educational.

This is an important point which has implications for the selection of problems, issues and topics for research, for if learning is to be built into the research process, it follows that tasks should be chosen where there is considerable, and perhaps continuing, uncertainty on the part of those involved, including the researcher. This too may seem to fly in the face of convention, which tends to see researchers as experts, and research as an activity exclusively carried out by those at the pinnacle of achievement in a field of knowledge. I am suggesting that, on the contrary, research should be carried out by people who do not know the answers to the problems they are investigating, that they should see their learning as involving their subjects in learning too, and that they should avoid foreclosing on recommendations whenever possible. But to state this view at this point is perhaps to run ahead of the text. I mention it here because I want to point to another appealing aspect of participant observation, which is its capacity as a means of learning.

One of the reasons for the widespread use of participant observation in recent years has been because it appears to offer a means of relating research to those in relatively low-status roles in the education system – particularly to teachers, and in a few cases to pupils. (Willis (1977), for example, offers us an appendix in which his book is reviewed by the 'Lads' who are its subject.) Measurement research of the kind conventionally used by educational research in the recent past, relying heavily on testing or survey methods, is invariably directed upwards within education systems. Its designed intention is to affect policy and policy decisions. Thus the work of sociologists of education in the 1950s and 1960s was often specifically intended as an attack on 11-plus selection, an attack formulated in terms of the rhetoric which the system used to defend itself. This research attempted to show that selection, intended to give working-class children access to grammar schools, in fact typically selected in terms of criteria that were primarily of a social class nature.

Such research was, and is, important and I do not want to minimize its significance. It is, however, research that is directed at those, mainly outside schools, who take decisions about what goes on inside. It was this research that created the basis, or at least the language, that in Britain made possible the establishment of a comprehensive secondary school system. It was research that in one sense raised no questions at all about the structure of the decision-taking system, but directed all its efforts to influencing one decision. In that sense it was both successful and limited to one kind of problem, albeit an enduring and important one.

Research that is directed in this way has more or less consciously to adopt a language, a style, and to find friends that lend it credibility. It has to develop a style that is convincing, credible and usable to those who constitute its audience. Carefully selected and well-packaged statistics are a prime case, and indeed in the eyes of many are synonymous with 'research'. Such statistics fit well the dialogues of politicians, administrators, managers and the press. They are less comfortable as part of the natural language of teachers or indeed of anyone else once the spotlight of public attention is turned away.

If the research problem is one that addresses relatively routine aspects of school and classroom practice, and sees teachers, pupils and perhaps parents as being the subjects and the primary audience for the study, then the use of other research forms becomes appropriate. The task, then, is to find forms of reporting and styles of presentation that easily enter the natural language, dialogue and styles of thought of those concerned. The sharp and selective use of statistics will often be inappropriate, as will the clipped and concise civil service style of report, or the heavy language of interpretive sociology. So, too, may be long, unedited transcripts or literally transcribed interviews presented without a helping text. The problem is a difficult and enduring one, and not easily solved. A participant observation role does however offer more of a basis for establishing dialogue between researchers and teachers, pupils and parents, and of providing some basis for making judgements about appropriate styles and forms of reporting, if only because these problems will have reoccurred throughout the research and will be familiar to the researcher. This is why I claim that the decision to adopt a participant observer role may in part be a political decision, for it relates to a decision to report sideways and downwards rather than upwards. Barry MacDonald, in his often quoted typology of evaluation models, terms this a 'democratic' model, to be contrasted with 'autocratic' and 'bureaucratic' models.

BUREAUCRATIC EVALUATION

Bureaucratic evaluation is an unconditional service to those government agencies which have major control over the allocation of educational resources. The evaluator accepts the values of those who hold office, and offers information which will help them to accomplish their policy objectives. He acts as a management consultant, and his criterion of success is client satisfaction. His techniques of study must be credible to the policy-makers and not lay them open to public criticism. He has no independence, no control over the use that is made of his information, and no court of appeal. The report is owned by the bureaucracy and lodged in its files. The key concepts of bureaucratic evaluation are 'service', 'utility' and 'efficiency'. Its key justificatory concept is 'the reality of power'.

AUTOCRATIC EVALUATION

Autocratic evaluation is a conditional service to those government agencies which have major control over the allocation of educational resources. It offers external validation of policy in exchange for compliance with its recommendations. Its values are derived from the evaluator's perception of the constitutional and moral obligations of the bureaucracy. He focuses upon issues of educational merit, and acts as expert adviser. His technique of study must yield scientific proofs, because his power base is the academic research community. His contractual arrangements guarantee non-interference by the client, and he retains ownership of the study. His report is lodged in the files of the bureaucracy, but is also published in academic journals. If his recommendations are rejected, policy is not validated. His court of appeal is the research community, and higher levels in the bureaucracy. The key concepts of the autocratic evaluator are 'principle' and 'objectivity'. Its key justificatory concept is 'the responsibility of office'.

DEMOCRATIC EVALUATION

Democratic evaluation is an information service to the whole community about the characteristics of an educational programme. Sponsorship of the evaluation study does not in itself confer a special claim upon this service. The democratic evaluator recognises value pluralism and seeks to represent a range of interests in his issue formulation. The basic value is an informed citizenry, and the evaluator acts as a broker in exchanges of information between groups who want knowledge of each other. His techniques of data gathering and presentation must be accessible to non-specialist audiences. His main activity is the collection of definitions of, and reactions to, the programme. He offers confidentiality to informants and gives them control over his use of the information they provide. The report is non-recommendatory, and the evaluator has no concept of information misuse. The evaluator engages in periodic negotiation of his relationships with sponsors and programme participants. The criterion of success is the range of audiences served. The report aspires to 'best-seller' status. The key concepts of democratic evaluation are 'confidentiality', 'negotiation', and 'accessibility'. The key justificatory concept is 'the right to know'.

(MacDonald and Walker, 1974, pp. 17–18)

Behind the somewhat provocative terms used here lies a concern with the inadequacy of an established pattern of research which reports upwards on those occupying relatively low status and having little power. This has become a major issue for social science research as well as for education. [. . .]

CONCLUSION

In most standard textbooks you will find discussions about the relative strengths and weaknesses of qualitative as against quantitative methods of research. Qualitative methods, it is said, are subjective, unreliable, unsystematic, lack adequate checks on their validity and are generally speaking unscientific. Quantitative methods, it is counter-argued, are technically inadequate in the face of real problems, usually inappropriately used and fail to explain most of the variance they do reveal. The argument is a pervasive one and in recent years both Cyril Burt and Margaret Mead have been accused by contemporary researchers, who have discovered that they both often failed to apply the methods they so strenuously advocated, and perhaps that they lied in reporting their results. The point that is less often made, and which I have emphasized here, is primarily concerned with different ways of conceiving the relationship between the researcher, the subject and the audience. I have asked, in terms of the political relationship between these different interest groups, whether the intention of the research is genuinely to learn and to encourage learning, or whether it is to propagate a particular view. The further question this raises, which will be taken up later, is whether it is feasible, or indeed wise, to advocate democratic research relationships within organizations that are essentially bureaucratic and hierarchical.

In his paper, 'What counts as research?' (Stenhouse, 1980), Lawrence Stenhouse dismissed the criticism of teacher research that sees teachers as too involved in professional action to be able to conduct objective research, adding, 'In my experience the dedication of professional researchers to their theories is a more serious source of bias than the dedication of teachers to their practice.' This chapter has been predicated on Stenhouse's assumption, but it is important to bear in mind that it is written by someone trained as a professional researcher.

Some time ago, at the conclusion of a long meeting with the head of a primary school to which I was trying to gain access to carry out a research study, the head said to me as I was leaving: 'You know, until I talked to you I thought you must be a sociologist.' The scarcely controlled contempt he brought to the final word does not translate into print. 'I thought you must be a *sociologist*.' The impact of the point did not really strike home until I realized that I had heard the same tone before. I had used it; but I had used it to refer to *headteachers*.

REFERENCES

Adelman, C. (1979) *Some Dilemmas of Institutional Evaluation and their Relationship to Preconditions and Procedures*, San Francisco, Calif. AERA.

Boehm, V. R. (1980) ' "Research in the Real World": a conceptual model', *Personnel Psychology*, 33 Autumn, pp. 495–503.

Faulkner, R. (1982) 'Improvising on a triad', in van Maanen, J. *et al.*, *Varieties of Qualitative Research*, Beverley Hills, Calif.: Sage, pp. 65–102.

MacDonald, B. and Walker, R. (1974) *Information Evaluation Research and the Problem of Control*, SAFARI Working Paper No. 1, Norwich, Centre for Applied Research in Education, University of East Anglia.

Stake, R. E. *Evaluating Educational Programmes: The Need and the Response*, Paris, OECD.

Stenhouse, L. A. (1980). 'What counts as research?' unpublished paper, Norwich, Centre for Applied Research in Education, University of East Anglia.

Webb, E. *et al.* (1966) *Unobtrusive Measures: Non-reactive Research in the Social Sciences*, Chicago: Rand McNally.

2.2 THE ART DEPARTMENT

PHILIP CLIFT

INTRODUCTION

This is a case study of a departmental review at a large Comprehensive school in the West Midlands. The review, of the Art Department, began in September 1981 and ended in January 1982 with the formal presentation, by the Senior Management Team, of a written report to the teachers concerned. The report was brief (only three sides of A4) and in three parts: a general description and evaluation of the department: a list of recommendations for actions to be taken by the teachers and a list of recommendations for actions to be taken by the Senior Management Team.

This case study is also in three parts: a brief introduction to the school and the review procedure: a descriptive account of the review procedure and an evaluation of the effectiveness of the review procedure in validly determining what were the salient strengths and weaknesses in the work of the department and in bringing about changes.

THE SCHOOL

The school is a coeducational school of over 1900 pupils of age 11 to 18 years, of 100 teachers and over one hundred ancillary staff. At the time of this review, the Senior Management Team consisted of the Head, the three Deputy Heads (First Deputy Head (Staff), Second Deputy Head (Curriculum), Third

Source: Clift, P. (1987) 'The Art Department', in Clift, P., Nuttall, D. L. and McCormick, R. (eds) *Studies in School Evaluation*, The Falmer Press, London, pp 110–135 (abridged)

Deputy Head (Administration)), and a Senior Teacher, the Director of Studies.

THE ART TEACHERS

The Art Department was quite small. There were four teachers fully committed to teaching Art, and one whose main responsibility was teaching Needlework but who also taught some Art. The four full-time Art teachers were

the Head of Department	Scale 3	
First Art teacher (AT1)	Scale 2	at the time of
Second Art teacher (AT2)	Scale 1	the review
Third Art teacher (AT3)	Scale 1	

The part-time Art teacher did not feature in the review.

METHODOLOGY

The role which I adopted for studying the process was that of non-participant observer. After considering the nature of the exercise and the people involved, I decided against asking to use a tape-recorder and instead noted the events in longhand as they occurred and, where it seemed to me to be significant, noted what was said, verbatim. I wrote up these notes immediately after each occasion and as soon as they were typed, sent copies to those involved with the request that they verify that the *substance* and the *spirit* of each occasion were accurately and adequately recorded. Prior to and during the review, I collected copies of all the relevant documents produced by the school. Before the review began, and immediately after the agreed report had been presented, I interviewed the various participants in order to find out what were their feelings about the review. The same procedure for verification was followed as for the records of the meetings. One month and again one year after the presentation of the final report, I revisited the school to find out what changes had occurred as a result of the review.

OUTLINE OF THE REVIEW

This was the first departmental review under new procedure agreed with Heads of Departments earlier in the year. The new style review consisted of three components:

　1　a Head of Department questionnaire concerning departmental matters as a preliminary to a series of meetings between members of the Senior Management Team and the Head of Department;

2 the observation, by members of the Senior Management Team, of lessons taught by members of the department;

3 Staff Appraisal interviews.

Based on these components, a draft report on the department was prepared by the Senior Management Team and presented to the Head of Department. After negotiation about its substance, a revised, agreed version was presented to the departmental team at a formal meeting. Formal minutes of the various meetings and appraisal interviews were not kept, although informal personal notes were sometimes made by members of the Senior Management Team.

The review procedure being studied was new at the school, but similar reviews are not. Much of a seven page appendix to the Head's progress report on his Five Year Plan 1974 to 1979 had been devoted to commenting on these earlier departmental reviews. It concluded that: 'Existing procedures do not go far enough. It should be turned into a dynamic activity.'

AIMS AND OBJECTIVES OF THE REVIEW

The revised procedure was set out in a discussion document and presented to the Heads of Department. It set out the following aims and objectives:

Document 1
The Aims of a Departmental Review
To investigate thoroughly the work of all departments within the school in order to encourage optimum performance.

The Objectives of a Departmental Review
1 To study the effectiveness of the teaching within a department and to assist in improving this if necessary.
2 To develop effective leadership in the department where necessary.
3 To improve the standards of work produced in the department where necessary.
4 To help to evaluate the syllabus of the department.
5 To provide a vehicle for an individual staff development programme within the bounds of their departmental work.
6 To help staff develop their own professional expertise and competence.
7 To study the assessment and evaluation procedure of pupils and assist in its improvement if necessary.
8 To help to improve stock and budgetary control within the department where appropriate.
9 To help with the planning of future strategies within the department.

As recorded in the minutes of the meeting of the Heads of Department held on the 11th March 1981, reaction to this document was anxious and ambivalent, with several threads of concern emerging. The Head stressed the benefits of 'insiders' versus 'outsiders' in the evaluation of their work. The Deputy Head (Staff) emphasised the staff development element. The minutes record a feeling amongst Heads of Department that the proposal was for 'inspection' and that evaluation should be confined solely to institutional matters, avoiding the evaluation of teachers. There was anxiety that judgments would be made about teachers' handling of classes, based on too few visits.

The detailed discussion of the review procedure at this meeting and the lengthy minutes devoted to it are in marked contrast to the brevity of its mention in the next meeting, under 'matters arising'. Assurances were given about the number of lesson visits on which judgments about teachers' competence would be based, and an attempt to make the procedure more 'egalitarian', or 'fraternal' was blocked. It was accepted that the review should go ahead as proposed. [. . .]

THE LESSON VISITS

Lesson observation by members of the Senior Management Team was semi-structured following the format set out in Document 2 below. Each teacher was observed on three separate occasions by different members of the Senior Management Team. I was able to 'double-up' once each with the Head and the Director of Studies. My main interests were how intrusive was the presence of the senior members of staff and how far I agreed with their evaluation of the lessons observed.

Document 2
Proposed Format for Lesson Report

Timing	Did pupils and staff arrive on time? Did the timing of the lesson provide a suitable division?
	Lesson content: was the lesson well prepared? Was there variety? Was the work suitable for the ability of the group? Was the lesson imaginative? Did the lesson deviate from the plan?
Materials Used	What materials and equipment were used? How were they distributed and collected?
Communications	What contact was made with pupils? How were the pupils involved in the lesson? Was there any link with previous work, recap and/or repetition? Was the questioning structured? What kind of rapport was there?
Pupil Learning	What skills were taught? What knowledge was gained? Did they enjoy the lesson?

Contingencies	How were any unplanned contingencies dealt with?
Marking and Records	Were the books satisfactorily marked? Were comments made on previous work? Was the mark book complete? Was the mark book used in the lesson? Were the records of work up to date?
Other Comments	What was the state of the classroom? How was it arranged? Is this the teacher's normal room? Any other points to be made? Summary of apparent strengths and weaknesses.

I 'doubled-up' on lesson visits with two members of the Senior Management Team. Neither took notes during their observation. One was the Head. He had the intrusive effect on the class predicted by AT3 in our initial discussion. Further, he failed to get satisfactory answers to questions which he asked pupils about the work in hand and why they were doing certain things. In his absence, I afterwards asked them the same questions, and they were able to explain quite adequately. Thus his 'perceived significance' biased the lesson evaluation. However, when I later discussed the matter with him, he agreed and presumably was able to make due allowance. The other lesson where I 'doubled-up' was observed by the Director of Studies, whose presence did not seem to be at all intrusive and distorting in effect.

THE STAFF APPRAISAL INTERVIEWS

The staff appraisal interviews were conducted by the Head and the Deputy Head (Staff), who claimed that the main benefits were: a report on individual teachers, *agreed with them,* on their personal file (to which the Head added 'they're helping to write their own references'), and clarification for the Senior Management Team as to what INSET actions they ought to take on the individual teacher's behalf. Prior to their appraisal interviews, the teachers were asked to consider the questions set out in Document 3 (below). These questions were then used to structure the interviews.

Document 3
Departmental Review Professional Development Questions
As part of the departmental review, you are invited to attend an interview with the Headmaster and Deputy Head responsible for Staff Development. This is arranged at .... on .... in the Headmaster's office. Before the meeting you are asked to consider the questions listed below which will form the basis of our discussions.
  1 Have you identified clearly defined objectives related to:
    a) your own development, b) your contribution to objectives of your department/school?
  2 What do you consider to be your achievements:

a) in relation to your own development,
b) in relation to the objectives of your department/school?
3 What appear to be your particular strengths and weaknesses?
4 Do you consider your job specification (the functions you are expected to carry out) exploit your strengths? Do any problems exist in relation to your job specification?
5 What modifications should be agreed to your job specification?
6 What other help/support is needed, for example, training:
a) at departmental level
b) at school level?
7 What objectives must now be set related to:
a) your own development,
b) your contribution to achieving the objectives of your department/school?
8 What would be a reasonable time span before we should review your position?

(Signed: Deputy Head (Staff))
November, 1981

The appraisal interviews, with the Head and the Deputy Head (Staff), took place after the lesson visits. The Head of Department was first. He is professionally ambitious, and is active in local politics. Originally a three-year trained teacher, by 1976 he had successfully completed a part time B.Phil degree and subsequently had tried, unsuccessfully, to obtain the pastoral experience which he considered to be necessary in order to move up the comprehensive school hierarchy. In response to Q1a (of Document 3) he said:

Head of Department: 'In 1976 I had a clear idea where I would like to be going: 1. get my degree; 2. get promoted to Head of Lower School, or Head of House. The second has not yet been achieved ... I'm beginning to wonder'.
Head: 'We're talking about professional development only. What about your *political* life? What are your objectives there, is it relevant to ask?'
Head of Department: 'I've achieved, or at any rate I'm likely to, a position of authority. But my ambitions are for *local* government only.'
Head: 'Are we saying that you get more personal satisfaction out of your political than professional life?'
Head of Department (hesitates): 'Yes, moving towards that.'
Head: 'Much of what we're discussing is going round the roundabout for the second time. We had a chat after the Head of House appointment about the Head of House role. I suggested then that you look rather *into* the Art department ...'.
Deputy Head (Staff): 'I discern less professional commitment than 3 years ago ... incentives lacking? ... opportunities not there?'
Head of Department: 'I'm happy as Head of Department Art.' (verified note of meeting)

The interview then moved on to the consideration of the Head of Department's departmental work, but kept drifting back to his ambition for wider experience.

> Deputy Head (Staff): 'Your desire for a pastoral commitment ... problem?'
> Head of Department: 'Yes, I'd have liked a deputy Head of House, without increment ... disappointed over that.'
> Head: 'Question 6 (Document 3) ... worries us ... teachers going nowhere ... need to provide a challenge, broaden experience, maximize job satisfactions. Are there any ways that we can support you: on the job training opportunities over the next twelve months?'
> Head of Department: 'Head of House role?'
> Head: 'Suppose you could be released for five half days, what area of experience would you like to explore? Don't be blinkered on Head of House.'
> Head of Department: 'I'd be capable of doing that well!'
> Deputy Head (Staff): 'in harness with Head of House already. You *can* do that ... no need to train you for that.' (verified note of meeting)

The Head of Department's persistence appeared to win a somewhat grudging concession from the Head:

> Head: 'Head of House ... not fully explored. The role is narrowly conceived by the present incumbent. What about considering counselling: relations, with outside agencies; parents, worried, angry; record keeping?' (verified note of meeting)

The Senior Management Team quickly returned to their former stance, however, pointing out the possibility of the Head of Department achieving status within the Art teaching fraternity in the LEA:

> Head: 'How can we help you to get job satisfaction within the Art department?'
> Deputy Head (Staff): 'Or you as Head of Department Art: of this school within the LEA ... should this be the objective for the future? ... are you a trend setter?'
> Head of Department: 'We're not trend setting, otherwise people would be coming here already.'
> Deputy Head (Staff): 'All visitors to the school invariably comment on the display of splendid painting here. Ought we to put up an exhibition in the local library, or outside the CEO's office?'
> Deputy Head (Staff): 'There's a brick wall on promotion. What's our duty to you? Lots of little things have been suggested. How long until we review how much movement has occurred?' (verified note of meeting)

After the Head of Department had gone, the Head said that it was interesting and pleasing that the interview had identified an objective for the Head of Department which was congruent with the institutional needs of the school: to extend the range of his activities with Art.

The Head of Department was subsequently regraded as Scale 4 Head of Department. He continued to regret the limitation on his career development imposed by what he saw as his confinement to Art teaching.

Head of Department (a year after the review): 'Scale 4 is probably my limit. I should have transferred to pastoral a while back. It's a bit late now and opportunities are very limited. (verified note of meeting) [...]

AT2: 'I've had to rethink. Originally I'd hoped to apply for Scale 2 posts ... but there are very few jobs, now. Had I applied earlier ... but then perhaps I'd have stood very little chance, but at least I'd have had interviews. I'm annoyed to see Head of Department for Art offered on Scale 2 nowadays, within Arts Faculties.' (verified note of meeting)

She was asked what she had done to merit promotion and what she might like to do:

AT2: 'In this school, *in* Art rather than outside it. There's not enough emphasis on the History of Art outside Sixth Form Work. I have suggested teaching it lower down the school to the Head of Department, who always says "Go ahead".'
Head: 'What about your achievements in relation to your own professional development?'
AT2: 'Well ... do you mean how far have I approached my Scale 2?'
Head: 'No, how far are you a better teacher?'
AT2: 'I can cope with kids ... get the best out of pupils ... motivate them ... too much towards exams perhaps, but that's partly their fault!'
Head (as revealed by the classroom observations): 'You're a lot better than we thought!' (verified note of meeting)

Unlike the Head of Department, AT2 denied any interest in broadening her role beyond Art teaching:

Head: 'Had we ought to be looking for courses to send you on?'
Deputy Head (Staff): 'Provide a broader base for you to gain satisfaction until promotion becomes possible?'
Head: 'Or broaden into a pastoral role?'
AT2: 'If that's the way, but my main interest is in Art.'
Deputy Head (Staff): 'Scale 2 is for additional responsibility, not just for services rendered over time.'
Head: 'Question 4 (of Document 3): does the job specification exploit your strengths?'

AT2: 'No written specification ...'
Head: 'Should we have one? What should we write for you?'
Deputy Head (Staff): 'The development of the History of Art?'
AT2: 'To gain a Scale 2?'
Head: 'Not that alone ... responsibility for job satisfaction.' (verified note of meeting)

Before the end of the interview, the Senior Management Team again referred to their new found knowledge of AT2's good qualities. For her part, she expressed much satisfaction with the review procedure and the extent to which, she felt, the Senior Management Team had obtained a valid picture of her work. She was subsequently promoted to Scale 2, with specific responsibility for Graphics for school publications and the display of Art throughout the school. [...]

The meeting [then] turned to considering the various recommendations, firstly those to the Art department:

An investigation to be made as to whether links can be made with the Craft and Needlecraft departments.

Deputy Head (Staff): 'Liaison demands effort. *Can* be cost-effective, but only when there's a *genuine* rationale and it doesn't have to be bureaucratic.'

To look at the place of 'Design' in the Art department.

Head of Department: 'We'll have a look at this.'

The department to examine their homework policy and look at what is being set to all pupils but especially the examination candidates. An explanation needs to be made to these pupils as to the benefits of providing their own paints and thereby gaining more experience with a wider range of materials.
A careful analysis needs to be made of the work of the Sixth Form Art students, O and A Level, and methods considered to improve this course.

Head of Department: 'I understand what's implied: more homework, a continuation of Creative Art throughout.'
Deputy Head (Staff): 'Someone in the department ought to mark O Level Art, in order to become familiar with standards.'
Head of Department: 'Difficult to get in. Art teachers three a penny!'

A member of the department should attend the Active Tutorial Work course next Summer term which promotes the notion of the teacher as an 'enabler and resource'.

Deputy Head (Staff): 'Fine, I'll arrange it.'

The department could look at the value of making use of the local environment as a resource for its teaching.
That the members of the department consider the value of using all the resources of the department, when, where and if necessary, for example, use of slides with groups lower down the school.

Head of Department: 'Need to discuss these within the department. There's a problem over blackout.' (verified note of meeting)

They then considered the recommendations to the Senior Management Team contained in the report:

The Deputy Head (Staff) to draft individual reports to members of the department as a result of their interviews with him and the Headmaster.

Deputy Head (Staff): 'Working on this.'

To investigate ways in which certain improvements can be made for storage space and blackout.

Deputy Head (Curriculum): 'Working on this.'

To discuss with the Caretaker the problems with the Pottery Hut and make improvements if possible.

Deputy Head (Curriculum): 'Deputy Head (Administration) will try again on this.'

To meet with the department to discuss how objectives can be passed on to pupils.

Deputy Head (Curriculum): 'We'll discuss this again after the department has had time to consider it.'

To investigate the movement of the department into adjoining areas.

The final comment in the report was attributable to the Head:

It seems to the Senior Management Team that the personal objectives of individual members of the department and institutional and departmental objectives are very largely congruent and that our recommendations are a way of achieving, we hope, both.

RETROSPECTIVE VIEWS

About a month after the presentation of the final report, I met the members of the Art department to discuss their retrospective feelings about the review. They were noticeably more outspoken than at the outset. The Head of Department said that they had already started to implement the recommendations to them. Some scepticism was expressed, however, about the extent to which the recommendations in the report addressed to the Senior Management Team would be implemented:

> AT1: 'Where's the money coming from to do all the things recommended in the report? Will the Senior Management Team become so preoccupied with other departments that they will forget all about us?' (verified note of meeting)

The Head of Department said that he was concerned that the recommendations for action by the Senior Management Team would be overlooked as a result of their going on to review the Maths department, 'which has 15 teachers'.

At a personal level, AT2 said that she now found the Head's attitude much pleasanter when she met him round the school. Indeed, it seemed to her that he now went out of his way to be pleasant and, on her part, she was 'no longer afraid of him'. AT1 said that she did not notice any difference in this regard but was nevertheless glad of the opportunity which the review had afforded to meet the Head personally, as she had not done so since her interview on appointment some years previously.

Both AT2 and AT3 thought that the Senior Management Team had been pleasantly surprised at what the review had revealed: that all the pupils liked Art and that classroom organisation was so efficient. [. . .]

EVALUATION OF THE REVIEW

The review may be evaluated generally by how effectively and efficiently it met the objectives set out in Document 1, on the basis of which it had been negotiated. It may also be evaluated more specifically in terms of: how effectively and efficiently it produced *evidence* about the state of Art teaching in the school; how *reliable and valid* that evidence was; how validly that evidence was *interpreted* in arriving at the conclusions embodied in the final report; and the extent to which the review process was an effective means of motivating those involved to act upon its conclusions.

The review of the Art department met Objectives 1, 3, 4 and 7 (Document 1) in the letter and in the spirit for the pupils, with the exception of the questionable assumption that the interests of the majority were best served by what best served the interests of pupils following O and A Level courses:

> Director of Studies: 'Setting high standards for the best will pull the others along.' (verified note of meeting, *op. cit.*)

With regard to the objectives which related to the teachers (5 and 6), the assistant teachers were perhaps better served than their Head of Department, despite his promotion. His aspirations for career development lie beyond the confines of Art teaching.

The meetings between the Head of Department and the members of the Senior Management Team, and the classroom visits produced *reliable* evidence about several matters of concern, in particular discrepancies between the curriculum-on-offer in Art, as set out in the syllabus, and the curriculum-in-action. The *validity* of this evidence is less certain. Scrutiny of the relevant case records reveals a number of questionable assumptions on the part of the Senior Management Team about the *nature* of Art teaching and a definite bias of concern towards the perceived needs of the more able pupils and towards performance in public examinations, particularly GCE O and A Level: a minority concern. Little serious attempt to evaluate the Art curriculum for the majority of pupils is evident in the case records, except by extension from the perceived needs of the more able.

For the assistant teachers, the lesson visits were of crucial importance. Whereas for the Head of Department, evidence concerning professional competence was additionally available from two other sources (examination results, curriculum management), for them the lesson visits constituted the only source of 'objective' evidence. They had access to the schedule to be used (Document 2) and thus were in a position to know what criteria would be used to observe and evaluate them. However, most of the criteria required the observers to make subjective judgments, for example:

> Did the timing of the lesson provide a *suitable* division?
> Was the lesson *well* prepared?
> Was the work *suitable* for the ability of the group?
> Was the lesson *imaginative*? etc. (Document 2, my italics)

The lesson observation pro forma ends with an open–ended section, 'Summary of apparent strengths and weaknesses'. The subjectivity of the whole procedure and particularly of this last section was alleviated to some extent by each teacher being observed by more than one member of the Senior Management Team and this aspect of the review may be deemed to be reasonably reliable. Its validity can only be judged in conjunction with Senior Management Team assumptions about the nature of Art teaching evident elsewhere in the review.

The appraisal of the assistant teachers was based on these classroom observations and what emerged in their interviews and on any preconceptions on the part of the Senior Management Team. The relative importance of these components is difficult to estimate. Careful perusal of the records of the interviews suggests that, as with the meetings with the Head of Department, preconceptions were very influential.

Several of the questions in Document 3 seemed to imply that 'professional development' included aspects and aspirations *outside* the department, whereas the objectives of the departmental review set out in Document 1 generally seem to be restricted to development *within* the department. However, the general managerial principle which the appraisal interviews seemed aimed to serve was the harmonising of teachers' professional development with the institutional needs of the school. During the interviews it became clear that the latter had primacy. The Head was constantly on the alert for the emergence of what he termed 'congruence'. This congruence took a somewhat arbitrary and procrustean form and led to conflicts of interest, particularly in the case of the Head of the Art Department.

It is noteworthy that the teachers in the Art department acted promptly upon most of the recommendations addressed to them. Thus much three-dimensional work was evident in the Art rooms a year later, homework had been given greater emphasis, a tentative start had been made to inter-departmental links with Craft and Needlecraft and the O and A Level courses were being revised.

In marked contrast with this ready compliance, virtually none of the recommendations for action to be taken by members of the Senior Management Team had borne fruit a year later. Individual reports to the Art teachers based on their appraisals had not been drafted, the problems of storage space, blackout, and the inadequate cleaning of the Pottery Hut remained unresolved, and the hoped-for move to adjacent rooms had not occurred. Even the modest recommendation that a member of the department should go on the Active Tutorial course had not been acted upon. The Head of the Art Department supposed that the promotion of the Deputy Head (Staff) to a Headship in another LEA might excuse some of this inaction. However, some six months had elapsed between the presentation of the report and his departure: time enough to have acted. In the light of his comments on the value of this aspect of the review (para 2.3), not to have dealt with the professional reports on the individual teachers might be seen as a serious breach of faith. Closer consideration of the other recommendations to the Senior Management Team suggests that they imply substantial resources, probably beyond the sanction of the Senior Management Team. Perhaps the one exception to this concerns the unsatisfactory cleaning of the Pottery Hut.

Overall, the review may be judged to have been *effective* in that it produced valid and reliable evidence of how things were in the Art department, on the basis of which prescriptions for *institutional* changes might be made, and it provided the necessary motivation for those changes of the most direct importance to the pupils to be acted upon. That some of the recommendations were for actions which were beyond the means of the school does not deny the effectiveness of the review procedure.

Views differed as to whether the review procedure was also an *efficient* means of arriving at prescriptions for changes and motivating their implementation. The Director of Studies expressed strong misgivings over the amount of his time (he claimed that it had 'cost' him 32 periods) which the review of this small department had taken. The Head of Department, however, said that he thought that the effort had been worthwhile and that he could not imagine any other means as effective.

Finally, a footnote on methodology. The process which I adopted for validating my accounts of the various meetings I attended, may have undermined my stance as a non-participant. The notes which I kept, and sent systematically for verification to those involved, amounted to a form of very detailed minutes. Remarks made by the Senior Management Team about the value of these 'minutes' in the absence of their own, points to the possibility that I may have slightly biased the proceedings by asserting my interpretation of events.

2.3 OUTDOOR PLAY

LINDA McGILL

Outdoor play is a vital aspect of Nursery Education. Young children are developing rapidly, not least physically, and need time and space to explore new ways of moving, exercise their developing muscles and begin to discover the power of their bodies. Many children, especially those who live in flats, also need outdoor play as a means of releasing excess energy, and all children need to be able to express themselves physically as part of their all round development. The garden or playground is also a place for fun and enjoyment, and should always be available as an alternative to indoor activities.

As a teacher committed to anti-sexist practice across the whole Nursery curriculum, I decided to look at outdoor play in relation to children's views of themselves as girls or boys, and this decision was spurred by the delivery of a new toy, a large, shiny, steerable, push-along engine. It appealed to all the children, so a rota had to be drawn up to give each a turn. It quickly became apparent that although girls were asking for and being given equal opportunity to play with the engine, they very quickly lost interest and gave up, whereas the boys sometimes had to be almost forcibly dragged off to give someone else a turn. One reason for the girls' lack of enthusiasm was that they lacked the skills required to steer the vehicle, so quickly became disillusioned with the toy and left it for others who could use it effectively. The girls were then relegated to 'pushers' and not 'drivers'.

To discover the reason for the girls' lack of skill, I began a series of observations of the outdoor area, to see exactly what the children were doing with their time outside. Initially, I observed only on a day when large, wheeled equipment was available, and used a time-sampling method, involving a checklist of all the activities offered to the children. This was completed every fifteen minutes over a period of one hour.

Source: McGill, L. (1986) 'Outdoor play', *Primary Matters 1986*, ILEA, London, pp. 57–58.

My exercise showed that boys were spending much more time than girls in activities which developed skills like hand/eye co-ordination and spatial awareness – required for steering wheeled toys, among other things. I also noticed that when a girl tried to use, say, a scooter, she was liable to be intimidated by one of a group of boys who virtually commandeered such equipment for their fantasy games. So two things were happening to the girls – they were not learning and practising certain skills and they were getting the message that this sort of toy was really for boys.

These findings were confirmed when I analysed other outdoor activities. The girls were always more likely to be found on the slide or in the sandpit directly beneath it, engaging in role-play or digging – relatively 'safe' activities – rather than actively engaging in play which involved the use of large muscles, like running, climbing or using the large wheeled toys. Outdoors many girls tended to be on the periphery, walking around the edge of the garden pushing a buggy or holding an adult's hand.

I was disturbed by the implications of my findings, but decided to investigate further by assessing the percentages of girls and boys using the garden. At the time there was a significant gender imbalance in the Nursery; we had twice as many boys as girls on roll. Analysis showed that the ratio of boys to girls was almost never represented in the gardens. Some girls spent most of their time indoors and some of the boys mostly in the garden. The average ratio was 24.5% girls to 75.5% boys. The implications of these findings need consideration. Girls are learning that boisterous outdoor play involving climbing equipment or large wheeled toys is not appropriate for them. They are also not using the opportunities to exercise and develop their large muscles which may influence their future as sportswomen. Finally, although the Nursery is providing equal opportunities in outdoor play, the girls are not taking up the option.

It is generally acknowledged that girls are more likely to give up sport and physical activity, particularly that involving the use of the upper body, at puberty. However, if my findings are true for girls generally, it can be assumed that fewer girls than boys are actually involved in physical activity using large muscles as early as three and four years old. This will obviously affect other spheres of development such as spatial awareness, hand/eye co-ordination, balance and mobility.

By spending time in the sandpit, walking around the garden or cuddling with adults, many girls are already exhibiting passivity, a style of behaviour less conducive to learning than one that actively engages the environment and interacts with it and with people.

This was not the case for all girls; some were involved in more active pursuits. Sabrina, for example, was observed running, skipping and climbing, and appeared in the garden five times in the eight observations. Sherifa and Antonya, however, appeared only once and then only on the periphery of activities. By contrast virtually all the boys were observed playing outdoors on more than one occasion and at a variety of activities, Leon six times and at six different activities, and Lloyd on every occasion, also at six different activities. (This must have implications for the learning experiences of some boys.)

After bringing the findings to a staff meeting, we discussed possible strategies to encourage the more active participation of girls in outdoor play to foster physical development, confidence and the learning of important skills.

First we tried a girls-only session outdoors, to take place after lunch for about ten to fifteen minutes. One or two of the Centre's staff expressed some reservations so it was decided to offer boys something special during the time, such as cooking or dancing. On the first occasion, all the girls came outdoors and immediately went for the toys favoured by the boys. With adult help, they had time and space to experiment and to develop and practise the necessary skills for scooter and tricycle riding, steering go-carts and the engine. Elizabeth expressed pleasure that no boys were present. She tended to spend her time outdoors in the sandpit, cuddling with an adult and only once skipping, but obviously now felt much safer and more relaxed, trying things she had not tried before.

When the boys then came out, they quickly re-asserted themselves and managed to gain control of equipment they wanted to use. They expressed no negative feelings about having been indoors for a short while. Obviously I would not normally allow boys or girls to persuade other children out of equipment they were involved with, but this time I wanted to see what the girls' reaction would be. After a week or so however, the girls had begun to realise that they had as much right to all of the toys as the boys, and felt safe in hanging on to scooters or tricycles even when boys demanded them. With time to practise in a safe and controlled environment, with no pressure from competent, confident boys, skills were developed and enjoyment was had by all the girls, who began to rush outside when girls-only time was announced.

After two weeks, the girls were clearly becoming more assertive in the garden, and had quickly learnt how to use the equipment, so the 'girls-only' sessions were ended. The staff were now far more aware of what was happening in the garden, and were able to ensure that girls, less confident boys and new children were given time and space to gain familiarity with all outdoor equipment and to practise their use. More sharing and collaborative play was to be fostered by careful choice of new equipment and the considered plans made for each day's lay-out of toys. The adults themselves were to present a positive role model for all children by being constructively involved in outdoor play and not huddled in a corner with a cup of coffee or sitting on a chair.

Next strategies we need to develop for encouraging boys who spend most of their time outdoors to become more involved in creative and quiet activities ...

|2.4| INSIDE THE LEGO HOUSE

ELIZABETH BURN

[...]

THE LEGO RESEARCH

The toy survey confirmed early differentiation in girls' and boys' interests. I therefore decided to look at a 'toy' that is also found in many classrooms and linked to early mathematical and scientific development. This resulted in observing one hundred children between 5 and 9 years of age building with Lego. In the toy survey far more boys than girls had selected Lego as a toy choice at home. My own teaching observations had shown clearly that, if given free choice, by 6 to 7 years of age, boys in classrooms dominated Lego play and girls had lost any initial interest and were often prevented from such play by boys.

I withdrew groups of three or four children and asked them to build a model with Lego, working either alone or with a friend. Three types of Lego were examined. The sample sizes for 1053 and 1030 (Technic) Lego were too small to draw any conclusions apart from the greater proficiency of the boys' constructional skills. The ordinary Lego research involved seventy-four children and showed wide gender-related differences in choice of model, construction skills and approach to the tasks set. In seventeen sessions, 83 per cent of girls built houses, whilst 83 per cent of boys built vehicles. When my own children at home helped me analyse these figures, it was suggested

Source: Burn, E. (1989) 'Inside the Lego house', in Skelton, C. (ed.) *Whatever Happens to Little Women?*, The Open University Press, Milton Keynes, pp. 144–488.

I should change them as nobody would believe they were not invented! The constructions mirrored toy choices and, for the boys, their models subsequently became incorporated into their fantasy play. All boys chose to work independently as they pre-planned their models carefully, quickly and quietly, showing clear task orientation. Even the younger boys would ask how long they would be able to work at their models, one 6 year old stating, 'It will take me about fifty minutes to build my spaceship properly ...' and it did! Thirty per cent of the girls chose to work in pairs and they saw building as a secondary activity with very little pre-planning and concentration on the task. The girls often changed their minds about their models and made no attempt to incorporate them into their play. Boys also employed what I called 'Lego language' in order to gather the appropriate bricks. They used the studs of the Lego as a guide and would phrase their requests accordingly, for example, a 6-year-old boy asked, 'Has anyone got a six-er?'

After 6 years of age, girls often commented on their own lack of interest in Lego:

> *7-year-old girl:* I used to play with the big Lego when I was little ...

> *6-year-old girl:* I've made houses before – they're dead easy ...

The eight single-sex groups revealed clearly that girls were judged by boys as not being very 'good' at Lego and indeed many girls accepted this evaluation of their abilities:

> *8-year-old girl:* The boys are the best ... you can say that again!

> *8-year-old boy:* Girls cannot build anything ... they just laugh, they are silly and play with houses and schools.

At the same time, several girls demonstrated a resentment towards this state of affairs and complained about the boys' behaviour in the classroom:

> *7-year-old girl:* The boys pinch it [the Lego] off me. They use it for the A Team ... and get wrong off the teacher for making a noise.

> *7-year-old girl:* I like playing but all the boys keep it and don't let us have it. They think girls can't use it.

Another worrying factor that emerged in the single-group sessions was that boys' derisory comments about girls' inexperience with Lego became more marked as children got older. For example:

> *9-year-old boy:* The girls won't want to come and build with Lego ... they're daft and play with Care Bears.

Boys who did not join in the abuse were taunted and ridiculed for playing with 'girls' toys'. One 8-year-old boy said of another boy in the class, 'He's soft ... he plays with his sister's Sindy doll.' Similar situations occurred in girl-only groups – a girl who did not participate was mocked for playing with He-Man, to which she responded by going bright red.

So, toys can be, and are, used to reinforce gender conformity. I was not surprised to be told by one mother that her son played with his sister's 'Wendy House' indoors but not outside in the garden for fear of being called a 'cissy'. The Lego sessions which I observed confirmed that gender differentiation certainly does influence the use of the Lego and unless teachers intervene then it is likely that girls' low level of interest and consequent technological underachievement will remain.

To summarise, the main points which emerged from the observation of children's play with Lego were very similar to those found in the toy survey. The models children chose to build were sex stereotypical with girls building houses and boys constructing vehicles which moved. The Lego play showed that boys appear to be more task-orientated, have developed superior construction skills and pre-plan models independently by 6 to 7 years of age. Girls, however, see Lego as mainly for boys, their models are more simple in design and are not incorporated into fantasy play. They appear to gain little satisfaction from such activities. Finally, as children move from 5 to 9 years of age the separation of girls and boys becomes more evident and members of the opposite sex are frequently ridiculed in peer group play if they do not conform to gender expectations.

CONCLUSION

This examination of children's early play patterns at home and at school showed clearly that girls are disadvantaged at an early age. Attitudes that are developed at primary level ensure that by secondary school girls undervalue their abilities and underachieve in physics, maths, computer studies and technology. Boys are able to obtain more teacher time and monopolise certain materials in many classrooms. The educational spin-offs of these behaviour patterns must be spelt out to teachers and parents. Unless they are given evidence of this imbalance, how can they be expected to try and redress it? Material by the Equal Opportunities Commission and the Genderwatch pack together with recent maths and physics reports (mentioned earlier) are important back-ups and help explain the reasons for concern. I would also recommend teachers to carry out simple research in their own schools to motivate and inform staff about what is happening in their own particular institution. For instance, I found the materials from the toy survey were very useful in parental and staff discussions. We tried to avoid allowing these discussions to become side-tracked into political arguments. Instead, the importance of widening all children's educational opportunities was the factor stressed.

My research indicated that very young children are well aware of gender 'rules' and they often welcomed the opportunity to openly discuss and sometimes challenge them. Children could easily carry out surveys of school life (playground behaviour for example) and reflect upon them. However, it is for individual schools to draw up action plans which cover all aspects of gender discimination in primary schooling. In one school I visited, staff had several meetings focusing on language and the 'gender messages' inherent in it. When a supply teacher arrived and started asking for 'strong boys' and 'well-mannered little girls', the staff realised how far their own understanding had increased. Teachers traditionally have used these terms to praise children and so have unfortunately contributed towards society's stereotyping, thus limiting a child's potential from an early age. In another school, older boys were encouraged to work in the nursery in order to develop the caring role that staff felt they lacked. I met teachers that informally monitored each other in the classroom to see if they could alter boys' dominance of their time. Once teachers realise the situation they can try out a variety of strategies which challenge gender differentiation, such as girl-only sessions for Lego and computer work. Yet, it is providing the opportunity for teachers to consider gender issues that has to be the first priority. All Newcastle schools have been directed to hold a Baker Day concerned with gender. These training days are run by women teachers rather than advisers. I am part of a team of three teachers and the sessions I have been involved in are proving an exciting way forward. When women practitioners themselves become involved in training, the shared teaching experiences mean that issues can be explored in more depth with the teacher/expert situation being replaced by colleagues enabling each other to look at classroom practice. These training sessions have allowed me to disseminate research findings in a way that is accessible to classroom teachers. Boys demanding teachers' attention and their disruptive behaviour are particularly commented upon! I have found that most teachers have generally no knowledge of gender research. However, when the teachers can be actively encouraged to become involved in research and discuss their findings with colleagues then curricular changes may be attempted. It seems to me to be far more productive to say to a teacher, 'What have you found?' than to say 'Do this ... do *not* do that.' I have read many guidelines for good practice but often they do not allow or invite teachers to explore the reasons why. Could this be connected to the issues raised in my introduction, when I referred to the lack of status given to the female primary teacher? Tackling gender issues effectively needs to be linked with women teachers gaining more confidence and becoming aware of their own position in society.

To see gender differentiation as only affecting girls is to misunderstand it and to focus in on guidelines for good practice alone could be counter-productive. Just as many children in my research were able to analyse gender barriers, so can teachers. Furthermore, I would argue that until they are encouraged to do so, the overall impact of Equal Opportunities shall remain limited.

TVEI IN CAISTER HIGH: A CASE STUDY IN EDUCATIONAL CHANGE

2.5

IAN STRONACH

INTRODUCTION

I could play safe and write this account in technical language, using words like Change Agent, Gatekeeper, Sponsor, and Client. But personalities and biographies are important: it would destroy understanding. And I would be cheating in a different kind of way – as a researcher, I would be using 'Science' to hide *behind* the account. Or I could write this account in everyday language, and use words like Stuart, the Head, MSC, and Tracey, and pretend that this was a story that told itself: I could hide *inside* the account.

Visible or invisible authority: these are the usual options in educational research. But I want to write myself into this account because there is no other way in which it can be written if it is to be fully educational – that is to say, if readers are to be given grounds for disbelieving as well as believing. If I am to de-authorise the account then I must be paradoxical and present the author so that the reader can see *from where I am seeing* and assess the validity of that perspective. (Educational research must present cases in terms of the problematics of their construction, and those problematics need to include the personal as well as the methodological and theoretical.) If we do not know the *who* of the writer, then we cannot know the *what* and *why* of the written.

So let's drop the pretence about objectivity. I saw, listened – and now write – as a person, a former teacher, a curriculum developer, as well as a researcher. A whole network of hidden comparisons underpins my thoughts about the school and about TVEI. Some go back into my own biography: for

Source: Stronach, I. (1988) *TVEI in Caister High: a case study in educational change*, CARE, University of East Anglia, pp. 2–34 (abridged)

example, in line 3 of the first fieldnote I wrote on Caister – 'very small-feeling school, like Gordon Schools, Huntly.' (19 Nov. 84) Later, 'compared with Johnstone High School queues are a feature – waiting to go to the canteen. Tight on crowd control – where are the dogs hidden?' A month after that, I was standing in the corridor outside the CDT department with the Head of Department (12 Dec. 84). He was saying to me,

'It's ethos, the kids, atmosphere – that's first. The rest's important but it comes second.' Then he asked what I thought of the school. I said,

'Reminds me of the school I first taught in – Huntly, 400 roll, small, warm, familiar.' And, of course, I compared Caister – rather more deliberately - with other schools trying similar vocational and consortium innovations, like the Clydebank schools I evaluated from 1978–82, or the project on community-based learning I ran at Johnstone. A last example of these myriad connections between biography and an understanding of the case – the 1984 Norfolk TVEI proposal to the MSC quotes me on the subject of Records of Achievement: my values are already directly represented in the case.

How deeply is my biography implicated in the interpretation of this case? I think the best clue I can give you is the strict/warm paradox that I argue represents the school ethos. I've taught in schools like that, and been happy teaching there. I liked Caister, and recognised some of the school paradox as a personal contradiction – as a teacher, I was a bit like that myself. It is an ethos against which I would argue, but towards which I feel a certain (warm) ambivalence.

That might help you criticise my interpretation of Caister TVEI. There is also a second personal point. How I 'got on' with the students and staff had a lot to do with the kind of data generated. And 'getting on with people' has nothing to do with objective methods. So I have tried to write in some indication of these things as well, to enable you to draw your own conclusions about the quality of access.

A final point. Am I writing a personal account rather than a researched one? Not at all – there is no such dichotomy, and I merely want to register that obvious but neglected point. I want to integrate the ethnographic and the personal in order to make this piece of research educational. The account is based on a large number of interviews and observations between 1984 and 1988, as well as documentary evidence. Its summative judgements rest mainly on a period of intensive fieldwork late in 1987, when I looked in detail at Caister and interviewed 19 of the staff. The notes and transcripts for that part of the research exceed 200 pages.

MAKING THE CASE

This narrative is an analysis and prescription in disguise.

The prescription is simple: Norfolk is centrally interested in the dissemination of TVEI innovations within the pilot schools and in the rest of the County as part of a £10.5 million TVEI Extension Project. That is why I chose to address the problem of dissemination.

The analysis is also simple. I want to portray the ethos of the school, as teachers and students experience it, and in its formal and informal manifestations. So 'assembly', 'supply cover', 'the staffroom' are presented as vignettes. That gives something of the *context*, along with the later sections on the 'old guard' and the 'young teachers'. Then I want to portray *policy* within that context – the Head, the TVEI Director. Finally, I need to portray something of TVEI *practice* with a detailed account of teaching and learning styles in the Business Information Studies course. I pick that aspect of TVEI for two reasons. It is an area of perceived success, and the overriding intention of TVEI Extension is to implement the 'active learning' to which it aspires.

I selected these dimensions of the school because I thought they were representative in terms of the data, and because they raised important dilemmas for dissemination in TVEI Extension. I hope that the school can use this account as part of its internal review dialogue, and have tried to write in a fairly conversational style.

Finally, I intend to use this detailed case study as a kind of 'template' against which to look at the different experiences of TVEI pilot schools in the Norfolk consortium, and the issues that these differences raise.

THE SCHOOL

The Norfolk TVEI submission to the MSC echoes the Caister 1984 school brochure – 'the school buildings are situated on a pleasant open site close to the village and holiday resort of Caister and adjacent to the beach.' (p. 7). The school is in a quiet cul-de-sac in a housing estate. It looks like a modern, urban primary school rather than a comprehensive – small, two-storey, brick-and-glass. From the car-park at the entrance, the school buildings seem makeshift. From left to right: a fenced playground, the light grey TVEI caravan beside the dustbins, cycle-sheds and kitchen, assembly hall linked to main entrance and the new Pascoe block. And a row of green mobiles on the edge of the playing fields, standing against a foreshortened horizon to the east – you sense the nearby North Sea.

Caister has been a four-year, all-ability comprehensive since 1979. Before that, it was a secondary modern. It has a roll of around 630 (1988), with a 6 FE in the second year (there is no 'first year'). Norfolk is a notably thrifty

LEA, and capitation allowed around £400 *per annum* for a Technical workshop. In contrast, annual TVEI expenditure on the 6-school consortium (equipment only) reached £194,396.

Second year pupils are banded A–C on the basis of Middle School reports and later in-school testing, and offered a conventionally broad curriculum, with setting in English and Maths. A-band pupils were expected to sit for GCE, while B and C sat for CSE. Results are regarded as good: there are a lot of long-serving staff, and the school catchment – which is competitive – is perceived to be a mix of middle-class and upper working class. [...]

Inside BIS

Within Caister, TVEI dissemination has failed to fight its way out of the 'enclave'. But dissemination is not development. The purpose here will be to look at TVEI development in the area of Business and Information Studies. This is a biased decision by the evaluation in that BIS is thought to be an area of success, oversubscribed by pupils in the school, and attracting a better cross-section of abilities. Other areas of TVEI in the school have failed to attract pupils thus far in the Project (micro-control technology has six students), or are being abandoned (Holiday and Leisure, Marine Studies).

In another sense, however, BIS is peculiarly representative of TVEI ideals in Norfolk. It has a pedagogical rationale (student-centred, active learning, team-teaching); it incorporates IT (a defining characteristic of consortium interests); and it expresses a vocational intention. Thus it seeks to represent in one course the T, V and E of the Initiative. In addition, it is a lynchpin of one of the major themes of TVEI Extension in the County – Relevance and Enterprise. Finally, it incorporates an INSET strategy ('curriculum led staff development') that is central to Norfolk's GRIST strategy. For all these reasons, it deserves careful scrutiny.

The development of the BIS course is reported in the Project publication 'Commerce and Retail' and will not be repeated here. So too are the favourable views of the teachers. Instead, I want to look in detail at pupil reactions to the BIS course in order to work out what processes seem to be involved and what outcomes are being achieved in a course that the BIS teacher in Caister regards as experimental '... tackling something completely different, completely new, not knowing where it's going to lead, what the pupils are going to get out of it ...' Such a focus will address a concern of the LEA: what criteria can act as relevant performance indicators of 'student-centred learning'?

STUDENT-CENTRED EVALUATION

'As far as school go it's lovely.'

The students at Caister generally are well-disciplined, polite, and obedient. Probably more of them think that they attend a 'good' school than is typical in the consortium. They even appreciate the discipline of the school:

'There's more discipline as well. And I think that discipline's one of the good things about this school.'
'But you learn a lot more off them teachers [strict ones] than what you do off the other ones.'

They identify 'normal' lessons as sitting down, being taught, writing, copying, listening. They often seem to subscribe to the child-centred approach that is peculiar to the school. That approach contains paradoxes. It is strict – 'they're really petty about what colour of grey you wear'; but it is 'nice'. It is formal, and also informal within its bounds – 'quite a few of the teachers are approachable and friendly and you can talk with them and have a laugh'. The formality and strictness of the regime tend to show most clearly in the school rituals, in beginnings and endings of lessons, assembly, breaches of the rules and norms. Thus even an informal, group- and discussion-based English lesson with a fourth year GCSE set and a 'young' teacher finishes with a report-back session – and with this series of injunctions:

Pens down and look this way
Face this way. Sit up straight.
Things away and stand quietly at your desks.
Stand quietly behind your desk.

In short, the distinctive child–centredness of the school seems to be based on conformity rather than individuality, and obedience rather than responsibility. It is from that implicit set of institutional criteria that students react to BIS and TVEI generally, and it is important that we read these reactions in those sorts of specific context rather than assume that students everywhere will respond likewise.

THE VOCABULARY OF BIS

I did not find the TVEI teaching and learning concepts helpful. 'Student-centred' started off in 1984 as a reference to teaching/learning style. It implied negotiation based on student learning needs; a holistic definition of those needs (cognitive and affective); and it stood in opposition to subject-centred or content-centred approaches. It referred to a process curriculum. But in 1988 the meaning of the word had changed – locally at least. 'Student-centred' did not imply any longer a certain teaching/learning style: it meant 'effective' learning. The most effective learning (whether active, passive, experiential or didactic) was by definition the most student-centred. Thus the term now lacked any prescription for the learning it was supposed to describe: it had become a tautology. Nor did 'active' learning help define the task. Did 'active' mean physical movement, intellectual activity of a certain sort, experiential sorts of social learning? The words were too vague to be useful.

A more precise vocabulary is offered by the Leeds TVEI national evaluation to categorise teaching styles as 'controlled', 'framed' and 'negotiated'. The last of these represents the BIS ambition and is defined as follows:

> A teacher who adopts a negotiated teaching style places a major emphasis on involving students in decision-making. Through continued discussion with individuals and group, teacher and students together make joint choices of content, issues to be confronted, problems to be solved, methods to be tried, and in particular the criteria to be used in determining success. (Barnes et al 1987 p. 29)

I wanted to see to what extent students experienced and were aware of these processes in BIS learning. (It was almost a condition of the process curriculum that they *should* be aware of *how* they were learning.) What follows is therefore based on interviews with BIS pupils rather than on observation or teacher interview.

THE ROLE OF THE TEACHER

> R. 'So there's a big difference between how you get taught in TVEI and how you get taught in the rest of the school?'
> P. 'Mm ... yeh, 'cos they treat you more as human beings in TVEI than what they do in some lessons. They think you're a soak, you know, sitting there soaking up a Maths lesson.'
> P2. 'Yeh, in other classes they treat you as a pupil and in TVEI they just treat you as somebody that wants to learn, somebody who's keen and is enjoying what they do learn.'

Students differentiated very clearly between what they took to be TVEI/BIS styles and 'normal' styles of teaching. The main points were that the teacher was a guide rather than an instructor, that more individual attention was given, and that it was collaborative – 'we're doing it together', 'discovering with them':

'I think Mr X's a good teacher, but then I think the TVEI people are, because Mr Y also teaches TVEI.'

P1. '... I like Mrs Brigham (the BIS teacher) 'cos she's fair and you can feel ... get very close to her without feeling she's a teacher. You can really talk to her.'

R. 'How can you manage that? Why's that possible?'

P1. 'She's just ... well a lot of teachers think that you're younger than them and they're in charge of you. I don't think that she feels like that. She tries to help rather than tell anyone what to do.'

P2. 'I think Mrs Brigham – you can talk to her a lot more because if you're wanting something, you can go up to her and just go and ask her something but if you were to ask another teacher in the class all the class hears what you're saying 'cos you have to put your hand up and you're not allowed to get up out of your seat and when you ask a question then all the others – all the class hears you. (...)'

P1. 'He says "oh," he says, "I'll have to go through this again. I'm not going round and explaining individually to all of you," but I don't learn so well when he's standing up there *shouting*. You know, I feel I learn when someone's just talking to me as a person rather than a thing listening.'

R. 'Uh-huh, right. Say more about Mrs Brigham as a teacher – why you think she's good.'

P2. 'I think it's because she sort of treats – she sort of treats you as if you're older – not older than what you are – but she sort of instead of being like saying "oh, you're lesser than what I am, I'm a teacher, you've got to listen to what I tell you, and I know it all" – like this. She sort of says, sometimes she'll say, "Well I don't know." She might say, she'll admit, that sometimes she don't know some things, or like I'll do something on the computer and she goes "Oh I didn't know how to do that." But with some teachers they'd probably never admit that.'

This guiding role of the teacher was explained in 'enabling' terms by students, although without that vocabulary. Mrs Brigham let you get on with it, made suggestions if you were stuck, put you on the 'right trail', 'get you going':

'... she'll set projects (...) and help you along them lanes, where Mr X'll help you along the computer paths.'

The personality of the teacher was also important to the students. Mrs Brigham was not seen to be 'moody', she was patient, allowed a joke, and she was understanding.

It was interesting that students could give such a clear account of the role and one that corresponded closely to the ideals of the course. Most of the student responses (unstructured small group interviews) were about *learning* rather than *teaching*. That in itself is unusual – students usually offer commentaries only on teaching (boring, good teacher, a laugh, helps you etc.). The BIS students, however, offered rich accounts of their learning, and spoke much more about learning than about teaching. On the basis of these accounts, four themes emerged as characteristic of the learning style. Students felt that they had a *responsible* role in learning; that learning was *integrative*, in the sense that it brought together social and cognitive, as well as practical and theoretical features; that it was *collaborative*, both in terms of teacher-pupil relations, and student group activities; and that it was *evaluative*, in that groups, pairs and individuals felt themselves required to reflect critically on their performance. These aspects did not apply to stages of learning, but to different dimensions of learning tasks.

RESPONSIBLE LEARNING

The main themes were about control. Students felt that they controlled the pace of the work to an extent, that they could order it in different ways – 'within reason' – and that this gave the work more interest, variety and flexibility. This was connected to the nature of the project work. It occasioned some uneasiness (of which more later) but the discipline remained – the system of deadlines was motivating. Deadlines were posted on the class noticeboard well in advance of completion dates. Students also appreciated the longer schedule attached to these projects ('know what's coming') in comparison with homework assignments in other subjects:

> P1. 'I was just going to say about if you could fall behind with your work. I don't think you can because every so often Mrs Brigham'll say "you've got a deadline to get some work finished" – say about a shop or something. Then she'll go through and check that you've done the work. Like, last Wednesday I was behind quite a lot. It weren't 'cos ... I weren't skiving off. We were doing something else and that was better. I'd rather do this what we were doing than doing other stuff so I spent more time on doing that – that was that advertising thing ...
> P2. 'Yeh, sometimes you think, oh, that's brilliant ...'
> R. 'Oh right.'
> P1. 'I spent more time doing that – shouldn't have done really, but I did, and I fell behind with the rest of the stuff then we'd TVEI all morning and I really got knuckled down and got all the work caught up then, so I'm not behind at all now.'

This kind of voluntary control resulted in breaks and lunch hours often being used to continue with work. It seemed typical that bells were ignored in the class, and that some students would work on for 5–10 minutes after the break. Students reported being motivated by the patterns of work, which were very varied. It was also usual for other students to turn up and get on with IT work of their own. There was not such a strong sense of 'class' in these lessons – the unit became the 'work-station' when individual work was going on.

Students also controlled their own movement to a greater extent. In a lesson, students might go to the library, form a group to discuss a piece of work, go to the other computer room, or do surveys in school or in town – 'spreading around all the time'. They experienced these various responsibilities as a kind of independence (perhaps *un*-dependence would be better), and this was the most prominent theme in the data:

P1. '(...) I suppose 'cos they're different to other lessons. You've got your computer and it's completely different. You don't have to sit there and listen to a teacher drone on. You get on with it yourself.'
R. 'Right. Do you all feel it's different?'
P2. 'Yeh because ...'
R. 'Give me a list of all the differences.'
P2. 'Well if you're in a Geography lesson or something, you feel more independent when you go into a TVEI lesson because if you're told what to do "alright, who's finished this? you go on and do this." Well then you go in there, you can – like – sit down as soon as you get in – and switch your computer on and whatever you need to do, you can do it yourself. You don't have to do the same as everyone else. You can do whatever you want to do instead of a teacher telling you what to do.'

EVALUATIVE LEARNING

A further aspect of the course that students commented on involved the need to evaluate what was happening in the learning process. Part of this came through experiment with the computer facilities. Trying it out, and then seeing the teacher or another student if you got stuck, seemed to be the norm:

P3. ''Cos I find that Mr X, he let me sit down in front of a computer and just told me what to do and I could do it myself and you learn a lot more like that. Instead of Mr X sitting down and doing it and you're watching, and I find that – just picked it up – and I went along. (...)'
P1. '(...) But it's different to writing it down.'
P2. 'That's 'cos you *use* it. You use what you're learning. The more you do it, the better you get at it. Same with everything. But in other lessons you don't practice.'

Sometimes evaluation was retrospective, rather than part of the learning process. Students made a project presentation to each other and to invited staff. The evaluation of the presentation was recalled:

'Well after we'd finished we all sat around in a sort of circle and Mrs Brigham sort of told us that we'd done well and then she said what groups found it hard and who needed longer and what did you find hard about it and where did you go wrong and we came – a lot of us didn't communicate in groups enough and some of us didn't put enough effort in . . .'

In another case, students had constructed application forms and judged their relative merits:

P1. 'And we handed these out to see what other people thought of it. We put some on the short-list and mine was put on the short-list and sorta I was surprised really 'cos I didn't think it was very good myself. But other people thought it was alright.'

P2. 'Yeah, mine wasn't put on the short-list and I learned a lot from that 'cos this other group who, er, looked at mine and summed it up, they told me a lot about what I could do to change it, and different things.'

P1. 'Yeah, it was our group. We told him he could, well, sort of look through it twice to make sure that there weren't no mistakes and that he could improve the information in his letter.'

INTEGRATIVE LEARNING

A third aspect of the learning brought together social and technical learning, as well as integrating business and IT curricula. In addition, the curriculum required students to deal with theoretical knowledge in practical situations and vice versa. A third kind of integration brought present and future together – in a kind of ideological resolution. To explain that last point, the students sometimes exaggerated this vocational intention. The course was about 'how to set up your own business'. It would 'help you in your life'. As early as the end of October (the course having started in early September) fourth year pupils were making instrumental connections between what they were doing and what it might mean later on. Val argued that it would be 'something to put down on my C.V.' (C.V.s were kept on disc and updated in profiling style.) She added that she would also like to have her own business – jewellery, clothes – not grotty like where she worked. I reacted with surprise at her phrase 'when I have my own business' and she added, 'as I do more of this course, I sort of realise that it could come true'. The phrase 'come true' relates to dreams, and, arguably, to the dream/hope/real sequence of ambitions that young people appear to hold under certain vocational conditions. Another aspect of the 'future' theme was that the usefulness of the course was often argued in a 'Tomorrow's World' kind of way. Computers were the coming thing, 'it's a computer world, innit?' – and 'my neighbour in her '20s is going to night school to learn how to use computers.'

So, fantasy or future, students saw this course as linking them to vocational possibilities in a way that other 'academic' subjects couldn't:

'... I think about it when I get home and think "oh, I am learning something" and I'll probably see job interviews in the paper that say 'computer work' needed, em, and I think I'm glad I took it 'cos I don't think History or Geography's [set against BIS in the Options] going to be ... don't see 'History Needed' on the bottom of a job application.'

The integration of social and technical learning has already been exemplified. There were also examples of theory and practice being integrated:

P1. 'Since I've been on the BIS my parents have bought me a computer to do at home, see, 'cos we sorta run a paper round. And they've sort of asked me to do the computing on that.'
R. 'So what have you done?'
P1. 'Well I've sorta put all the names of the houses on it and the money. And I just add things on to it. And it's easier to work things out on it. And they learn off me. So when I'm not there they can do it themselves. So I'm making them – my parents – learn as well as me. 'Cos they didn't know nothing about computers, they didn't even believe in 'em, 'till I started coming home and telling them what I've been doing.'

COLLABORATIVE LEARNING

Teachers of IT and BIS often commented on the change in students' attitudes – from notions of 'copying' to helping or cooperating. Sometimes the collaboration was between students and involved 'chains of expertise' where students who had mastered, say, the Apple Mac would instruct other students, or solve problems in other students' activities.

P1. '(...) At first I didn't get the gist of it. And Tom here he had learned from another person.'
P2. 'A while back – graphs. And then Mrs Brigham said, "Right if you want to know anything, just ask Simon."'
P1. 'Yeh, he taught someone else how to use it, and then another person ...'
P2. '... it was a sort of chain. Smithy told somebody else and it just went on like that. Not everybody knows how to use the graphs.'
P1. 'Yeh, we all know now how to do it.'
R. 'Is that only you that does that? Can you give me examples of other people doing that?'
P1. 'Er, yeh, em, Val Sterling, she was the first to, what was it, do the Macintosh, I think. Learn on the Macintosh. (...)'
P2. 'But I, Val taught me and I sorta taught somebody else. People are gradually learning how to use it from other people. And sorta, it takes a lot of, um, off Mrs Brigham as well because then she doesn't have to have

people keep coming up to her and saying how to use this, and how do I use that . . .'

The verdict of the students was that 'it was like a team really'. Neither teacher nor students reported that such interactions caused problems. The students felt that discipline was adequately replaced by responsibility:

'. . . 'cos we have the chance to mess about, we don't.'

CONCLUSION

IS THIS STUDENT-CENTRED LEARNING?

Student-centred learning is difficult to define. But the BIS initiative defines the intended switch in teaching and learning styles in some detail:

Teaching style A
Traditional Pedagogy?

Tending towards

1 *Passive learning*
   – listening, taking notes, memorising;
   – depending on teacher input and direction;

2 *Individualised learning*
   – working alone on parallel tasks;
   – most talk is teacher-pupil(s);

3 *Factual, theoretical learning*
   – using learning as a description of or preparation for experience;

4 *Knowledge-for-its-own-sake*
   – intrinsic ends;
   – little reference to utility.

Teaching style B
The aspirations of TVEI?

Tending towards

1 *Active learning*
   – problem-solving, doing projects;
   – developing skills, taking responsibility;
   – emphasis on equipment, resources;

2 *Collaborative learning*
   – group work on shared tasks;
   – class discussion, much pupil-pupil talk

3 *Experiential learning*
   – using experience as a stimulus to reflection and learning;

4 *'Relevant' knowledge*
   – emphasis on practical application and future relevance/utility.

The direction of the changes is clear enough, and there are strong indications from the pupil interview data that key aspects of the teaching/learning innovation are perceived by the students. The categories that I would stress on the basis of the student data are:

responsible learning
evaluative learning
integrative learning
collaborative learning

There is clear evidence that the students believe in the effectiveness of those sorts of learning. They also believe that other subjects could follow suit. There is some evidence that the competencies engendered on the course are transferable – they are confident about presentations in the future, teach each other IT skills, and occasionally teach others – parents in one instance, the headteacher in another.

How convincing is the evidence? I think it is convincing in terms of the group of BIS students interviewed, but that is not necessarily a representative experience of BIS. Valid in itself but not generalisable – that would be my conclusion. Other teacher data and school data shows similar reports, however, and it would be reasonable to infer that fourth year BIS experiences across the TVEI consortium are similar in some respects at least. It will not surprise anyone that this sort of outcome can be highly dependent on the personality of the individual teacher.

IS IT DIFFERENT?

Teachers often want to say, 'But I've been doing that. It's just new words for old practices.' But in this case students distinguished very clearly and precisely between what happened in 'normal' classes and what happened in BIS. ('We're always writing, writing, writing.') In addition, the kinds of 'child-centredness' that the school traditionally supported were very different from the version promoted by TVEI – so a surface similarity could be very deceptive.

Evidence of the strangeness of the pedagogy to students can be seen in the uneasiness they sometimes expressed: was this really learning? Sharon's account mentioned this theme, and it came up powerfully elsewhere:

R. 'Right. Why do you think you feel uneasy about it though?'
P. 'Em, well it's like these two subjects went in option boxes with Chemistry and History (i.e. BIS double option) – and sort of really subjects where you have to do a lot of work, think a lot about, and a lot of my friends now are in the History lesson and they'll say 'oh, I've got a load of homework for the weekend and I've got all this to do and I've done all this' and they'll be talking about all these things that ... and I'll think "well, I ain't got any homework over the weekend and I ain't learned a real lot" but I *have*, you know, I mean I've learned a lot this morning already – we've been doing something else on the computer but she just can't sort of have it written down – and say I've done all this in my lesson.'

Some students also felt that other teachers did not value their IT skills, and resisted the possibilities for their own subject:

'Plays and different things, em, she says: "I'd sooner it be in your own handwriting. To show what you can do.' In Maths or anything, er, History, and a few other things like that you're not allowed to use a word processor.'

A final indication of that strong boundary of difference between BIS and other subjects can be seen in the strange mixture of behaviours the students sometimes showed in the BIS classroom. An informal and open discussion of business plans would be accompanied by punctilious use of 'sir', 'miss' and raising the hand in order to speak. Similarly, although students went to and from the two computer rooms and the library, gentle knocks accompanied each entry into the computer room. (Stuart: 'I don't tell 'em, they just do it.') Thus, the students found it different. Although GCSE styles are claimed to be similar to TVEI, there was no indication from the students that this was the case. I had expected to hear more parallels drawn by the students – but it was not a theme that cropped up at all except in so far as BIS was a GCSE course itself.

How does the BIS data connect with the evaluation questions asked by Norfolk?

Norfolk asked 3 questions to which these data are relevant:

1 In the context of TVEI what performance indicators are appropriate in measuring achievement and attainment of the student?
2 To what degree and in what manner has TVEI developed new teaching and learning styles?
3 What has been the contribution and value of the TVEI consortium arrangements in effecting curriculum change?

I feel that the notions of *responsible, collaborative, integrative* and *evaluative* learning are less vague (in a conceptual sense) and more real (in an empirical sense) indicators of TVEI pedagogy. There is considerable evidence that BIS intentions have been realised in the case examined. The contribution of the consortium teacher group and advisory teacher support seems to have been absolutely central – but this issue will be discussed in the second part of the final report, as indeed will other issues relating to BIS development.

POSTSCRIPT 22 APRIL 1988

I felt that I was taking a big risk in writing the case study in the way I had. It was quite personal about some of the staff, and about my role. For the first time, I had tried to describe the 'feel' of a school and to build that into the explanation of a project. How would the audience react? Beforehand I imagined an ascending ladder of anger and scorn rising from the 'younger teachers' to Stuart and the Head, and a plateau of apoplexy beyond that, in the LEA. I got it quite wrong. The Head and Stuart had suggestions and criticisms to make, but they appreciated what I was trying to do – there was no objection in principle to the personal approach. The Head felt that I had got Stuart and TVEI about right, but that the tone of the piece was too sceptical about the school. Was I mocking the assembly? But he thought that I'd caught the atmosphere of the staffroom and the school, and he recognised the voice and qualities of the 'old guard'. The image of glacial change was right – long-established staff, conservative parents and pupils, and a successful school all made for slow and cautious attitudes to change. He accepted that TVEI hadn't become 'whole-school' yet. Then he surprised me: he cared a lot about the ghost of headmasters past.

Stuart wondered if I'd used a magnifying glass – caught the detail and missed some of the picture. He felt the tone was sceptical, but accepted both the problems for TVEI that the account outlined, and the way staff saw him. Perhaps there was too little on what was possible in these circumstances, given the time and the context.

I spoke to three other teachers on the 'phone and felt quite euphoric. They recognised the school, had no objections to the approach: it was pretty accurate, and easy to read. I began to get carried away with myself and imagine that case studies like this could help a school discuss what it was and what it wanted to be . . . be quite powerful in a formative as well as a summative way . . . maybe even . . .

The Head was courageous. He set up a special staff meeting in directed time, where small groups discussed the report and then gave feedback to the evaluator. I thought that if the Head and Stuart accepted the report, as well as the other individuals I had spoken to, then I was home and dry – after all, it was a sympathetic and carefully researched account based mainly on the staff's own perceptions, wasn't it?

I was wrong. The spokespersons were critical. Generally, it was thought that I had been well-intentioned, but had got it wrong. The report was readable, but I'd not stressed sufficiently the 'good atmosphere' and positive values of the school, and perhaps sniped at them – in reference to obedience and discipline, and especially in the account of the 'assembly'. The 'colour and feel' of the school was there in the account, but somehow undervalued both by humour that came over as sarcasm, and by the implication that the school ought to be more like TVEI. The account also misled because a lot of it was about TVEI, yet TVEI had been a small affair in the school, for the 'less able' on the whole, and very 'separatist'. Other school initiatives were not reported either; nor was the 'special breed' of Caister pupils. The biggest surprise for me was to realise that some of them saw me as a representative of TVEI, rather than as an independent commentator. That was a fairly critical public reaction, but it seemed to centre on rebalancing rather than rejecting the account. I felt that only one teacher had 'rubbished' the report. He saw it as a 'Sun reporter job', 'over-selective', 'badly written', based on 'eavesdropping' and 'cheap humour'.

I went back to the school the next morning, wanting to ask individuals who had not spoken at the meeting what they thought. I also wanted to understand in more detail the objections of the 'old guard', which I had not expected. The tone was different – friendly, informal. Some of the reactions were different as well. One problem was that many resented the compulsory meeting to discuss a report on a reform that had touched few of them. Several said that they could not speak up at such meetings, but thought that the report was about right – and that was a problem for some people. It was 'pretty factual really', 'compelling', more or less 'accurate'.

I began to think that this was more than a postscript, included so that outsiders could read my version against the school one and make up their own minds. The meeting had been formal, and in the presence of the senior management. The group reporters were 'old guard'. The tone of the meeting had been cold. There had been consensus. Yet some of the themes from the data had disappeared – there were no criticisms of leadership for change, and no challenge to the status quo. When I asked what the 'younger teachers' thought there was a silence. And other themes had stepped forward in prominence. You could feel the solidarity of staff when one teacher said 'This is a very, very traditional school. The "old guard" is to be thanked by the school for all they have established.'

The following day had been informal, friendly even where critical. Silences from the day before were filled in. Different opinions were expressed. The polarity between group/individual, formal/informal, official/unofficial, cold/warm generated discrepant accounts. I then realised that I'd started this account with an idea about the strict/warm paradox within the school. Perhaps discrepant accounts were not to be resolved by further negotiation or research. When people said (or did not say) one thing in one context, and something else in another, they were not contradicting themselves so much as they were reflecting the nature of the community of their school, and one of the contradictions that lay at its heart.

There was also an educational footnote to go with that speculation. One-third of the case study was about how different an experience pupils had found learning in one TVEI class compared with their normal classrooms. In all my conversations about the case study, no-one mentioned it.

REFERENCES

Barnes, D. et al., (1987) *The TVEI Curriculum 14–16. An interim report based on case studies in 12 schools.* University of Leeds for MSC.

Fiddy, R. and Stronach, I. (1987) 'Fables and Futures: cases in the management of education' in Gleeson D. (ed.) *TVEI in Secondary Schools: a critical appraisal.* Milton Keynes: Open University Press.

INSPECTION AND ITS CONTRIBUTION TO PRACTICAL EVALUATION

2.6

BRIAN WILCOX

[...]

RECENT EMPHASIS ON INSPECTORATES AND INSPECTION

Increasing emphasis is being given to the importance of inspection and inspectorates as major means of monitoring and evaluating educational (and training) provision. This can be seen in the changing fortunes of Her Majesty's Inspectorate (HMI) (Lawton and Gordon, 1987). Since the war there had been an increasing trend away from the use of the most familiar of HMI activities, namely the full inspection. During the 1950s and 1960s the influence of HMI was, perhaps, at its lowest point. Indeed a Select Committee in 1968 recommended that full inspections should cease and the number of HM Inspectors be reduced (Select Committee, 1968). However, this was the time when the educational consensus which had lasted from the postwar period began increasingly to fall away. The 1970s was a decade marked by an accelerating disquiet about the state of the public education system, financial crises and cutbacks in education, and the emergence of educational accountability as a key issue. In this new climate HMI was able to re-establish successfully an influential national role in which, in particular, inspection was central. Not only was the rate of full inspections increased, but the notion of inspection was significantly extended to encompass national surveys of

Source: Wilcox, B. (1989) Inspection and its contribution to practical evaluation. *Educational Research* 31.3.

educational provision and expenditure and the assessment of whole LEAs. The importance of HMI and its inspection activities were unequivocally endorsed by the Rayner Committee (DES/WO, 1982), the most recent of the periodic attempts over the years to review the Inspectorate's role. Undoubtedly, the subsequent decision to publish HMI reports on inspections has had the effect of raising the profile both of the Inspectorate and the process of inspection. Also it is significant to note that the current complement of inspectors, just under 500, is greater than in the pre-Rayner period.

The notion of a national inspectorate has also commended itself to the Manpower Services Commission (MSC), now the Training Agency (TA). The MSC recommended to the government in 1985 the setting up of a Training Standards Advisory Service (TSAS) to provide an independent assessment of the quality of training in the Youth Training Scheme (YTS). The service was established in September 1986 and currently consists of approximately 40 officers called Training Standards Inspectors (TSIs). In due course, it is intended that TSIs will inspect both YTS and Employment Training Schemes (TA, 1988).

The period following local government reorganization in 1974 resulted, *inter alia*, in the establishment of larger local education authorities (LEAs) and more coherently organised teams of educational advisers (sometimes called inspectors). The period which followed has been regularly punctuated by debates reflecting an uncertainty about the exact nature of the adviser role. The government attempted a clarification of this vexed matter in a draft statement on advisory services (DES, 1985). The statement emphasized the function of support and development to teachers, institutions and local initiatives, and the responsibility for monitoring and evaluating the authority's services. Since then, and particularly in the wake of the Bill which has now become the Education Reform Act (Great Britain, 1988), the Secretary of State for Education and the Department of Education and Science (DES) have been at pains to underline the importance of the latter fuction:

> The local inspectorates will need to monitor and evaluate school perform-
> ance. They will need to provide LEAs and the schools themselves with
> trusted and informed professional advice, based on first hand observation
> of what schools are actually doing. Doing all these things well requires
> inspection in all its forms. (Secretary of State, 1988, paras. 10–11)

Financial support is available to LEAs, under the Education Support Grant (ESG) programme, from 1989/90 to help them develop coherent inspection policies and to appoint extra advisers (DES, 1988a). The programme should provide over a five-year period for the appointment of 300 advisers additional to those already in post (estimated to be in excess of 2,200 in 1986 (Stillman and Grant 1989)).

HMI, the TSAS and LEA advisers are but three examples of the several dozen inspectorates found in local and national government. Rhodes (1981) classifies inspectorates as either enforcement or efficiency ones. *Enforcement* inspectorates are concerned with ensuring compliance with statutory requirements using, if required, action through the courts. Examples include the inspectorates for mines, health and safety, and weights and measures. In contrast, *efficiency* inspectorates are appointed to secure, maintain and improve standards of performance. They do not have legal sanctions available to them and their formal powers seldom extend beyond a basic right to inspection. Consequently, efficiency inspectorates are highly reliant on their powers of persuasion. HMI is a clear example of an efficiency inspectorate, as is the more recently established TSAS. LEA advisers may also be said to be examples of a *local* efficiency inspectorate.

INSPECTION AND ITS RELATIONSHIP TO EVALUATION

The legal basis of inspection in the education sphere is contained in Section 77 of the 1944 Education Act. Although there has never been a rigid definition of inspection, there are conventions, instructions and guidelines (Browne, 1979). It is possible therefore to identify the main general elements which are likely to apply to all inspections whether conducted by a national or a local inspectorate; they include:

1 the involvement of experienced professionals with some independence from the institution or programme being inspected;
2 the observation of various aspects through formal or informal visits involving one or more inspectors;
3 the preparation of a report on a formal visit for the institution or programme and those responsible for it;
4 the expectation that inspectors have intimate knowledge and continuing experience of what is inspected;
5 the inspectorial function of not only pronouncing judgement, but also encouraging and developing the institution or programme (after McCormick and James, 1983).

It should be noted here that the definition is given in terms of institutions and programmes rather than of individuals. This is in line with the main concern of HM Inspectors, who except in special circumstances, inspect teaching rather than individual teachers. Considerations of the teaching competence of individuals and related issues, such as teacher appraisal, are regarded as separate matters and are not included in this review.

Inspection is of course an example of a method of evaluation. Evaluation as an explicit activity may be defined as 'the systematic collection and interpretation of evidence leading, as part of the process, to a judgement of value with a view to action' (Beeby, 1977, quoted by Wolf, 1987, p. 8). In particular, inspection is a form of *external evaluation* – i.e. one which is carried out by people who are not part of the institution or programme involved; in contrast, evaluation conducted by those within is known as *internal evaluation*. Educational evaluation has emerged as a separate discipline over the last two decades or so and has a voluminous literature, which describes a variety of styles, approaches, methods and techniques. Recent reviews of the field of evaluation are provided by Tyler (1986); Murphy and Torrance (1987); Simons (1987); and Wolf (1987). However, the evaluation literature usually omits any reference to inspection as a mode of evaluation; and, where it does, provides very little guidance about the methods actually used. In the case of the American literature, this neglect is perhaps not surprising since inspection, as understood in Britain, is not a feature of the public education system. In the USA evaluation has been largely conducted by specialist external evaluators appointed to funded programmes. The lack of recognition of inspection in the English literature is perhaps surprising since the main efforts in evaluation have been made by inspectors and advisers who, to some extent, occupy the role and use of resources allocated to external evaluators in the USA (Kogan, 1986, p. 141). Part of the explanation may lie in the fact that the main contributors to evaluation theory and methodology in this country have been academics and educational researchers. They may not therefore have recognised the work of inspectors and advisers as falling within the legitimate parameters of evaluation as they understood them. Another relevant factor is that, apart from HMI reports, the outcomes of inspections have not generally been available in the public domain. Consequently, inspection has tended to be a hidden form of evaluation. Brief descriptions of the different types of inspection undertaken by HMI have been provided by former HMIs (e.g. Blackie, 1970, 1982); Thomas, (1982) and, more recently, by HMI itself on current practice (DES, 1986).

In the case of the inspection of maintained schools, the following categories are identified.

1 *Informal visits* are carried out by inspectors, individually or in groups, and often confined within a single day; no formal report is produced, but they contribute to HMI knowledge of the education system and publications on provision.
2 *Full inspections* cover the whole life and work of the school, including the standards of work in each subject and aspects of the curriculum; and a report is subsequently issued.
3 *'Short' secondary inspections* deal with the general quality of the school's life, work and organization, not with individual subjects. The report is much briefer than that for a full inspection.
4 *Surveys* can be concerned with an aspect of the curriculum, a whole phase, particular year groups or a combination of these. They may involve computer-chosen samples of institutions and will lead to one or more reports (DES, 1986).

The arrangements for full and short inspections follow a standard pattern (arrangements for surveys however are more varied). A 'panel' of inspectors is involved, led by a reporting inspector (RI) who is responsible for the inspection as a whole, including the drafting of the report. The size of the panel will vary according to the type and size of school and whether the inspection is a full or short one. A full inspection of a large secondary school will involve 12 or more members. The time spent in the school will range from three to five days, depending on the type of inspection. The RI makes a preliminary visit to the school to explain the background to the inspection to the head and, if required, to the staff. Before the inspection, information is provided by the school, partly through the completion of standard questionnaires. Whilst in school the inspectors spend as much time as possible observing the work of pupils in the classroom and elsewhere. In addition, they will talk to pupils and staff, look at samples of pupils' work and attend assemblies, registration and tutorial sessions, and a selection of extra-curricular activities. Towards the end of the inspection the findings are fed back to the head and other senior staff. The school is encouraged to make clear any factual inaccuracies or interpretations which are considered ill-founded. After the inspection, a meeting with the governing body is convened to hear and comment on the main findings before the report is written. The report appears, if possible, within six months of the inspection. Reports, although they do not follow a standard pattern, do tend to contain a number of common elements. In the case of maintained schools, copies of the report are sent to the chief education officer, the clerk of the governors and the head. Fourteen days later the report is published and becomes freely available. The LEA (and the governors in the case of a voluntary-aided or special agreement school) is required to indicate, within three months, what action is to be taken in the light of the report's findings.

The TSAS inspection programme of YTS seems to follow quite closely the HMI model of full inspection (TA, 1988; Murphy and Henderson, 1988). The inspection of a scheme is carried out by a lead TSI who collects together details of the scheme and the Approved Training Organisation (ATO) responsible for it. The TSI may have preliminary meetings with TA area office staff and scheme managers to explain the inspection procedure and identify any aspects of the scheme requiring particular attention. Inspections involve, on average, five days on site visits. Large, multi-scheme ATOs or multiprogramme schemes may involve two or more TSIs. During the visit inspectors talk to scheme organisers, trainees, work experience providers, supervisors, off-the-job training providers, tutors and others. At the end of the visit the lead TSI gives an oral report on findings jointly to ATO and TA Area Office (AO) representatives. An inspection report is then produced, summarising the main findings and setting out the recommendations. Six months after the issue of the report, AOs are approached about progress on implementing the recommendations. Some differences from HMI procedures appear to be: use of smaller teams; more specifically formulated recommendations for follow-up action: quicker production of final report; and possibly proportionately less time spent on observation of the training/learning situations.

In the case of LEA advisory services and inspectorates, as already indicated, inspection is much less generally developed as a major activity than for HMI and the TSAS. There are, however, enormous differences between LEAs, and a small number do appear to have implemented HMI-style inspections (Winckley, 1985) and others will certainly follow suit as a result of the 1988 Act. Apart from full inspections, Pearce (1986a, 1986b) identifies the *review* – usually confined to a department or a section – as another feature of LEA inspections. However, many advisers probably gain an intimate knowledge of schools more from making a variety of regular visits than from formal inspections. Few LEAs require advisers to record and report such visits, and even fewer make any attempt to collate such information to provide an advisory service view of individual schools. Stillman (1989) identifies a bewildering range of methods which chief advisers claim their advisory teams use in evaluating the performance of schools. Thus information on schools may be directly collected by activities variously described as inspections, evaluations, in-depth visits, surveys conducted through visiting, specific team visits, general team visits, advisory team reviews, chief and senior adviser visits. He also finds an even larger number of activities which involve indirect, distant, or school-produced information for evaluation. The package of evaluation methods used will differ in number, type and formality from one LEA to another. The field of LEA evaluation would seem to be in a considerable degree of conceptual disarray.

If inspection is to become a more prominent feature of public evaluation, then there is a strong case for making what is known about it more widely available. Apart from the description of inspection types of the kind identified above, there is a surprising dearth of information about the methods, techniques and assumptions which they involve. What information is available will be found in documents accessible only to members of the inspectorates to which they apply. Several commentators (Nisbett, 1979); Walker, 1982; Pearce, 1986b; Kogan, 1986) have made the point that inspectors tend to be sceptical of the use of specialised research or evaluative techniques, preferring subjective and non-technical methods – the credibility of which is based on the inspectors' ascribed status. However, there is evidence that HMI, in particular, have increasingly since the mid-1970s made use of some of the technical paraphernalia of the specialist evaluation – e.g. sampling techniques, survey questionnaires, observational schedules, and the like, for some of their activities. Although HMI would tend to reject the suggestion, there is some justification for regarding them – at least, for part of their work – as members of the research community (Wilcox, 1986). A good example representing both the justification and the limitations of this claim is provided by the HMI's most recent study of secondary schooling in England. The report of this study (DES, 1988b) is replete with quantitative data and has a style which is close to that of a research report. If a document is regarded in that way, inevitably it attracts the scrutiny of researchers, who may raise methodological queries not answerable from a consideration of the document alone. Thus statements in the document of the type 'two thirds of the work seen was of a satisfactory standard' imply an agreed set of criteria being used consistently by many different inspectors. Moreover, the report as a whole represents the aggregation of nearly 200 individual secondary school inspections. The processes involved in combining such a vast amount of data into generalisable judgements are of great methodological interest. Neither of these two issues is adequately illuminated in the report.

CONCLUSION

This article was produced in the context of the author's work as Director of the Inspection Methodologies for Education and Training (IMET) Project. He is grateful to the members of the Project Steering Group (and particularly to Professor John Gray) for helpful comments on an earlier draft.

REFERENCES

Blackie, J. (1970). *Inspecting and the Inspectorate*. London: Routledge and Kegan Paul.
Blackie, J. (1982). 'HM Inspectorate of Schools 1839–1966.' In: McCormick, R. and Nuttall, D. L. (Eds) *Curriculum Evaluation and Assessment in Educational Institutions*. Block 2. Part 3. Milton Keynes: The Open University Press, pp. 7–13.
Department of Education and Science (DES) (1985). *A Draft Statement on the Role of Local Education Authority Advisory Services*. London: DES.
DES (1986). *Reporting Inspections: Maintained Schools*. London: DES.
DES (1988a). *Education Support Grant*. Draft Circular. London: DES.
DES (1988b). *Secondary Schools: An Appraisal by HMI*. London: HMSO.
Department of Education and Science/Welsh Office (DES/WO) (1982). *Study of HM Inspectorate in England and Wales* (Raynor Report). London: HMSO.
Kogan, M. (1986). *Education Accountability: An Analytic Overview*. London: Hutchinson.
Lawton, D. and Gordon, P. (1987). *The HMI*. London: Routledge and Kegan Paul.
McCormick, R. and James, M. (1983). *Curriculum Evaluation in Schools*. London: Croom Helm.
Murphy, K. and Henderson, S. (1988). *The Early Inspections: An Evaluation of the Training Standards Advisory Service*. Sheffield: Training Agency.
Murphy, R. and Torrance, H. (Eds) (1987). *Evaluating Education: Issues and Methods*. London: Harper and Row.
Nisbet, J. (1979). 'The role of evaluators in accountability systems.' In: Murphy, R. and Torrance, H. (Eds) *Evaluating Education: Issues and Methods*. London: Harper and Row, 1987, pp. 49–56.
Pearce, J. (1986a). 'School oversight in England and Wales'. *European Journal of Education*, 21, 4, pp. 331–4.

Pearce, J. (1986b). *Standards and the LEA: The Accountability of Schools*. Windsor: NFER–Nelson.

Rhodes, G. (1981). *Inspectorates in British Government: Law Enforcement and Standards of Efficiency*. London: Allen and Unwin.

Secretary of State for Education (1988). *Speech to the SEO*. London: DES Press Office.

Select Committee (1968) *Report on Education and Science. Part I, Her Majesty's Inspectorate*. London: HMSO.

Simons, H. (1987). *Getting to Know Schools in a Democracy*. London: The Falmer Press.

Stillman, A. B. (1989). 'Institutional evaluation and LEA advisory services'. *Research Papers in Education*, 4, 2, pp. 3–27.

Stillman, A. B. and Grant, M. (1989). *The LEA Adviser – a Changing Role*. Windsor: NFER–Nelson.

Thomas, N. (1982). 'HM Inspectorate.' In: McCormick, R. and Nuttall, D. L. (Eds) *Curriculum Evaluation and Assessment in Educational Institutions*. Block 2. Part 3. Milton Keynes: The Open University Press, pp. 13–34.

Training Agency (TA) (1988). *Training Standard Advisory Service: First Annual Report 1987–88*. Sheffield: Training Agency.

Tyler, R. (1986). 'Changing concepts of education, evaluation'. *International Journal of Education Research*, 10, 1, pp. 1–113.

Walker, R. (1982). 'Reflections on Block 2, Part 3.' In: McCormick, R. and Nuttall, D. L. (Eds) *Curriculum Evaluation and Assessment in Educational Institutions*. Block 2. Approaches to Evaluation. Part 3. Inspections. Milton Keynes: The Open University Press, pp. 42–4.

Wilcox, B. (1986). 'Research communities, the White Paper chase and a new research ecumenism.' *British Education and Research Journal*. 12 1, pp. 3–13.

Winkley, D. (1985). *Diplomats and Detectives; LE Advisers at Work*. London: Robert Royce.

Wolf, R. M. (Ed.). (1987). 'Educational evaluation: the state of the field'. *International Journal of Education Research*. 11, 1, pp. 1–143.

2.7 | DEVELOPMENTS IN THE APPRAISAL OF TEACHERS

DEPARTMENT OF EDUCATION AND SCIENCE

THE CONTEXT OF THE SURVEY

'Staff appraisal involves qualitative judgements about performance and although it may start as self-appraisal by the teacher, it will normally involve judgements by other persons responsible for that teacher's work – a head of department or year, the headteacher, a member of the senior management team or an officer of the LEA. This appraisal may well (and usually does) include the identification of professional development needs.' This definition of appraisal is taken from *Quality in Schools: Evaluation and Appraisal*[1] a short report by HMI published in 1985. The report resulted from enquiries and visits made in 1983 and 1984 to local education authorities and schools where school self-evaluation and staff appraisal were known to exist.

Since then interest and activity in the appraisal of teachers have increased substantially. Teachers' conditions of service now envisage an agreed national framework for appraisal, and the Government has indicated that it intends to make Regulations in Autumn 1989 under Section 49 of the Education (No 2) Act 1986 to give effect to such a framework. Pilot work on school teacher appraisal has been funded by education support grants (ESG). Between 1987 and 1989, six authorities (Croydon, Cumbria, Newcastle-on-Tyne, Salford, Somerset and Suffolk – hereafter termed 'pilot' authorities) were funded to undertake the development of appraisal in schools.[2]

This report assesses the work of authorities, schools and colleges on appraisal and the extent to which they (especially the non-pilot authorities and the institutions located in them) are prepared for the implementation of

Source: DES (1989) *Developments in the Appraisal of Teachers, Department of Education and Science*, pp. 3–36 (abridged)

a national appraisal system. Differences between institutions in the primary, secondary and further and higher education (FHE) phases are also referred to, as is the pace at which authorities and institutions are preparing themselves for a national system.

Between summer 1987 and spring 1989, we visited both pilot and non-pilot LEAs. Discussions were held with officers in each of the pilot authorities and visits were made to 27 schools and four colleges of further education. Discussions were also held with officers in 63 non-pilot LEAs in England and visits were made in these authorities to 125 schools (49 primary, 73 secondary and three special) and to 67 FHE institutions. We did not attend lessons or interviews where teachers were being appraised, but the views of many staff, both appraisers and appraisees, were heard, and the documentation associated with many developing appraisal schemes was read. In addition, in the course of other visits to local authorities, schools and colleges, we noted developments in teacher appraisal, and information and opinion arising from these sources have been incorporated in the report.

Local authorities and individual institutions were asked about:

1 the context for the development of appraisal, especially the origins, aims, guidelines, administration, participants, relationship to other policies and costs;
2 the process of appraisal such as the sources of information; classroom observation; components, for example self-appraisal, interviews and the associated preparation and outcomes; records; and arrangements for monitoring and evaluating the impact of appraisal;
3 training;
4 the effects of appraisal upon: the policies and management practices of authorities and institutions; the work and professional development of teachers, both individually and more generally; and the quality of teaching and learning.

The picture emerging from the non-pilot authorities is probably reasonably representative of all authorities. Officers and advisers were found to be generally positive about appraisal and confident of their ability to implement a scheme. Several however expressed concern about the costs in time and money of a full appraisal system. Because we were guided to schools and colleges where work on appraisal was thought to be in hand, the appraisal activity in the institutions visited is probably more advanced than in the generality of schools and colleges.

THE GROWTH AND ADMINISTRATION OF APPRAISAL

THE ORIGINS OF POLICIES AND SCHEMES

Policies for the implementation of teacher appraisal have been developed in the six pilot authorities, although in all but one their work was delayed by the effects of teachers' industrial action in 1987. In addition to these six authorities at least eleven others have official policies for the appraisal of staff in schools and at least one has a policy for appraisal of staff in further education. Some of the schemes in non-pilot LEAs pre-date the six pilots and three were formally introduced over the period 1982–5. Following the issue on 12 August 1988 of the DES letter informing LEAs of the probable timetable for the introduction of a national scheme for the appraisal of school teachers, several more authorities have set up pilot schemes or working groups. At least twelve non-pilot authorities have allocated LEA funds to initiate appraisal schemes.

Factors which have contributed to the growth of activities connected with staff appraisal include the adoption of the GRIDS project,[3] the process of formal inspection by LEAs, initiatives taken by individual chief education officers, the introduction of the Local Education Authority Training Grants Scheme (LEATGS) and the appointment of advisers or development officers within whose remit appraisal is included. As part of the pilot project, one LEA has introduced the NFER/IMTEC[4] method of school review; another has linked appraisal with GRIDS.

Many schools and colleges in non-pilot LEAs have introduced schemes either formally as part of an LEA scheme or at the initiative of senior staff in the institution. The great majority of these institutional schemes have been introduced in the last three years. One hundred and four schools and sixty-four colleges visited in non-pilot authorities had staff development schemes and over half of these included appraisal. In the institutions visited since autumn 1988 an increased proportion of such schemes refers explicitly to appraisal. In many institutions, staff development schemes were introduced in response to LEAs' requests for consultation with teachers and the identification of needs in the context of the LEATGS.

At the institutional level the origins of staff development or appraisal schemes are varied. In many institutions schemes were introduced as a result of heads, deputies or other senior staff attending courses of training where staff appraisal was one of the topics covered. Encouragement from, and participation by, industry have helped in a few cases. Some senior staff experienced appraisal in industry or commerce before entering the teaching profession and this experience was influential in the initiation and shape of the scheme introduced. In many institutions, appraisal was introduced through experimental schemes involving working groups, usually on a voluntary basis. Initiatives taken by heads, especially new heads on appointment, have commonly been at the origin of appraisal schemes. The establishment of new schools, the reorganisation of schools, mergers or the re-structuring of institutions have enabled elements of staff appraisal to be introduced.

The nature of appraisal schemes in non-pilot authorities varies widely. In one county, the scheme involves most of the senior staff in all departments of the administration, including education: the scheme for appraising all teachers is presently at the discussion stage. In another county, the scheme includes both schools and colleges of further education and the authority's expertise has been used by the Service Children's Education Authority (SCEA) in training appraisers. In a third county a modest pilot scheme involving ten secondary schools began in 1988 and has been further extended to include an additional ten secondary schools and 25 primary schools. Many authorities deliberately avoid the use of the term 'staff appraisal', preferring 'staff development' or 'staff review'. In one, a staff development scheme has been introduced which may help pave the way for an appraisal scheme. A growing number of institutions are developing their own schemes, in some instances with the encouragement and guidance of the LEA. Several authorities have seconded teachers to investigate work on appraisal and some have used their LEATGS monies to fund the appointments of staff development tutors and to facilitate aspects of appraisal such as the provision of supply cover for classroom observation.

In the pilot authorities, central teams, including seconded teachers or heads, have been set up to design the schemes and documentation. In 18 of the non-pilot authorities visited, teachers likewise were involved in the design of appraisal schemes. Several referred to formal consultation with teachers' organisations. Seventeen of the non-pilot LEAs have consultative or steering groups and in nine authorities the scheme is administered by a small central team. Outside the pilot LEAs the development of administrative structures and processes proceeded slowly until summer 1988. The emphasis at the pre-scheme stage has usually been on consultation. In one county the development officer wrote to schools inviting an expression of interest and in another links were established with all six pilot authorities before its guidelines were drawn up. Since the issue of the DES letter in August 1988 and the inclusion of training for schoolteacher appraisal among the national priority areas in the LEATGS for 1989–90, there has been a perceptible quickening of pace. [...]

MAIN FINDINGS

Outside the pilot LEAs there is a great deal of experience of appraisal – both officially at LEA level and in individual schools and colleges. There has been a substantial increase in work on appraisal since the issue of the Department of Education and Science (DES) letter to LEAs in August 1988.

The aims of appraisal are rarely stated clearly; where they are stated they relate to individual teachers' professional growth, institutional management, or the quality of teaching and learning. Many LEAs are waiting for the DES to issue guidelines before drawing up their own. However, some authorities, and many individual institutions, have drawn up sets of guidelines.

Usually appraisal is carried out by heads, especially in primary schools. In colleges, heads of department are the main appraisers and in secondary schools deputy heads are also involved. Line management appraisal is the norm.

The majority of institutions in all phases see appraisal as contributing to their plans for INSET and staff development. They are much less likely to see appraisal as part of planning for curriculum development and whole school evaluation.

The costs of appraisal are a worry to LEAs but few have evaluated them very precisely. Funds provided through the local authority training grants scheme (LEATGS) are often used to finance training costs.

The process of appraisal varies greatly in scope and detail between phases and across institutions and LEAS. Self-evaluation is more commonly found in schools than in colleges and established procedures for the observation of teaching are more evident in pilot than in non-pilot LEAs. The views of college students are more frequently taken into account than those of school pupils. All institutions give prominence to the interview.

Virtually all schemes include a written record but there is no consensus on ownership and access, lifetime or even use of the record.

The most common intended outcome of appraisal is in-service training, but job modification and change of jobs are also common outcomes.

Consistency has not figured as a major concern: the most common means used to achieve it are standard training courses and guidelines and a core of experienced appraisers.

In the pilot authorities appraisal schemes are being systematically monitored and evaluated but in the non-pilot authorities there is little formal monitoring, and even less evaluation.

Training for appraisers has generally been more extensive than that for appraisees. Training has been more comprehensive and systematic in pilot than in non-pilot authorities. A wide range of agencies is used for training, including higher education; LEA officers and advisers; seconded heads and other teachers; and industrial and commercial organisations.

The major effect of appraisal is on the development of in-service strategies but a wide range of other effects was also found. These included job change; improved communications and morale; better management of institutions; modification of curriculum plans; and improved teaching and learning.

COMMENTARY

Experience in both the pilot and non-pilot authorities indicates that the appraisal of teachers can be introduced and operated in a positive and systematic way, and that among the outcomes of such healthy schemes are improved self-management and better morale among teachers involved. But a record of substantial success in pilot initiatives, supported by cooperative LEAs and teachers, while a good basis on which to build, does not guarantee that a national system can be implemented as smoothly. For that to be achieved several issues need to be resolved and a number of measures taken.

THE PURPOSES OF APPRAISAL

There is general agreement in both the pilot and non-pilot authorities that two principal aims of appraisal are to facilitate the professional growth of the individual teacher and to effect institutional improvement. Those broad aims subsume a wide range of other more specific purposes, which include the deployment of staff; institutional and curriculum change; implementation of policy; and career development. Essentially, however, appraisal is about the judgement of performance. Consequently one aim of a national system of appraisal might be to use such judgements to measure the performance of individual teachers against what is expected of them, and to inform decisions about what action is appropriate to meet their needs. Inevitably, a spectrum of teacher performance will emerge from any such activity and poor as well as exceptionally good performance will be identified. It is not clear how far such judgements might be used also to inform decisions about rewards or measures affecting teachers experiencing difficulties. The effective operation of a national system will require clarity about such matters.

THE TIMING OF THE INTRODUCTION OF A NATIONAL SCHEME

The current preoccupations of most teachers lie with the introduction of the Education Reform Act 1988. The introduction of the National Curriculum and of a new system of pupil assessment requires a great effort on the part of individual teachers and an extensive programme of in-service training. LEAs are heavily involved in the implementation of the Education Reform Act and in particular the local management of schools and colleges. In the circumstances, appraisal has understandably had a low priority for teachers, advisers and officers.

In both the pilot and non-pilot LEAs there is a great deal of experience already of the operation of appraisal schemes, both at LEA level and in individual schools and colleges. Many of these initiatives have been sensibly conceived and sensitively implemented at a carefully judged pace. But they have been undertaken mainly with teachers who are willing volunteers and have touched only a fraction of the 433,000 teachers and 23,000 schools who will be involved in a national system for England and Wales. For the very many teachers outside those schemes the appraisal of performance will require an openness to external and self-evaluation; a change that will take time to be accomplished.

We estimate that the operation of a national appraisal system in schools which allows for release for the process itself and some on-going training will require the equivalent of 1,800 additional teachers. This is based on the assumption that every teacher is formally appraised every two years, that each appraisal includes at least two hours of classroom observation, and that both appraisers and appraisees will be trained. The current shortages of teachers in some parts of the country and in some subjects, while not large in themselves, suggest that the additional staffing may not be readily available. In addition the rapid turnover of staff in some parts of the country will make the operation of appraisal difficult in those areas. These two factors raise questions about the timescale for the implementation of a national system.

MEASURES WHICH WOULD EASE THE INTRODUCTION OF A NATIONAL APPRAISAL SYSTEM

The definition of appraisal and the purposes of a national system should be made clear. Underlying the purposes will be the crucial question of what are reasonable standards to expect of individual teachers. If nationally agreed competencies are developed these may provide a baseline for what is expected of experienced staff. In any case, some consistency of practice and expectation is desirable in itself but particularly so given the mobility of the teaching profession.

National guidelines will need to cover: the participants; the components of the appraisal process; the frequency of appraisal; the range of information to be gathered; procedures for classroom observation and the conduct of interviews; the preparation and retention of records and access to them; training; alternative models for implementation; and monitoring and evaluation.

A balance will have to be found between the firm guidance which many authorities are looking for, and the opportunity for the institutions concerned to contribute to the creation of a scheme and thereby have a sense of involvement and ownership. Equally a national system will need to be flexible in order to build on the experience of appraisal which already exists and to allow for different school cultures, intakes and the different phases: primary; secondary; 16–19.

All LEAs will need to develop strategies for the introduction and operation of appraisal that include arrangements for: consultation with teachers and governors; the appointment of co-ordinators; the organisation of training, and the setting up of monitoring, evaluation and appeal systems. A realistic assessment of the role of the advisory services will be essential. Effective appraisal should lead to better identification of INSET needs and more focused and efficient use of what is available. But some consideration needs to be given to the demand that may be generated when the INSET needs of all teachers are identified on a regular basis within a national system of appraisal.

Individual institutions will need to relate the local authority's scheme to their own circumstances. Particular attention will need to be given to identifying those institutions where appraisal might be introduced first and to the phasing in of training for different groups of staff. Classroom observation will be an essential part of the process and institutions will need to ensure that appraisers have sufficient credibility with appraisees. The procedures adopted will need to meet the needs of all teachers, including those of exceptional ability and those experiencing difficulties.

All teachers, whether as appraisers or appraisees, will need to be prepared and trained. Their early experiences of the operation of the scheme are crucial as these will convince them of its benefits or otherwise.

Sufficient time must be allowed for the introduction and implementation of the system. That is essential for a good scheme and a good scheme will not be cheap.

There should be real returns from appraisal as well as costs. Better classroom performance, better deployment of teachers, more effective preparation of lessons and a greater degree of cooperation are potential gains. But there will be costs and those will depend upon a range of factors including:

1 the characteristics of the scheme, for example: the frequency cycle, the ratio of appraisers to appraisees and the amount of supply cover needed to allow for observation and interview;
2 the training pattern to be adopted, for example: the number of training days required by different groups of participants, including heads, teachers and trainers; the costs of employing expert trainers; follow-up to the initial training; supplementary training to allow for wastage and turnover; and the amount of training arranged within teaching time;
3 manpower needs for co-ordination and administration;
4 the costs of monitoring and evaluation using internal or external agents;
5 the pace at which the scheme is to be introduced and the proportion of the teaching force to be trained in successive years. In the first year of a four-year introductory period perhaps ten per cent might be trained and then appraised. In each of the second, third and fourth years 30% of the teachers might be trained and appraised. On a biennial cycle, however, the first cohort will need to be reappraised in the third year, and the second cohort reappraised in the fourth. Thus costs grow rapidly up to the fourth year. Thereafter, training costs will diminish and subsequently stabilise.

Naturally, if some of the training takes place on non-contact days, costs will be proportionately reduced.

Given these assumptions and those mentioned in paragraph 2, p. 130, we estimate that the equivalent of 1,800 additional teachers will be required to operate a national system and that annual costs would level out in the region of £35m.

Finally, it is important that appraisal is not done for its own sake but is seen as a tool integral to the management of other initiatives and strategies. That is especially important in the context of the implementation of the Education Reform Act 1988.

REFERENCES

[1] HMSO, (1985) *Quality in Schools: Evaluation and Appraisal.*
[2] From April 1989, Barnet, Croydon, Cumbria, Hertfordshire, Kent and St Helens have begun pilot work in further education.
[3] Guidelines for Review and Internal Development in Schools (a School Curriculum Development Committee project on whole school evaluation).
[4] National Foundation for Educational Research/International Movements Towards Educational Change.

EVALUATION OF TEACHER AND PUPIL PERFORMANCE

|2.8|

JOAN SALLIS

No discussion of the 'client' view of the parents' role would be complete without a reference to the growth of interest and experience in the appraisal of teachers and the testing of pupils. Many would argue that if parents are to be assured that the service is sufficiently self-critical to afford their children the best education, there must be formal means for measuring the competence of teachers, which means consequently measuring also the attainments of pupils.

Like most observers of the scene I have been very impressed by the range and quality of work now going on to establish fair and constructive ways in which schools can evaluate their performance and that of their staff as individuals. Nobody who attended the DES Conference on *Better Schools: Evaluation and Appraisal* in Birmingham on 14 and 15 November 1985, or read the report subsequently published could doubt that the service has advanced in leaps and bounds in recent years both in its enthusiasm for better techniques of appraisal, and progress in developing them. This process seemed to be going on so well without government intervention, that it was regrettable that the government had soured the debate by introducing alien associations into appraisal. For months every Ministerial statement on appraisal of teachers was made in the same breath as a suggestion that there were too many incompetent teachers, with the implication that the only point in more self-critical techniques was to identify and purge the schools of a number of poor performers. It was also unfortunate that the subject was linked with the long teachers' pay dispute of 1985 and 1986, and acceptance of appraisal not only made a condition of pay awards but also linked to incremental progress. It was at that Birmingham Conference that Sir Keith Joseph, then Secretary of

Source: Sallis, J. (1988) *Schools, Parents and Governors: a new approach to accountability*, Routledge, London, pp. 37–40.

State, chose to recant both the punitive view of appraisal and its link with pay, but it was too late to heal all the bitterness.

The Education (no 2) Act of 1986 while not abandoning appraisal, now contains the seemingly innocuous statement:

> The Secretary of State may by regulations make provision for requiring local education authorities, or such other persons as may be prescribed, to secure that the performance of teachers to whom the regulations apply ... is regularly appraised in accordance with such requirements as may be prescribed.

Pilot studies were then initiated by the DES in six LEAs, coordinated by the National Development Centre for School Management Training based at the University of Bristol and evaluated by the Cambridge Institute of Education.

What is being developed will be sounder and more durable if it has the understanding and trust of teachers themselves and if it is seen to be positive and constructive in intention and fair and participatory in practice. It is good to see so much emphasis on whole school appraisal, since many of us who have as outsiders become familiar with schools know how much more an individual teacher's performance depends on the teamwork, the leadership, the structures of support within a school than on private talent. This is why the appraisal/pay direct link is so wrong.

This is not the place, and I am not the writer, for expert commentary on the techniques of evaluation and their future, but in any discussion of the part they might play in parents' relationships with schools some very important issues emerge. First, there are some useful benefits for parents and governors. As I noted, parents generally would be very encouraged to know that schools had arrangements for appraising teachers, and even if the information they were given and the involvement they were offered went no further than that it would increase confidence. I see it as essential, as schools introduce such arrangements, that they should describe the system to the general body of parents as well as communicating in more detail with governors. A further benefit is that governors, who often have very difficult staff problems to consider from time to time, would be less likely to be faced with them too late for much constructive action if difficulties were identified routinely in a teacher's early career. At present such issues, by the time they come to governors, are fraught with emotion. Finally in the catalogue of benefits to parents and governors one should mention the help regular appraisal would afford to all those involved in staff appointments. At present much reliance is placed on confidential reports, and all concerned know that they can sometimes be unrevealing and at worst misleading. Those who write them want to support staff seeking promotion, so give them the benefit of the doubt. Occasionally they yield to the understandable temptation to write over-generous comments on one they would like to be rid of. This would be less serious in the context of a properly documented career. Most outsiders know vaguely that there is a code in reports. We are meant to laugh at 'It would be a very fortunate head who got this teacher to work for him', but how do we know the difference between 'worthy of consideration' and 'worthy of serious consideration'? More soberly, a well-documented career affords some safeguard for governors against unhelpful references, but it is also a protection for the teacher against the occasional real or imagined malice or simple human incompatibility. I do not want to suggest that teacher appraisal will solve all the problems of schools, but if we can divest it of some of its dramatic overtones it will surely be a modest help with some of them.

I have heard representatives of the teachers' unions become almost apoplectic about any suggestion that the time might come when governors might take part in appraisal processes. Yet if governors are to have a responsibility for determining a school's aims, and for satisfying themselves as to the methods to be adopted to achieve those aims, if they are to be involved in the appointment and promotion of staff, is it logical to exclude them completely from the school's arrangements for career review? Obviously, if being a governor is not to become a full-time job, there must be limits to the detail with which they can concern themselves, but I suggest that as a minimum they should be thoroughly familiar with the system, should have access to the records, should from time to time have the experience as individuals of observing the process, and should be enlisted to support the head in any particularly difficult or important task arising from that process.

What of parents? I have suggested that it is very important for them to know in general terms what structures exist in the school to review the performance of teachers and to promote their professional development in an orderly way, while supporting any who have difficulties. This is probably all that the majority would wish to know, and I don't think we are yet ready to see teachers' records open as well as those of pupils! The question of parent and pupil input to teacher appraisal is bound to generate heat, but parents and older pupils *do* have very clear impressions of teacher effectiveness, and I would hope we could give some thought to how we might incorporate them as a part of the total process once it has become routine to have appraisal at all. I should not want to impede such routine acceptance by going too fast, but I do look forward to a time when 'I am not a perfect person' is as unremarkable a statement in teaching as elsewhere. [. . .]

part three
EFFECTIVE SCHOOLING: OLD AND NEW ISSUES
PREPARED BY JOHN ISAAC

INTRODUCTION TO PART 3

JOHN ISAAC

These three readings illustrate views from different parts of the education system and the writers take contrasting positions as they write. The first reading is by Tim Brighouse, written when he was the Chief Education Officer for Oxfordshire. The responsibility of the LEA is made clear and the study goes on to link effectiveness with a shared value system, the importance of leadership from the Headteacher and a focus on the pupil. There is also a critical review of the way in which recent central government initiatives may hinder the development of effective schools.

David Reynolds, a leading figure in the series of international conferences that have done so much to generate interest and academic debate around the effectiveness issue contributes in the second reading an informative and analytical survey of literature in the field.

The third reading is taken from a book reporting a funded research project. This extract raises some of the key issues that appear in this kind of research and some of the dilemmas that face the researchers. It also introduces the latest concept of the measurement of effectiveness that has been applied and which raised some debate when it was published. But Smith and Tomlinson finish this section by pointing out that none of the methods used so far take account of the way that the school organisations are *live* and constantly changing.

Source: Specially commissioned for this volume. Copyright © 1990 The Open University.

3.1 | EFFECTIVE SCHOOLS AND PUPILS' NEEDS

TIM BRIGHOUSE

INTRODUCTION

The first part of this chapter attempts to provide an impression of an effective school and suggests a classification of schools. I want to go on to describe what I think are the processes through which schools become effective. We can then look at the evidence which schools themselves use to judge their effectiveness. Finally, I want to examine some of the implications of the government's proposals to legislate for a national curriculum, the retrenchment that will take place if teachers are required to engage in assessing pupil learning at ages seven, 11 and 14, and the way this will have a considerable effect on the majority of pupils who are not engaged in learning directed towards formalised state examinations which in reality is a provision for the select few. Included amongst this number is a significant proportion of pupils with special educational needs.

It is ironic that, apart from the HMI document 'Ten Good Schools' (1977) there is practically no consideration of the effective school in all the many HMI and DES documents of the last ten years. Even the White Paper 'Better Schools', which might have been expected to give attention to the issue, failed to do so. There are, of course, other studies from different agencies and such research findings as found in Rutter *et al.*'s (1979) publication.

This omission is explained in part by the diversity of opinion about what is a good or effective school and, therefore, the elusiveness of the topic. In some strange way the sum of the parts of the effective school is exceeded by the totality of what it stands for.

Source: Brighouse, T. (1989) Effective schools and pupils' needs in James, N. and Southgate, T. (eds) *The Management of Special Needs in Ordinary Schools*, Routledge, London, pp. 5–18.

Nor is this a topic which can be tackled by an examination of the obverse side of the coin: it is easy to identify the really ineffective school. Perhaps that is why the media concentrate on bad schools in the hope that by identifying their qualities other schools would know what to avoid. Merely to avoid evil, however, does not guarantee virtue; indeed it might be argued that a preoccupation with adequacy, incompetence and downright inefficiency involves such close scrutiny of its qualities that one is, as it were, adversely affected by the experience. One thing that is certain, however, is that schools which look over their shoulders too often, schools which seek to interpret the latest whim of society, are uncertain schools. They are schools that do not know for what they stand. Such schools – just like complacent schools – will never be good or effective schools. Just as the good citizen is not simply one who avoids crime, so the good school is not merely to be defined by being safely indistinguishable from the next. Nevertheless to establish effective schools and colleges constitutes the major part of a local authority's business. If it could get that right, the LEA would have reasonable claim to being itself effective in the major part of its business.

THE EFFECTIVE SCHOOL

Some of the best literature on the topic is illuminating and positive, descriptive, and relies little on quantified evidence and research, preferring instead a subjective impressionistic view of quality. It is none the worse for that.

An effective school can first and foremost be recognised through its pupils, its staff and its community. Recognition is not solely from the office, from the headteacher or the newspaper; nor will it be necessarily through brochures or speech days – important though they may be – that you know of the effective school. It will be rather from parents who say 'My child simply cannot wait to go to school ... We are doing this survey with Jane because she has brought it home from school and is so insistent that we take part in its completion.' It will be from the kitchen staff or the cleaners who comment, 'It's alright up at Bluebells. Their head is a real good sport. I go there for the people and not the money and I wouldn't miss it for the world.' Or it will be from the community represented perhaps by the local employer's comment, 'We'd always take one from St Thomas. They always seem to produce such willing and confident youngsters.' Such are the comments that will be heard about the effective school in its local community.

Litmus tests of outstanding schools, therefore, are not just public occasions or examination results but also and importantly private witnesses. Of all connected with the school, the non-teaching staff can tell the depth and the quality of the relationships in the school and can readily see whether the school truly celebrates all its constituents. They see beyond the honours board to the consistency of treatment of one another. Ultimately the effective school is discerned in the confidence of its pupils and their commitment to future personal development. They are not merely happy, they are unafraid, free, self-disciplined and autonomous. So often the ordinary school celebrates the few and misleads or even disables the many.

SHARED VALUES

The outstanding and effective school will have a set of articles – not of course the Articles of Government which every school must have – but almost articles of faith, a kind of collective creed. The jargon phrase often used to describe this phenomenon is a 'shared value system'. The school as a whole, especially the teaching and non-teaching staff, will have a high level of agreement on the purpose of the school.

I do not mean unexceptionable and vague generalisations which adorn education text books but the certainty of a shared value system. Such schools know where they stand on race, the equality of the sexes, on the place of the family in society, matters of prejudice and educational philosophy, because they have discussed these issues sometimes to the point of exhaustion. From this certainty the important everyday rules and habits of the community flow. The certainty informs the marking system, the personal records, arrangements for games, time given to music and residential trips – in short, every activity of the school community.

SELF EVALUATION

One of the means of achieving such a shared value system is the sensitive use of the processes of self evaluation – eschewing perhaps initially the accountability end of the spectrum with associated implications of self-justification or defensiveness – in favour of an emphasis on common school purposes which depend on interdependence and collegiality.

Such shared value systems are more difficult to achieve in a society which has become more pluralist and tolerant of diversity and where perhaps the pervasive and powerful influences of institutions such as the church and the extended family can no longer be assumed. Moreover, the purpose of schooling has simultaneously become more ambitious. In former times it was more straightforward to achieve a shared value system in primary schools which would be judged by their success rate at eleven-plus or in the grammar school, with the view of ability which was narrowly intellectual – even if monocularly ungenerous – and based on flawed research for its justification. The shared value systems achieved may have been flawed – they may, for example, have undervalued the wider range of human ability and have depended for their existence on the failure of the majority, many of whom had talents which were never uncovered and for whom schooling was an experience to be got out of the way as soon as possible – but they were at least clear and realisable.

A SET OF PRINCIPLES

It is more difficult to espouse the value systems of the comprehensive, primary and secondary schools especially when most of the organisational features are inherited from the previous selective system. The teachers of one school, during a reconsideration of their self-evaluation, expressed their value system – which is, of course, distinct from their aims and objectives – broadly if idealistically as follows:

- children should be treated as they might become rather than as they are;
- all pupils should be equally valued;
- teachers should have the expectation that all their students have it in them to walk a step or two with genius, if only they could identify the talent to find the key to unlock it;
- the staff unitedly should stand for the successful education of the whole person;
- the staff should contribute to the development of mature adults for whom education is a lifelong process and proposed to judge their success by their students' subsequent love of education;
- the staff should try to heal rather than to increase diversities, to encourage a self-discipline, a lively activity to breed lively minds and good health, a sense of interdependence and community.

The effective school will test all its practices – its systems of marking, recording, appointments, publications, its staff development systems, its curriculum, its communications system, structure and system of community relationships – against these principles. It will necessarily find mismatch but will ceaselessly attempt to bring its practices closer to its principles.

LEADERSHIP

In this task the school will depend on successful leadership. In the DES document 'Ten Good Schools', and all other literature, there is the underlying importance of the presence of an outstanding headteacher. The importance of leadership was brought home when a colleague commented on the paradox in one primary school where all the teachers were good, even outstanding, and yet the school could not be called effective. What had happened was the departure of an outstanding headteacher who had been replaced by a very ordinary, even inadequate, newcomer. Slowly the edge was disappearing from the school. Conversely we agreed there was another school which was outstanding although a few years ago we would have thought it ordinary, even humdrum. The collective growth in the school's imperatives seemed to have spurred on all staff to the point where ordinary teachers were performing above themselves, the children had new-found confidence and assurance. Of course, a new and skilful headteacher had arrived.

Our leadership in schools may be divided into three categories. The *first category* displays a style which leads researchers into classroom practice to call its practitioners 'perceptive professional developers'. Such headteachers would see their role above all as requiring experience and insight based on a deep understanding of their own position on educational and social issues; they would, however, eschew imposing views on others. They regard their role as enjoyable and enriching to themselves as they develop their own skills as well as those of others. They are sharp at identifying the necessity for change and have a deep understanding of its nature. Galton (1980), in the 'ORACLE' survey, gave high marks for success to classroom teachers who were 'infrequent changers'. Every now and then such teachers changed their arrangements, changed their style, the style of the classroom organisation, and improved the quality of children learning. So it is for the first category of school leadership.

The 'perceptive professional developers' give attention to and have an active interest in the curriculum where the change needs to be most frequent. It needs to be most frequent because the teacher must meet individual needs and catch the interests of a multitude of different young people. New materials, new courses, a new environment (in the sense of being new to the teacher or the department concerned) are justified by the expansion of information and the consequential need to replace the old and irrelevant with the new and relevant.

New skills are also cherished but the older ones are cast off only after a deliberate reflection of outworn usefulness. In the curriculum, therefore, the 'perceptive professional developer' knows that information needs to change more frequently than skills and that attitudes need to be fairly consistent in the school as a derivative of their shared value systems. Such leaders see themselves as conductors or perhaps the first violin and the staff basically as colleagues in an orchestra. They may be flamboyant or you may not notice them – styles are legitimately different after all. Such headteachers recognise teachers' different strengths and work so as not to produce a false model to those teachers. Such leaders have the breadth of vision in their appointments to bring to their orchestra new instruments and new performers. They are often good at improvisation: they look for harmony rather than discord to see the necessity for hard argument and debate.

Such leaders have a keen interest in others and see themselves as facilitating the development of those people. Such headteachers will not be absent too long from the school. Such a category of school will change the organisational structure less frequently – perhaps only to give a new perspective for teachers and other staff and the learners themselves in order to maximise the opportunity of shared perceptions. So the timetable, pastoral systems of posts and responsibilities, and the departmental arrangements are changed, but only with enormous care since they provide the everyday bearings of support and stability on which the community depends.

The 'perceptive professional developers' see the importance of the bits and pieces: the note of thanks, the particular potential and failing of each member of the community and his or her different need of support, the chronic and acute personal problems of his or her senior colleagues, none in themselves important in the grand scheme of things but every one, however, vital for the performance of the school as a whole. Such leadership is of course a plural quality. It is exercised at all levels, heads of department and co-ordinators, for example, and for all the people there are in the school.

The *second category* of leadership produces people who can best be called 'the system maintainers'. They are characterised by their wish 'to keep things on an even keel' and to preserve the existing order of things in order to maintain high standards. They fear precedents which might weaken previous success and are alarmed by change which might precipitate declining standards. They eschew virtually all change. They do not take risks. They like order in all that they do. In establishments run by 'system maintainers' you will find comments like these:

'We tried that in so-and-so's time and it didn't work.'

'Why do you want to upset everything that has worked for so long?'

'Yes, that is a good idea: if only we could consider it but I fear we cannot because ...'

'That would set a precedent which would have alarming implications.'

Such schools have some way to go to be really effective. They will achieve success of a sort but they will never have that sharp observation which will find the talent of every child. You can tell when they are getting near to moving towards success. It is when they try something different and confess to the thrill of unexpected enjoyment. You can also tell when they are *en route* towards the third category. It is when you hear more frequently the comment 'Things are not what they used to be' or 'Many leaders are instinctively system maintainers'. They are too distrustful of change.

The *third category* of leadership is thankfully very rare nowadays. One may simply term it as inadequate. Security has become a way of life. Such leaders fear their insecurity. They are left with enjoying a status to which they adhere for their own salvation: they use the post not for what can be done for others but solely for themselves. In such schools good teachers become worse and if they have sense they leave. In the end only those either at the beginning or at the very end of their careers are left in such schools. Such leaders do not recognise anything but the temporary glorification of their own position.

QUALITIES OF LEADERSHIP

Among the leadership qualities in effective schools – and these qualities can be found collectively in the senior management team – the following recur: being cheerful and optimistic even in adversity; showing welcome; obviously enjoying the achievements of others especially amongst all the staff and not just the teaching staff; being a good listener; taking the blame and showing fallibility; being able to see time in perspective and being able to organise that in relation to the various constituents; having a fairly well thought out philosophy and understanding of the differential nature of change.

Lastly, you will recognise the effective school by its appearance. It will be environmentally – but especially visually – aware. In this, of course, schools are blessed for better or worse by their natural inheritance; few can be better placed than some of the famous schools in the private sector. Nevertheless all effective schools make the best of their circumstances, even those in less promising ones, by using the internal walls and the background of the school as an additional subliminal factor. Schools for years have displayed children's work but the nature of that display will tell the perceptive visitor much about the effectiveness of the school. Does it, for example, represent a range of work from different children? Does it support the school's policies and practices across the whole range of the curriculum – maths, science, language as well as art and craft? Are there unfinished pieces of work, problems unsolved, puzzles to pose questions? Are the images reflective of the school's set of beliefs on the family, the role of women in society, for example?

There is a multitude of questions to ask when entering the school. A responsible and confident school often lets the pupil speak for it in showing visitors around, in answering the telephone and in welcoming a visitor at a school entrance which will be clearly marked. Some schools have gone further. There has been a conscious attempt to overcome the institutionalised feel of the school by the use of carpet, material and the abolition of the pervasive bell. In one instance it was even noticed that a school occupied its non-lesson time with orchestral, choir and other musical practice in the main thoroughfares of school activity. Noise as well as appearance affects the quality of learning.

So will the visitor, especially the professional visitor, with half an observant eye recognise the effective school: by its shared values, its treatment of one another, its cheerful leadership, its appearance and perhaps by the small talk of a staffroom where people exchange opinions about pupils, papers on the curriculum, and share ideas from the professional journals. Such evidence lies outside the lessons where the quality of the student's learning can be assessed. But how are such schools achieved?

PROCESSES WHEREBY SCHOOLS BECOME EFFECTIVE

It has already been remarked that the effectiveness of a school is closely related to the quality of its leadership. Such leaders have to be chosen and the responsibility for that process rests on the local education authority and the governing body in a balance of partnership which is laid down by the 1986 Education Act. Once appointed, headteachers need to be valued and supported, through induction and appropriately timed periods of in-service refreshment, during the tenure of their office.

The school's leadership – the wise headteacher ensures as wide a sharing of this function as possible – will give early attention to collective processes of self-evaluation, sometimes drawn from the concern of staff and the wider community itself. Shared vision for the school is gradually established. Self-evaluation will be a tool to keep under review the match of declared principles to actual practices not only in the curriculum but in the school's organisation.

A visual policy for the school, for example, is maintained only by hard work and a systematic scheme in which all share. Particularly impressive recently was the example of one secondary school which had involved almost a quarter of its pupils and staff in devising different strategies for changed display in the public parts of the school.

PROCESSES OF SCHOOL ORGANISATION

The effective school does not ignore the bits and pieces of administration. One very famous headteacher remarked 'I take my stand on detail.' This will lead the effective school to list all the various administrative tasks and functions from their beginning to their end and to identify alongside each the person who is responsible for worrying over the timely completion of the various tasks being undertaken by others, but which collectively will lead to the successful completion of the operation. It matters not at all whether the task is a regular news-sheet to parents, a parents' evening, a play, a collection of option choices, a careers convention or a duty roster.

The effective school gives careful attention to its system of assessing the pupils' work. It is essential that the staff compare children's work amongst themselves in order to moderate and calibrate their own perceptions of standards and expectations of achievement so that they are not too low or too high. They must take care not to depend on norm-referenced marking systems but to make sure that marking is a further means of 'conversing' with the pupil. It is unlikely that teachers professing to be child-centred will be true to that belief unless they can demonstrate that they mark the children's work both in a timely fashion and in a way which is positive.

The principles of assessment in the effective school have informed the requirements of the Oxford Certificate of Educational Achievement (OCEA). They provide a set of principles as applicable to primary as to secondary schools for they will stimulate schools – their teachers, parents and pupils – to devise explicit maps of learning and chart the progress of all students in their journey of learning. They will have a policy for homework which is understood and followed by pupils, staff and parents. The involvement of these in a shared contract of learning can often be established whether in a survey or project work or in the attention to revision and further practice of examples. Parents can help enormously with memory tasks and practices established to foster mental agility, besides of course being supportive, understanding, giving of their time and trying to enable youngsters to have interesting experiences whether close at hand or far away from the home.

The school will typically have a set of expectations by which all agree to abide; a sanctions system will be understood and administered with sensitivity to the circumstances of the individual. The organisation of pupils in groups, classes or sets is closely examined to avoid inevitable expectation of failure and negative self-image which can result from streaming by ability in a general way. Nor should it be thought that such arrangements are to be found exclusively in the secondary sector where forms of setting based on interest and aptitude according to task, information and skill are again necessary as the youngster grows older; the colour coded tables in a reception class may have within them the seeds of future problems. The school gives close attention to its practices of consultation with parents, recognising their capacity as prime educators in their own right.

The last major process of achieving school effectiveness lies in staff development policy and practice. It will of course apply to all staff whether teachers or not and will range from an adequate system of induction (which should lead naturally to a form of individual personal review of plans and discussion of the realisation of those plans without all the paraphernalia and difficulty of an appraisal scheme) through to ensuring adequate time for personal reading, development and further training. There will be great care to differentiate between a collective staff development plan and that of the individual.

INDICATORS BY WHICH A SCHOOL JUDGES ITS EFFECTIVENESS

The school evaluation process has revealed a wealth of measures – collections of evidence if you like – by which effective schools assess themselves. It will range from scores in tests of, for example, reading and mathematics, to the number and quality of school performances and events. There will be a check, pupil by pupil, on the opportunity for residential experience and involvement in service to the community and outside. Attendance rates of staff and pupils alike will be monitored. When it comes to examination results the school, with an eye to each youngster's achievement, will monitor not just the proportion of youngsters in the age group year on year getting higher grades, but the score per pupil over a range of subjects. The local educational authority may seek to compare schools of differing backgrounds. However, it is more important for each school to set up its own indices of performance in order to build ever higher achievement over the years.

ROLE OF THE LEA

The role of the LEA in the process of achieving school effectiveness is complex but important. It includes, of course, the provision of adequate resources but it also covers much more. The LEA can set a climate and exercise its duties sensitively to stimulate the questioning, developing, self-confident school. It will tolerate individually different practices within a framework of principles; it trusts and praises in public but will vigorously 'police' in private rather than *vice versa*. Above all an LEA can create a professional and communal climate in which schools are more rather than less likely to be effective. Such an LEA will find its staff sought by others and it will publish its practices nationally. It will be particularly careful in its appointment procedures. It will have support service personnel – whether administrators, advisers or development officers – who demonstrate in their actions their understanding and encouragement for the subtle nature of change in schools.

The challenge to the LEA in this task has now become more formidable. It will be tempting, but wrong, to copy central government's top-down activity on the curriculum. Indeed, the advisers in particular will be busy acting as consultants or brokers to hard-pressed schools which must deal with the ill-timed incursions of Whitehall into the curriculum. Unless they are assisted, our effective schools will be undermined or overwhelmed by such activity which inevitably will interrupt the carefully considered development plan which is the feature of any school that has justifiable claims to effectiveness.

EFFECTIVE SCHOOLS AND GOVERNMENT POLICY

The government in the early part of 1987 took a significant wrong turning in its educational policies. The signs of it were there in the 1986 Act with its last minute accretions such as the requirement for headteachers and governors to take account of the Chief Officer of Police when drawing up curriculum statements and in other clauses on matters such as political indoctrination. What these sections revealed was a government which was intent on general legislation as a result of particular and isolated incidents. Hence a few failing inner-city schools and one or two local education authorities failing in their task were dealt with, not as they might be through decisive intervention by the Secretary of State using his existing powers under the 1944 Act, but by punishing all schools and all local education authorities.

No matter that the standards of achievement are improving faster in the United Kingdom than in any other western European country. 'Spare us the facts, just feed our prejudices' seems to be the principle on which future educational planning is to be based. Hence the proposals for tests at seven, eleven and fourteen to ensure, as the Prime Minister said (Torquay 1987), not merely that 'we are clear what children should learn but that we are sure that they are actually learning it'. The dangers of tests so far as school effectiveness is concerned are too obvious to mention. The pupils are either standardised by reference to the average performance of an age group thereby causing teachers to attend to those close to the average; or are differentiated so that youngsters become labelled early and perform according to that expectation. One director of education has actually spoken of holding children back a year in order that they should master the subject matter of the test. A sideways glance at the United States will reveal the logical outcome of these processes. There, they have such problems in their inner-city schools that armed police stalk the corridors and the cream of a generation cannot be tempted at any price into teaching. Teachers themselves in the United States confess that they cheat when their students take the tests, either by giving their children more time, or by asking if they really meant to give that answer, or simply by doing the questions for them. It has all the inevitability of mediocrity of the Revised Code in the latter part of the nineteenth century. In the United States, for all their fine words about integration of children with special educational needs, they stop short of mainstreaming as a result of their strict adherence to age and grade.

Central government in England and Wales, with its promise of city technology colleges, its determination to allow popular schools to escape the system and its espousal of assisted places, not to mention tests related to age, demonstrates that it does not believe in the right of all children to enjoy a place in an effective school. For the structure it plans requires there to be at least three categories of school to which I have earlier alluded. The implications for all children with special educational needs are too obvious to emphasise. They are doomed to grace and favour treatment but are most likely to be in the state-maintained 'division-three' schools that will be created by the new arrangements.

Such a system, if indeed it is created, will last as long as the fissured society it creates does not erupt. It will simmer like a city perched on the continental shelf waiting for the inevitable earthquake – creating its ghettoes, ever-widening the gap between the rich and the poor, paying through the nose for its intolerance and increasing the size of its police force. It will, moreover, reverse half a century of development towards a different set of values.

References

DES (1977) *Ten Good Schools*, London: HMSO.

Galton, M. and Simon, B. (eds) (1980) *Progress and Performance in the Primary Classroom*, London: Routledge & Kegan Paul.

Rutter, M., Maugham, B., Mortimore, P., Ousten, J. and Smith, A. (1979) *Fifteen Thousand Hours*, London: Open Books.

School Effectiveness and School Improvement: A Review of the British Literature

3.2

David Reynolds

It is important to make clear at the outset that only in the last decade has a body of research findings in this area begun to emerge, a marked contrast with the United States, for example, where both school effectiveness and school improvement have been large and established disciplines from the early 1970s onwards. There is not space to consider the detailed reasons for this here (see Reynolds, 1985) but a few explanations for this state of affairs may be instructive:

1. There has been great difficulty in gaining access to schools in Britain for comparative research purposes as shown by the unhappy experience of Michael Power (1967, 1972) in Tower Hamlets, where research access to schools was refused after large differences were found in schools' delinquency rates.
2. Early research findings in the United States (Coleman, 1966; Jencks *et al.*, 1971) and in Britain (Plowden Committee, 1967) showed very limited school effects on academic outcomes and created a climate of professional educational opinion which believed that variation in individual school organisations had minimal effects upon pupils' development.
3. The absence of well-developed and reproducible measures of institutional climate, again in marked contrast to the situation for researchers in the United States, hindered the understanding of within-school processes and the measurement of the characteristics of effective organisational processes.
4. The rise of determinist sociology of education, as reflected in the work of

Source: Reynolds, D. (1988) 'School effectiveness and school literature: a review of the British literature' in Reynolds, D., Creemers, B. P. M. and Peters, T. (1988) *School Effectiveness and Improvement Proceedings of the First International Congress London 1988*, School of Education, University of Wales, and Rion Institute for Educational Research, Groningen

Bowles and Gintis (1976) and Bourdieu and Passeron (1977) led to a neglect of the school as an institution independent from the wider society that lasted throughout the 1970s and early 1980s, with the result that the pioneering work into school organisational processes of Hargreaves (1967) and Lacey (1970) had no further elaboration or development until the studies of Ball (1981) and Burgess (1983).

5 The intellectual hegemony of traditional mainstream British educational research, with its psychologically determined stress on the primacy of individual, family and community based explanations for children's 'educability' created a professional research climate hostile to school effectiveness work, a hostility which showed in some of the critiques of the Rutter *et al.*, (1979) study *Fifteen Thousand Hours* (see, for example, Acton, (1980), and Goldstein, (1980)), and in some of the reception given to our early work from South Wales, which for example Musgrove (1981) called 'widely applauded but highly implausible'!

Organisational or school effectiveness research is therefore still in Britain very much a 'fledgling paradigm', with a relatively limited number of people engaged on research work, a still quite recent history and a lack of established firm relationships with other educational disciplines such as sociology of education or educational administration. Both the major British school effectiveness studies of secondary schools in fact emerged from a *medical* research environment (Rutter at the Institute of Psychiatry, Reynolds at the Medical Research Council) rather than from mainstream educational research or from educational administration, a situation which again may reflect on the strength of individualised psychological explanations and of individualised policy concerns within mainstream British educational research.

The remainder of this paper will now look at the literature and research in this area, attempting to outline those areas where there are agreed and consistent findings across the various British studies (relatively few in number), and also to outline areas where there is a continuing debate and a lack of agreement when studies and findings are compared with one another (a somewhat larger number).

DO SCHOOL ORGANISATIONS HAVE EFFECTS UPON PUPILS?

Early work in Britain, such as the regression analyses conducted for the Plowden Committeee (1967), suggested that individual school organisations had few differential effects upon pupils. Whilst clearly schools mattered in affecting children's academic and social development, it was the *uniformity* of schools' organisational effects which was emphasised in the 1960s and 1970s by reports such as those by Coleman (1966) and Jencks *et al.* (1971).

The early British school effectiveness studies (Reynolds, 1976; Reynolds and Sullivan, 1979; Rutter *et al.*, 1979) sought to show that the outcomes of individual schools were not determined by the academic and social background of their intakes of pupils, yet there was in many people's minds the considerable doubt noted above as to whether enough detailed information on the intakes of pupils had been collected to ensure that the large differences in the outcomes of the schools studied did not only reflect the effects of unmeasured differences in the quality of the intakes of pupils.

More recently, however, studies which have collected a very wide range of data concerning the intakes into different schools have still found large differences in the outcomes of the schools, even when allowance has been made for differences in intakes. The recent ILEA Junior School Project of Mortimore *et al.*, (1988) has data on the ability, social class, sex and race of pupils on entry to their junior schools and still finds that this detailed individual information is a poor predictor of what progress the children will make over their next four years, without further data on the organisational character of their schools. Further methodologically sophisticated research studies which also show that schools have substantial effects are considered below.

WHAT IS THE SIZE OF A SCHOOL'S EFFECTS ON ITS PUPILS?

Early studies showed – in the views of their authors – very large school effects. Power *et al*, (1967) reported a twentyfold difference in the delinquency rates of London schools, a difference which he argued was virtually independent of catchment area characteristics, and Gath (1977) reported substantial variation in the child guidance referral rates of Oxfordshire schools. Reynolds (1976) reported large differences between schools in their effectiveness which were again argued to be virtually completely due to the effects of the schools themselves. The variation in delinquency rates across the schools was three-fold; in further education entrance rates, it was from 50 per cent participation amongst school leavers down to 8 per cent, and in attendance rates it was from 90 per cent attendance at the 'top' school to only 77 per cent at the 'bottom' school. The Rutter team (1979) also emphasised the scale of their school effects, and the early work of Gray (1981) using already available local education authority databases produced an estimate that the 'competitive edge' possessed by the most effective tenth of state secondary schools as against the least effective tenth amounted to approximately the equivalent of one and a half 'O' level public examination passes per child. Substantial school effects on examination results were also reported by Gray *et al.*, (1983) in their analysis of data from secondary schools in Scotland and by Brimer *et al.*, (1978) using school 'O' and 'A' level examination passes as their measurement of effectiveness.

After these early studies, however, came a large number of British studies that showed much smaller school effects, although these studies have in turn now been followed by a further wave of research in the last few years which again suggests the existence of quite substantial school effects. The research suggesting only small school effects was as follows:

1 Comparisons of local education authorities showed that social, economic and environmental factors accounted for up to 80 per cent of the variation in pupil academic attainment (Department of Education and Science, 1983, 1984; Gray, Jesson and Jones, 1984).
2 Comparisons of schools which were selective with those which were comprehensive showed minimal differences, as in the National Children's Bureau Studies (Steedman, 1980, 1983) and as in the work from the Scottish Education Data Archive (Gray *et al.*, 1983).
3 Comparisons of individual schools showed small differences in effectiveness, as shown by the Scottish data of Willms (1986) in which schools only explained two per cent of the variation in the academic achievement of pupils. The more recent work of Gray, Jesson and Jones (1986) suggested also much more limited school effects than their earlier study, with the difference between the most effective and least effective schools being only a very low grade CSE public examination pass in size.

More recent work, however, has begun to support the earlier suggestions of large school effects. Cuttance's (1989) recent Scottish data suggests that up to 8 per cent of the variance in pupils' examination attainments is school related and that the difference between the 'most effective quarter' and 'least effective quarter' of schools is of the order of two 'O' level examination passes. Reynolds *et al.* (1987) have recently reported large school system effects upon pupils, in particular a major deficiency in the non-academic outcomes of comprehensive schools when compared to pupils from the selective system. Mortimore and his colleagues (1988) also report substantial school effects not upon attainment at a point *in time* but upon progress *over time* where, in the case of mathematics, for example, the influence of the school was ten times more important than the influence of the home. Even in reading, which is likely to be more dependent upon the general cultural background of the child's family, the school's influence on pupil progress was four times greater than that of the child's home. Aitken and Longford (1986) report that seven per cent of the variation in pupils' examination results may be due to the effects of their schools and Willms' (1987) analysis of local education authorities suggests up to ten per cent of the variation in academic achievement is due to the effects of school.

ARE SCHOOLS EQUALLY EFFECTIVE UPON DIFFERENT ASPECTS OF PUPIL DEVELOPMENT?

The early work of Rutter *et al.*, (1979) and Reynolds (1976) reported high inter-correlations between schools' academic effectiveness and their social effectiveness as measured by attendance and delinquency rates. However, more recent work has suggested that schools may be differentially effective in different areas. Gray *et al.*, (1983) showed that social outcomes such as liking for school or attending school were partially independent of schools' academic outcomes, as did the National Children's Bureau research on comprehensive/selective system comparisons, where the comprehensive schools were performing academically as well as those of the selective system, but were under-performing socially. Our own work (Reynolds *et al.*, 1987) shows small academic, but large behavioural and attitudinal, differences in the effectiveness of the same two systems. The ILEA study (Mortimore *et al.*, 1988) shows that schools can be differentially effective upon their pupils' academic and social outcomes.

Even if we look only at one discrete area of schools' effectiveness – the academic outcomes from schooling – there is substantial variation in the recent Mortimore (1988) study between schools' effectiveness on one academic outcome like oracy (heavily influenced) and reading skills (less heavily school influenced). Cuttance (1989) even notes large differences between the effectiveness of different *subject* departments within the same school, with the differences equivalent to of the order of one to two 'O' level public examination passes in several cases.

ARE SCHOOLS CONSISTENTLY EFFECTIVE OR INEFFECTIVE OVER TIME?

Early work suggested that effective schools had been so for a long time period (Reynolds, 1976) and that schools were consistent in their effectiveness (Rutter *et al.*, 1979). More recently, however, Gray and Jesson (1985) have noted that individual schools and individual teachers within a school can vary markedly in their academic effectiveness from year to year, which suggests to them a possible lack of school consistency. Blakey and Heath (1989) also show substantial change in effectiveness over time in their sample of Oxfordshire comprehensive schools.

DO SCHOOLS HAVE THE SAME EFFECTS UPON ALL PUPILS?

Early work (Reynolds, 1982; Rutter *et al.*, 1979) suggested that a school was equally effective or ineffective for all types of pupil in the school, irrespective of their social background or their ability.

More recently, however, Aitken and Longford (1986) found that schools can differ in their regression line slopes (the line reflecting the statistical relationship between their intakes and outcomes), with some schools having particularly steep ones which indicate that a very small increase in initial intelligence is associated with a very large increase in 'outcome'. Also, Cuttance (1989) notes that disadvantaged pupils from low socio-economic status homes are more affected by their schools than pupils from an 'average' background whereas Gray, Jesson and Jones (1986) note the opposite – that high ability pupils were more affected by their schools than those of lower ability. McPherson and Willms (1987) argue that the effects of comprehensivisation in Scotland varied considerably according to the social class of pupils, with working class pupils gaining more than others. All these recent studies suggest that schools may not have consistent organisational effects across all their pupils, but may have different size effects upon different kinds of pupils, a finding supported by the Willms and Cuttance (1985) evidence of the existence of a few schools being very effective for high ability children and a few for lower ability children.

WHAT ARE THE CHARACTERISTICS OF EFFECTIVE SCHOOL ORGANISATIONS?

It is important to note that we know at present far more about what factors are associated with academic effectiveness than those factors which are associated with social outcomes. Rutter *et al.*, (1979) identified over twenty factors associated with academic effectiveness, yet could only identify seven factors associated with social effectiveness as measured by a school's possession of a low delinquency rate. The recent ILEA study of Mortimore *et al.*, (1988) found only six school factors associated with behavioural effectiveness (such as low rates of misbehaviour) and thirteen school factors associated with academic effectiveness judged in terms of good reading scores, even though the schools' overall effect *sizes* were the same on the two different outcomes. Our relative ignorance of the factors making for social effectiveness is also unlikely to be remedied by work from abroad, since virtually all the North American studies (with the notable exception of Brookover *et al.*, 1979) look only at *academic* effectiveness (see reviews in Anderson (1982), Purkey and Smith (1983)).

It is also important to note that we have only three studies in Britain which have been able to systematically collect data on the school processes of effective and ineffective organisations, two on processes in secondary schools (Rutter *et al.*, (1979); Reynolds, (1976), (1982)) and one on primary school processes (Mortimore *et al.*, (1988)). The Rutter study found that certain factors are not associated with overall effectiveness, amongst them class size, formal academic or pastoral care organisation, school size, school administrative arrangements (i.e. whether a school was split site or not), and the age and size of school buildings.

The important within-school factors determining high effectiveness were argued by Rutter (1980) to be:

1 The balance of intellectually able and less able children in the school since, when a preponderance of pupils in a school were likely to be unable to meet the expectations of scholastic success, peer group cultures with an anti-academic or anti-authority emphasis may have formed.
2 The system of rewards and punishments – ample use of rewards, praise and appreciation being associated with favourable outcomes.
3 School environment – good working conditions, responsiveness to pupil needs and good care and decoration of buildings were associated with better outcomes.
4 Ample opportunities for children to take responsibility and to participate in the running of their school lives appeared conducive to favourable outcome.
5 Successful schools tended to make good use of homework, to set clear academic goals and to have an atmosphere of confidence as to their pupil capacities.
6 Outcomes were better where teachers provided good models of behaviour by means of good time-keeping and willingness to deal with pupil problems.
7 Findings upon group management in the classroom suggested the importance of preparing lessons in advance, of keeping the attention of the whole class, of unobtrusive discipline, of a focus on rewarding good behaviour and of swift action to deal with disruption.
8 Outcomes were more favourable when there was a combination of firm leadership together with a decision-making process in which all teachers felt that their views were represented.

Our own work in South Wales, although undertaken in a group of secondary modern schools and in a relatively homogeneous former mining valley that is very different in its community patterns from the communities of Inner London, has produced findings that in certain ways are parallel to those of Rutter and his team. Our work involved the collection of data on the pupil inputs, pupil outgoings and school processes of eight secondary modern schools, each of which was taking the bottom two-thirds of the ability range from a clearly delineated catchment area. We found substantial differences in the quality of the school outputs from the eight schools, with a variation in the delinquency rate of from 3.8 per cent delinquent per annum to 10.5 per cent, in the attendance rate of from 77.2 per cent average attendance to 89.1 per cent and in the academic attainment rate of from 8.4 per cent proceeding to the local technical college to 52.7 per cent proceeding on to further education.

Our early analysis (Reynolds, 1976) of our intake data showed no tendency for the schools with the higher levels of performance to be receiving more able intakes on entry. In fact, high overall school performance was associated with *lower* ability intakes as measured by the Ravens Standard Progressive Matrices test of non-verbal ability. Although subsequent full analysis of our full range of intake data revealed a tendency for the higher performance schools to have intakes of higher verbal and numerical ability, the personality variables for these intakes (higher extraversion and higher neurotrism scores) suggest, on the contrary, a poor educational prognosis. Simply, the intake scores still seem to be unable to explain the variation between our schools.

Detailed observation of the schools and the collection of a large range of material upon pupils' attitudes to school, teachers' perceptions of pupils, within school organisation and school resource levels has revealed a number of factors within the school that are associated with more 'effective' regimes. These include a high proportion of pupils in authority positions (as in the Rutter study), low levels of institutional control, low rates of physical punishment, small overall size, more favourable teacher pupil ratios and more tolerant attitudes to the enforcing of certain rules regarding 'dress, manners and morals'. Crucially, our observation has revealed differences between the schools in the ways that they have attempted to mobilise pupils towards the acceptance of their predetermined goals that are associated with their effectiveness. Such differences seem to fall within the parameters of one or other of two major strategies, 'coercion' or 'incorporation'. Five more effective schools that took part in the research appeared to be utilising the incorporative strategy to a greater (three schools) or lesser (two schools) extent. The major components of this strategy are twofold: the incorporation of pupils into the organisation of the school and the incorporation of their parents into support of the school. Pupils were incorporated within the classroom by encouraging them to take an active and participative role in lessons and by letting them intervene verbally without the teacher's explicit directions. Pupils in schools which utilised this strategy were also far more likely to be allowed and encouraged to work in groups than their counterparts in schools utilising the coercive strategy. Outside formal lesson time, attempts were made to incorporate pupils into the life of the school by utilising other strategies. One of these was the use of numbers of pupil prefects and monitors, from all parts of the school ability range, whose role was largely one of supervision of other pupils in the absence of staff members. Such a practice appeared to have the effect of inhibiting the growth of anti-school pupil cultures because of its effects in creating senior pupils who were generally supportive of the school.

It also had the latent and symbolic function of providing pupils with a sense of having some control over their within-school lives; the removal of these symbols also gave the school a further sanction it could utilise against its deviants. Attempts to incorporate pupils were paralleled by attempts to enlist the support of their parents by the establishment of close, informal or semi-formal relations between teachers and parents, the encouraging of informal visits by parents to the school and the frequent and full provision of information to parents that concerned pupil progress and governor and staff decisions. Another means of incorporation into the values and norms of the school was the development of interpersonal rather than impersonal relationships between teachers and pupils. Basically, teachers in these incorporative schools attempted to tie pupils into the value systems of the school and of the adult society by means of developing 'good' personal relationships with them. In effect, the judgement was made in these schools that inter-internalisation of teacher values was more likely to occur if pupils saw teachers as 'significant others' deserving of respect. Good relationships were consequent upon minimal use of overt institutional control (so that pupil behaviour was relatively unconstrained), low rates of physical punishment, a tolerance of a limited amount of 'acting out' (such as by smoking or gum chewing, for example), a pragmatic hesitancy to enforce rules which may have provoked rebellion and an attempt to reward good behaviour rather than punish bad behaviour. Within this school ethos, instances of pupil 'deviance' evoked therapeutic rather than coercive responses from within the school.

In contrast, schools which utilised the 'coercive' strategy to a greater or lesser extent (three ineffective schools) made no attempt to incorporate pupils into the authority structure of the school. Furthermore, these schools made no attempt to incorporate the support of parents, because the teachers believed that no support would be forthcoming and they exhibited high levels of institutional control, strict rule enforcement, high rates of physical punishment and very little tolerance of any 'acting out'. The idea, as in the incorporative schools, of establishing some kind of 'truce' with pupils in these schools was anathema, since the teachers perceived that the pupils would necessarily abuse such an arrangement. Pupil deviance was expeditiously punished which, within the overall social context of these schools, was entirely understandable; therapeutic concern would have had little effect because pupils would have had little or no respect for the teacher-therapist.

The most likely explanation of the choice of different strategies is to be found in the differences (in the two groups of schools) in the teacher perceptions of their intakes. In schools which have adopted a 'coercive' strategy, there was a consistent tendency to over-estimate the proportion of pupils whose background can be said to be 'socially deprived' – in one such school, teachers thought such children accounted for 70 per cent of their intake whilst in one of the incorporative schools teachers put the proportion only at ten per cent – and a consistent tendency to under-estimate their pupils' ability. In these coercive schools, teachers regarded pupils as being in need of 'character training' and 'control' which stems from a deficiency in primary socialisation, a deficiency which the school attempts to make good by a form of custodialism. Such perceptions are germane seeds for the creation of a school ethos of coercion.

The characteristics of effective primary school organisations have recently been identified that are associated with high performance in cognitive areas such as reading and writing and in non-cognitive areas such as low truancy levels (Mortimore *et al.* 1988):

1 Purposeful leadership of the staff by the head. This occurs where the head understands the school's needs, is actively involved in it but is good at sharing power with the staff. He or she does not exert total control over teachers but consults them, especially in decision making such as spending plans and curriculum guidelines.

2 Involvement of the deputy head. The deputy head can have a crucial role in whether a school is effective or not. Where the deputy was usually involved in policy decisions, pupil progress increased.

3 Involvement of teachers. In successful schools, the teachers were involved in curriculum planning and played a major role in developing their own curriculum guidelines. As with the deputy head, teacher involvement in decisions concerning which classes they were to teach was important. Similarly, consultation with teachers about decisions on spending was important.

4 Consistency among teachers. Continuity of staffing had positive effects but pupils also performed better when the approach to teaching was consistent.

5 A structured day. Children performed better when their school day was structured in some way. In effective schools, pupils' work was organised by the teacher who ensured there was plenty for them to do, yet allowed them some freedom within the structure. Negative effects were noted when children were given unlimited responsibility for a long list of tasks.

6 Intellectually challenging teaching. Not surprisingly, pupil progress was greater where teachers were stimulating and enthusiastic. The incidence of 'higher order' questions and statements was seen to be vital – that is where teachers frequently made children use powers of problem-solving.

7 A work-centred environment. This was characterised by a high level of pupil industry, with children enjoying their work and being eager to start new tasks. The noise level was low, and movement around the class was usually work-related and not excessive.

8 A limited focus within sessions. Children progressed when teachers devoted their energies to one particular subject area and sometimes two. Pupil progress was marred when three or more subjects were running concurrently in a classroom.

9 Maximum communication between teachers and pupils. Children performed better the more communication they had with their teacher about the content of their work. Most teachers devoted most of their time to individuals, so each child could expect only a small number of contacts a

day. Teachers who used opportunities to talk to the whole class by, for example, reading a story or asking a question were more effective.

10 Thorough record-keeping. The value of monitoring pupil progress was important in the head's role, but it was also an important aspect of teachers' planning and assessment.

11 Parental involvement. Schools with an informal open-door policy which encouraged parents to get involved in reading at home, helping in the classroom and on educational visits, tended to be more effective.

12 A positive climate. An effective school has a positive ethos. Overall, the atmosphere was more pleasant in the effective schools, for a variety of reasons. There was less emphasis on punishment and criticism and more emphasis on rewarding pupils. Classroom management was seen to be firm but fair in the effective schools.

Whilst there are some clear differences between the three British studies in their respective findings, the degree of communality in the findings on the factors responsible for organisational effectiveness is quite impressive. Also impressive is the extent to which American research into school organisational effectiveness suggests similar factors to be responsible in their elementary and high schools. Comprehensive reviews of this literature are available elsewhere as we noted above and all we have space to do here is to take one 'meta-analysis' of all American findings conducted by two Canadians (Renihan and Renihan, 1984) to compare with the British findings. They found that the following factors were important in creating an effective organisation in the studies they reviewed:

1 *Leadership*. This point is reinforced in studies which highlight several key leadership qualities. These include assertive administrative instructional leadership, assumption of responsibility, high standards, personal vision, expertise, and force of character.

2 *Conscious attention to climate*. In effective schools specific attention is given to the creation and maintenance of a climate which is conducive to learning. In short, very specific rules, regulations and guidelines are laid down and they are clearly understood by everyone.

3 *Academic focus*. Several authorities identify a marked emphasis on basic academic skills as a common characteristic of effective schools. Further, the importance placed upon basic skills is reflected in the major portion of school time allocated to them.

4 *Great expectations*. Central to the notion of positive ethos in the school is the duality of high expectations for student performance on the one hand and high expectations that students can achieve on the other. In effective schools, performance is monitored to ensure that students meet pre-established standards which are made well known to them.

5 *Sense of mission*. Successful schools project a consistent philosophy and a sense of mission which are always shared by teachers, pupils and administration. Such a focus on mission is reflected in the following characteristics:

- shared norms and consistency throughout the school;
- agreed-upon ways of doing things;
- clearly stated goals known to all;
- a high degree of acceptance of the importance of goals;
- joint planning.

Central to this notion is the critical element of ownership, for when staff, students, and community are involved in charting a direction they become committed to its success.

6 *Positive motivational strategies.* Studies at both the school and the classroom levels of analysis have repeatedly indicated that in successful schools there is a greater conscious reliance on praise rather than blame. In addition, successful schools evidence strategies which are designed to enhance their students' self-image and to foster a friendly and supportive atmosphere.

7 *Feedback on academic performance.* Effective schools provide consistent and continuous feedback to students on their academic achievement. Furthermore, student evaluation is tied to monitoring of teaching performance and the appropriateness of curriculum level objectives. More specifically effective schools use the results of standardised (preferably criterion-referenced) achievement tests to make significant decisions regarding programme and modes of instructional delivery.

It is important of course not to overemphasise the extent of the agreement between the various British studies and between these studies and the American literature. Rutter *et al.*, (1979), for example, find that high levels of staff turnover are associated with *effectiveness*, a completely counter intuitive finding that is not in agreement with the Reynolds' (1976, 1982) findings of an association between high levels of staff turnover and *ineffectiveness*. Similarly, the consistent American findings on the link between frequent monitoring of pupil progress and academic effectiveness is not in agreement with the recent findings of Mortimore *et al.*, (1988) that monitoring which involves frequent testing of children is a characteristic of ineffective schools. Nevertheless, the degree of similarity on the issue of effective school processes between the various international findings is quite impressive.

FUTURE DIRECTIONS FOR SCHOOL EFFECTIVENESS RESEARCH

Detailed prescriptions of the research agenda that remains to be tackled are available elsewhere (Rutter, 1983; Reynolds and Reid, 1985) and we have only space here to outline the most important areas in which further investigations are necessary to develop the knowledge base on effective school organisational practices:

1 We need research undertaken in more typical samples of schools, (since early work has been exclusively urban, has been undertaken either in London or in South Wales, and has been based in highly disadvantaged communities, to see if the same factors are associated with effectiveness in different areas. Larger sample sizes (like Mortimore's fifty schools rather than Reynolds' eight or Rutter's twelve) are also needed. More studies of primary school effectiveness are also needed.

2 Some British studies, particularly those from the Centre for Policy Studies (Cox and Marks, 1983, 1985), have been highly defective in their measurements of pupil intakes into schools, which may have led to invalid assumptions being made about schools or systems of education being more effective simply because full allowance had not been made for the intake quality of their pupils. Analyses based only on measures of home background (as with Cox and Marks above) or background and ability (as with Rutter *et al.*, 1979) are unlikely to be adequate. What is needed in the future are multiple indicators of intake in order to see if these variables together explain variation in outcome.

3 'Means-on-means' analyses, where school averages for all pupils are used, as in the Reynolds' (1976, 1982) work, make it impossible to analyse the school experience of different groups of pupils and also lower explanatory variance. Individual pupil level data rather than group data is now widely agreed to be necessary both on intake and at outcome (Aitken and Longford, 1986).

4 Further work is required into the school processes that are associated with effectiveness. We are still not completely sure *which* processes are associated with effectiveness, and also *how* the school organisational factors have their effects, through pupil self-concepts or by direct modelling for example. We need to know what *creates* the organisational factors, which may require a degree of historical study since there are those who insist that what makes an effective school is in part the history of being an effective school. We need to know also whether the same school factors are equally effective with very *different* types of teacher personality or teachers with different educational philosophies, or by contrast whether different methods may be *equally* effective when used by different persons. Simply, the 'person/ method' interaction and the 'person/method' fit are both areas that will undoubtedly repay further investigation. Most important of all, we need to investigate *which* of the school organisational features are the most important and which factors (like the headteacher perhaps) may determine other features. No existing British studies have attempted to do this at the present time.

5 Areas that have been seriously neglected by the existing body of British research need future attention. The leadership or management style of the headteacher is seriously neglected in both the British secondary school studies, since in both cases the researchers felt that it was politically impossible in the mid to late 1970s to give this factor the attention it potentially deserved. The content of the curriculum, the books and

materials used, its relevance to children's culture and the world view the curriculum imparts have also received minimal attention, no doubt because of the difficulty of classifying and measuring 'knowledge' (Wilcox, 1985) and no doubt because of the destruction of the utility of Bernstein's attempted classification (King, 1983) of curriculum and organisation.

The classroom environments of effective school organisations have also not been studied in detail in either of the secondary school studies, an omission which hampers the integration of the bodies of knowledge on effective schooling and effective teaching. The pastoral or welfare aspects of education and the within-school practice and ethos of care and guidance are also not areas that have received sufficient attention. Our last serious omission in terms of areas to be studied is the actual administration, management and decision taking process within schools, an area where school effectiveness work would clearly benefit from a closer knowledge of the real worlds of educational practitioners. In part because of the neglect of the headteacher's role in the two secondary studies, we are still unclear about the precise nature of the leadership to be found in effective organisations, although the portrait to be found in the recent Mortimore *et al.*, (1988) study of the effective head as both a purposive leader and at the same time also as concerned to involve staff in the running of the school takes our knowledge some considerable way further. What is the departmental or middle management structure of an effective school organisation, or the relations with outside supportive agencies, or the appraisal process or the school self-evaluation process in use? What are the actual mechanics of the administration in terms of *behaviours* as well as reified organisational *structure*? In these key areas – very important for practitioners or policy makers who might want to directly attempt to change school practice – school effectiveness work is still deficient in knowledge.

FROM SCHOOL EFFECTIVENESS TO SCHOOL IMPROVEMENT: THE NEED FOR A RELATIONSHIP

In one other area also, the future development of school effectiveness research needs to be different from its past, namely the interrelationships with the areas of school change and school improvement. Overall, the translation of school effectiveness work into programmes of detailed school change in Britain using those factors identified in the various research studies has been pitifully poor and the 'take up' of knowledge by practitioners very limited indeed, with the exception of specific Inner London Education Authority initiatives such as the 'Inspectors Based in Schools' who directively attempted to bring good practice to schools. In part, this may be because school effectiveness research in Britain is heavily academically dominated, unlike the United States for example where practitioners have undertaken most of the research and where the school effectiveness 'movement' was launched by a black American school board superintendent and practitioner, Ron Edmonds.

In part, though, it is the actual character of the research itself that has probably contributed to poor levels of implementation by practitioners or by policy makers. There are high levels of abstraction and a lack of detail in some of the concepts utilised in the research like 'academic press' or 'balanced control orientation'. Practitioners are still heavily content- or curriculum-orientated whereas school effectiveness work is mostly concerned with the organisation of the school. The school effectiveness research is weak on issues of management and organisation and weak – as we noted earlier – on the 'technology' of schooling. The research is quite strong on school environments but weak on the precise curricular and organisational arrangements that are the *means* to attain effective school environments.

The limited practitioner relevance and limited 'take up' have been magnified in their effects also because the academic study of school improvement, school review and school change has been a very separate discipline in Britain with a distinctively different history and set of traditions. School improvement in Britain probably began with the teacher researcher movement (Elliott, 1977, 1981), moved on to school self evaluation and review (Clift and Nuttall, 1987) and later attempted to ensure that the review process was linked to an improvement policy (as with the Hargreaves report on *Improving Secondary Schools* (1984), the GRIDS scheme of McMahon *et al.*, (1984) and the International School Improvement Project of Bollen and Hopkins (1987).

Overall, though, this school improvement effort in total has continued to be concerned more with individual teachers than with the organisation of their schools, has rarely empirically evaluated the effect of changes in the schools, has often indeed been more concerned with the journey of undertaking school improvement than with reaching any particular destination and has often celebrated practitioner knowledge whether it is itself a valid improvement strategy or not, leading to a futile reinvention of the wheel in each project. The sociology of education has been particularly good at the latter (e.g. Woods and Pollard, 1987). The lack of 'mesh' between the school effectiveness and school improvement literatures and research communities – seen for example in numerous disparaging comments about school effectiveness work by the school improvers Holly and Hopkins in Reid, Holly and Hopkins (1987) – can be argued to have damaged school improvement work and to have again reduced the potential practitioner impact of school effectiveness work (see Reynolds, 1988, for elaboration of this theme). The lack of knowledge about school change strategies within the school effectiveness community has probably – with other factors mentioned above – also been responsible for the rather disappointing results that have occurred when school effectiveness researchers have attempted to *directly* change schools themselves. The London research team of Rutter and his colleagues attempted to bring their knowledge derived from their research into some of their original sample of schools, as described elsewhere by Ouston and Maughan (1989), yet were disappointed in their effects on pupil outcomes, probably because of the somewhat 'top-down' knowledge transfer process, the lack of technological applicability in their research base and the neglect of the important 'headteacher factor' in the original study. In Wales, we tried a rather different consultancy-based method of bringing the results of school effectiveness work to schools, in which the school staff owned the change process, which was exclusively 'bottom up' in orientation. This too had disappointing results in the short term (Reynolds, 1987). More recently there are occasional examples of the successful translation of school effectiveness work into school improvement programmes, as in the case where teachers attending in-service training as school 'change agents' generated over four major organisational changes per person, over eighty per cent of which had survived in a six-year follow-up study (see Reynolds *et al.*, 1989, for an outline of the project results and philosophy).

Overall, though, school effectiveness research has had much more to say about what makes a 'good' school than about how to make schools 'good'. An improvement in knowledge and appreciation of the practical issues of school and practitioner management and school administration would seem to be an urgent necessity if school effectiveness research is to be more successfully linked with school improvement.

REFERENCES

Acton, T. A. (1980) 'Educational criteria of success: some problems in the work of Rutter, Maughan, Mortimore and Ouston', *Educational Research*, Vol. 22, No. 3, pp. 163–173.

Aitken, M. and Longford, N. (1986) 'Statistical modelling issues in school effectiveness studies', *Journal of the Royal Statistical Society, Series A*, Vol. 144, No. 1.

Anderson, C. A. (1982) 'The search for school climate: a review of the research', *Review of Educational Research*, Vol. 52, No. 3, pp. 368–420.

Ball, S. J. (1981) *Beachside Comprehensive*. Cambridge: Cambridge University Press.

Blakey, L. and Heath, A. (1989) 'Differences between comprehensive schools: some preliminary findings', Reynolds, D. and Cuttance, P. (eds) *New Directions in School Effectiveness and School Improvement*. London: Cassell.

Bollen, R. and Hopkins, D. (1987) *School Based Research: Towards a Praxis*. Leuven, Belgium: ACCO Publishing.

Bowles, S. and Gintis, H. (1976) *Schooling in Capitalist America*. London: Routledge and Kegan Paul.

Bourdieu, P. and Passeron, J. C. (1977) *Reproduction: in Education, Society and Culture*. London: Sage.

Brimer, A., Madaus, G. F., Chapman, B., Kellaghan, T. and Wood, R. (1978) *Sources of Difference in School Achievement*. Slough: NFER.

Brookover, W. B., Beady, C., Flood, P., Schweitzer, J. and Wisenbaker, J. (1979) *School Social Systems and Student Achievement*. New York: Praeger.

Burgess, R. G. (1983) *Experiencing Comprehensive Education: A Study of Bishop Macgregor School*. London: Methuen.

Clift, P. and Nuttall, D. (eds) (1987) *Studies in School Self Evaluation*. Lewes: Falmer Press.

Coleman, J. (1966) *Equality of Educational Opportunity*. Washington: U.S. Government Printing Office.

Cox, C. and Marks, J. (1983) *Standards in English Schools: First Report*. London: National Council for Educational Standards.

Cox, C. and Marks, J. (1985) *Standards in English Schools: Second Report*. London: National Council for Educational Standards.

Cuttance, P. (1989) 'Evaluating the effectiveness of schools', Reynolds, D. and Cuttance, P. (eds) *New Directions in School Effectiveness and School Improvement*. London: Cassell (in press).

Department of Education and Science (1983) *School Standards and Spending: Statistical Analysis*. London: D.E.S.

Department of Education and Science (1984) *School Standards and Spending: Statistical Analysis. A further Appreciation*. London: D.E.S.

Elliott, J. (1977) 'Evaluating in-service activities from above or below?' *Insight*, November.

Elliott, J. (1981) *School Accountability*. London: Grant McIntyre.

Gath, D. (1977) *Child Guidance and Delinquency in a London Borough*. London: Oxford University Press.

Goldstein, H. (1980) Critical notice – Fifteen Thousand Hours by Rutter *et al.*, in *Journal of Child Psychology and Psychiatry*, Vol. 21, No. 4, pp. 364–6.

Gray, J. (1981) 'A competitive edge: examination results and the probable limits of secondary school effectiveness', *Educational Review*, Vol. 33, No. 1, pp. 25–35.

Gray, J., Jesson, D. and Jones, B. (1984) 'Predicting differences in examination results between Local Education Authorities: does school organisation matter?', *Oxford Review of Education*, Vol. 10, No. 1, pp. 45–68.

Gray, J., Jesson, D. and Jones, B. (1986) 'The search for a fairer way of comparing schools' examination results', *Research Papers in Education*, Vol. 1, No. 2, pp. 91–122.

Gray, J., McPherson, A. and Raffe, D. (1983) *Reconstructions of Secondary Education*. London: Routledge and Kegan Paul.

Hargreaves, D. H. (1967) *Social Relations in a Secondary School*. London: Routledge and Kegan Paul.

Hargreaves, D. (1984) *Improving Secondary Schools*. (Report of the Committee on the Curriculum and Organisation of Secondary Schools). London: ILEA.

Jencks, C. *et al.* (1971) *Inequality*. London: Allen Lane.

King, R. (1983) *The Sociology of School Organisation*. London: Methuen.

Lacey, C. (1970) *Hightown Grammar*. Manchester: Manchester University Press.

McMahon, A., Bolam, R., Abbott, R. and Holly, P. (1984) *Guidelines for Review and Development in Schools (Primary and Secondary Handbooks)*. York: Longman/Schools Council.

McPherson, A. and Willms, D. (1987) 'Equalisation and improvement: some effects of comprehensive reorganisation in Scotland.' Paper presented to the Annual Meeting of the American Educational Research Association, May.

Mortimore, P., Sammons, P., Ecob, R., Stoll, L. and Lewis, D. (1988) *School Matters: The Junior Years*. Salisbury: Open Books.

Morton-Williams, R. and Finch, S. (1968) *Enquiry 1*. London: HMSO.

Musgrove, F. (1981) *School and the Social Order*. Chichester: John Wiley.

Ouston, J. and Maughan, B. (1989) 'Innovation and change in six secondary schools', Reynolds, D. and Cuttance, P. (eds) *New Directions in School Effectiveness and School Improvement*. London: Cassell (in press).

Plowden Committee (1967) *Children and Their Primary Schools*. London: HMSO.

Power, M. J. *et al* (1967) 'Delinquent Schools?', *New Society*, Vol. 10, pp. 542–3.

Power, M. J., Benn, R. T., and Morris, J. N. (1972) 'Neighbourhood, school and juveniles before the courts', *British Journal of Criminology*, Vol. 12, pp. 111–132.

Purkey, S. and Smith, M. (1983) 'Effective Schools: A Review', *Elementary School Journal*, Vol. 83, pp. 427–52.

Reid, K., Hopkins, D. and Holly, P. (1987) *Towards the Effective School*. Oxford: Blackwell.

Renihan, F. I. and Renihan, P. J. (1984) 'Effective schools, effective administration and effective leadership', *The Canadian Administrator*, Vol. 24, No. 3, pp. 1–6.

Reynolds, D. (1976) 'The delinquent school', Woods, P. (ed) *The Process of Schooling*. London: Routledge and Kegan Paul.

Reynolds, D. (1982) 'The search for effective schools', *School Organisation*, Vol. 2, No. 3, pp. 215–37.

Reynolds, D. (ed) (1985) *Studying School Effectiveness*. Lewes: Falmer Press.

Reynolds, D. (1987) 'The consultant sociologist: a method for linking sociology of education and teachers', Woods, P. and Pollard, A. (eds) *Sociology and Teaching*. London: Croom Helm.

Reynolds, D. (1988) 'British school improvement research: the contribution of qualitative studies', *International Journal of Qualitative Studies in Education*, Vol. 1, No. 2, pp. 143–54.

Reynolds, D. and Reid, K. (1985) 'The second stage: towards a reconceptualisation of theory and methodology in school effectiveness research', Reynolds, D. (ed) *Studying School Effectiveness*. Lewes: Falmer Press.

Reynolds, D. and Sullivan, M. (1979) 'Bringing schools back', Barton, L. (ed) *Schools, Pupils and Deviance*. Driffield: Nafferton.

Reynolds, D., Phillips, D., and Davie, R. (1989) 'An effective school improvement programme based on school effectiveness research', *The International Journal of Educational Research*.

Reynolds, D., Sullivan, M. and Murgatroyd, S. J. (1987) *The Comprehensive Experiment*. Lewes: Falmer Press.

Rutter, M. (1980) *Changing Youth in a Changing Society*. Oxford: Nuffield Provincial Hospital Trust.

Rutter, M. (1983) 'School effects on pupil progress – findings and policy implications', *Child Development*, Vol. 54, No. 1, pp. 1–29.

Rutter, M. *et al* (1979) *Fifteen Thousand Hours*. London: Open Books.

Steedman, J. (1980) *Progress in Secondary Schools*. London: National Children's Bureau.

Steedman, J. (1983) *Examination Results in Selective and Non-Selective Schools*. London: National Children's Bureau.

Wilcox, B. (1985) 'Conceptualising curriculum differences for studies of secondary school effectiveness', Reynolds, D. (ed) *Studying School Effectiveness*. Lewes: Falmer Press.

Willms, J. D. (1986) 'Social class segregation and its relationship to pupils' examination results in Scotland', *American Sociological Review*, Vol. 51.

Willms, J. D. (1987) 'Differences between Scottish educational authorities in their examination attainment', *Oxford Review of Education*, Vol. 13, No. 2, pp. 211–32.

Willms, J. D. and Cuttance, P. (1985) 'School effects in Scottish secondary schools', *British Journal of Sociology of Education*, Vol. 6, No. 3.

Woods, P. and Pollard, A. (eds) (1987) *Sociology and Teaching*. London: Croom Helm.

3.3 STUDYING SCHOOLS AND THEIR EFFECTS

D. J. SMITH AND SALLY TOMLINSON

It has been shown that the proportion of school leavers who have attained a modest standard of basic number skills is considerably lower in Britain than in some other European countries, for example, West Germany.[1] This kind of comparison is rather limited. It is quite possible that there would not be the same contrast in the proportion of school leavers attaining a much higher level of skill, and that British schools, particularly those in the private sector, do as well or better at training an élite as those in other countries. However, a relatively low standard among the majority of children is a significant failing because of its implications for the personal development of the mass of the population and for the performance of the British economy. As an economic power, Britain has been in long-term secular decline since about 1870. There is wide agreement among economic historians that since industry has become dominant over agriculture, no country has transformed its economic performance without first radically improving its education system. In the present phase of development, fewer and fewer jobs requiring a minimum of education or training are available. Methods of working will continue to change rapidly, so people need to be equipped with the language, reasoning and number skills that will enable them to absorb new information and thereby adapt to change. These are strong arguments for the belief that making schools more effective should be a high priority for any present-day government.

However, until recently, the strongest tradition of thinking about school effectiveness has not been primarily concerned with improving personal development and economic performance. Instead, it has concentrated on inequality of attainment between individuals, and has examined the question whether better schools would significantly reduce these individual differences. This focus of thinking and research was a response to political programmes

Source: Smith, D. J. and Tomlinson, S. (1989) *Studying Schools and their Effects: A study of multi-racial comprehensives*, Policy Studies Institute, London, pp. 18–27.

that saw education as a means of achieving greater equality; the two best examples of such programmes are the abolition of selection at 11 plus and the Educational Priority Areas, an attempt to use extra educational resources to compensate for multiple deprivations in particular localities.

Two American studies strongly challenged the view that education could make an important difference to inequality: these were James Coleman's report, published in 1966, on *Equality of Educational Opportunity*[2] and Christopher Jencks's reanalysis of Coleman's and other material, published in 1972 in the book *Inequality: a reassessment of the effect of family and schooling in America*. Jencks concluded that 'equalizing the quality of high schools would reduce cognitive inequality by one per cent or less' and that 'additional school expenditures are unlikely to increase achievements, and redistributing resources will not reduce test score inequality'.[3] Essentially, the basis of this claim was that a child's test scores or examination results could be predicted far more accurately from knowing the family background than from knowing which school the child went to. From the way the conclusion was phrased, it is clear that it was a direct response to the compensatory education programmes that were favoured in the 1960s both in the US and in Britain. However, it was interpreted as meaning that education had no effect. As Michael Rutter has put it 'these conclusions were both widely quoted and interpreted as meaning that schooling had such minor marginal effects that the educational process was scarcely worth the relatively large resources poured into it'.[4] Whereas Coleman and then Jencks had concluded that schooling was not effective as a means of reducing individual inequality, their conclusions were taken to mean that schooling has little influence on whether or not children can read, write and do arithmetic.

Over the past ten years, this view has increasingly been challenged, both in America and in Britain. Our own research is one of a number of projects that have set out to demonstrate that different schools have different effects, and have looked for explanations of these differences. The two most important British projects are *Fifteen Thousand Hours*, by Michael Rutter and his colleagues, a study of 12 secondary schools published in 1979; and *School Matters*, by Peter Mortimore and his colleagues, a study of 50 junior schools published in 1988. There is, in addition, a large body of other research and writing that is concerned with effective schooling and related matters. In 1983, Purkey and Smith produced a review of the American evidence, and Michael Rutter produced a review of American and British evidence.[5] Here we will not try to summarise the results of past research. Instead, we will make some general points about the analysis of school effectiveness, and about the associated methods of research. It would be good to be able to say that this discussion of the problems involved in understanding school effectiveness prepares the way for the presentation of findings, which will show how these problems can be solved. However, that would be a distortion on two counts. First, our research was only partially successful in terms of the objectives as originally defined, because we met with serious practical difficulties which could not all be overcome within the time and resources available. More important, to the extent that a conceptual framework can now be sketched, this is an outcome of the project. It is not the same as the framework that shaped the original design.

THE MEANING OF EFFECTS

The basic problem in measuring the effectiveness of schools is that the level of attainment reached by children is influenced by a wide range of factors in addition to the school. Hence it cannot be assumed that the attainment of the children (or their responsiveness or sense of social responsibility) is a product of their schooling, or, therefore, a measure of its effects.

This problem is common to all attempts to measure the effectiveness of social institutions. In fact, in most other cases, the links between the activities of the institutions and the desired results are far more difficult to trace. For example, the police aim to keep the peace, to prevent crime and to catch and prosecute offenders. However, the level of public order, the crime rate and the proportion of offenders who are caught are all the result of complex social processes. Among all these influences, it is extremely difficult to trace the effects of policing.

In looking for a way of defining the effects of institutions, one approach is to consider how far the outcomes would be changed if the institution did not exist at all. At first, this sounds like a definition of the total effect of an institution. However, it is not very useful in practical terms. According to Rutter, the available evidence suggests that children's cognitive development is, in fact, affected by whether or not they attend school. Also, 'the evidence on the effects of school closure in Western societies, either as a result of war ... or attempts to avoid racial integration ... are in keeping with that conclusion – as are the findings on the benefits of continued schooling during late adolescence'.[6] But it is difficult to use this kind of evidence in an ordered way to provide a quantitative assessment of the effects of normal schooling; and of course this approach is no use at all in showing what kinds of schooling work best, and why. Apart from the practical problems in obtaining good evidence, there is an interesting structural problem with this line of argument. A society minus a particular institution is one of two things: either it is managing temporarily without that institution (as in the case of school closures to avoid racial integration) or it is an entirely different kind of society that does not value what that institution does, or achieves it by entirely different means. An example of the second case would be tribal societies without writing or mathematics which pass on an extensive repertoire of skills, knowledge and oral history and secure close cooperation from children without any formal schooling. In the case where schools are temporarily closed, they may be partially replaced by something else; for example, parents may teach their children at home. More generally, other social processes and institutions will not remain fixed when the schools are temporarily closed, but will adapt to the new situation. In the case of a society that has not yet developed schools, it will be radically different in so many ways from a more technically developed and socially differentiated society that it would be difficult to make any useful comparison. It may seem to be common sense to think of the effect of schools as the difference it would make if there were none, but on closer analysis it is hard to attach any definite meaning to this idea, either in principle or in practice.

Most research and analysis of effectiveness adopts one of the many approaches having an important family resemblance: that they try to measure or analyse the differences between the results achieved by different schools (or other institutions). How 'the results achieved by different schools' is defined and analysed is crucial (the point will be discussed below). But given an appropriate definition and analysis, studying the differences between the results achieved by different schools is a promising approach, and it does bear on the most general questions of effectiveness. If no difference could be found between the results achieved even by schools adopting contrasting styles of teaching and methods of organisation, then this would, indeed, suggest that schools have little or no effect. The reason is that if schooling does have some effect, then the amount and nature of the effect is bound to vary between one school and another, unless the schools are extraordinarily homogeneous. This is enough to show that school differences are a promising starting point for the analysis of school effectiveness. But there remains a problem in defining how much effect a school has.

THE PERSISTENCE OF MENTAL CAPACITIES

The groundwork for research on school effectiveness has been done by the mental testing movement. A huge range of test instruments has been developed to measure many different mental skills and aptitudes. Compared with the measures used in much social research, the best of these instruments have been developed by rigorous and refined methods. They have been shown to have a high level of reliability (the same person, if tested twice, would obtain closely similar scores). There is also a huge body of information relating to the validity of the main tests, which have been used in many different studies; for example, different tests of reading comprehension do appear to be measuring reading comprehension, because the score that a person obtains on one such test is highly correlated with the score he obtains on another.

Discussion of the subject of mental testing has been clouded by the controversy over 'IQ tests' and 'intelligence'. IQ tests are merely composite tests that cover a range of mental skills and depend as little as possible on knowledge of any specific subject matter. There is no particular reason to describe them as tests of intelligence, except that scores on the component sub-tests, which cover more specific mental skills such as verbal or non-verbal reasoning, are quite highly correlated, so that, for example, someone who has a high verbal reasoning score tends quite strongly to have a high non-verbal reasoning score too.

IQ tests have been discredited among many sociologists because they were associated with the theory that intelligence (or effectively the IQ test score) is largely determined by genetic factors. For the purpose of analysing school effectiveness, there is no need to enter into this controversy. It is important to recognise, however, that independently of their theory of the origin of individual differences, the mental testers had discovered at least two very important facts: that mental capacities vary widely between individuals, and that there is a very strong tendency for the mental capacities of an individual adult to persist over time and for the mental capacities of an individual child to develop in a predictable way. With the use of the refined and reliable instruments that have been developed, if a child is tested in mathematics and reading at the age of eight, it is possible to make a surprisingly good prediction of the scores that the same child will achieve in mathematics and English (but on different tests) at the age of 15. Furthermore, in seeking to predict the child's test scores at 15, a knowledge of his or her scores at eight will be far more useful than any other piece of information; much more useful, for example, than knowing what socio-economic group the family belongs to or, indeed, what kind of school the child attends.

Thus mental capacities develop in a relatively predictable way, and having developed they tend strongly to persist. Also, individual differences in mental capacities are strongly related to family background (how far this is because of genetic inheritance is not important for the present discussion). Because children's test scores tend to grow in a predictable way, a test score at any one age (from about five onwards) is a very good basis for predicting the score at a later age. Family background factors are a fairly good basis for predicting the scores obtained on a range of tests at any one age. At the same time, of course, a substantial part of the variation in scores between individual children is not related to family background: there are many low-scoring children coming from privileged families, and many high-scoring children coming from disadvantaged families. Still, family background is quite a powerful predictor.

Jencks *et al.*, concluded that about 50 per cent of the variance between individual children in scholastic attainment was attributable to family background, while only 2 to 3 per cent was attributable to school variables. Essentially, this was a re-statement of the very well-known facts summarised above. Individual differences in attainment are large; attainment is strongly related to family background; and individual performance shows considerable stability throughout the process of child development. School effects will appear small in relation to the very wide range of highly stable individual differences.[7]

It is correct to conclude from this (as Jencks did) that improving the standard of schooling in the poorer schools will not significantly reduce individual inequalities. (As Rutter points out, lowering the standards of the better schools would probably be a rather better method of reducing individual differences, but even so it would not reduce them much.) However, it does not in the least follow from this that schools have little effect, or that an improvement in school effectiveness (by an amount equivalent to the difference between the best and the poorest schools) would not produce a significant improvement in attainment. There are two reasons for this.

1 If there were no school differences this would suggest that schools have little effect, but it is not true that the proportion of variance attributable to schools is a good indicator of the size of school effects. This is because the proportion of variance attributable to schools depends on how hetero-geneous the schools are. There are strong pressures towards homogeneity (such as school inspectors) and it is likely that many schools have much the same effects, but a few schools are much better or much worse than the majority. The difference between the best and worst schools would be a much better indicator of the effects of schooling than the proportion of variance attributable to schools, since this latter figure would be mostly determined by the mass of relatively homogeneous middling schools. In any case, no measure of school differences is a quantitative measure of the total effect of schooling, since the schools actually existing at any time do not represent the complete range from the best possible schooling to no effective schooling at all.

2 There is no justification for using individual differences as the yardstick for measuring school differences. Differences between schools may be small compared with differences between individuals, but may still be very important. A small increment in the average score in mental arithmetic, for example, may take a large proportion of individuals across the threshhold needed to be able to retain a score at darts.

A NEW APPROACH TO MODELLING SCHOOL EFFECTIVENESS

Our research project is one of three that adopt a new approach to modelling school effectiveness (the other two are the ILEA junior school project, published as *School Matters*, and the Thomas Coram infant school project). This new approach developed from the pioneering work of *Fifteen Thousand Hours*, but incorporates important improvements in statistical procedures developed through the work of Murray Aitkin and Nicholas Longford, for-merly of the University of Lancaster, and Harvey Goldstein of the University of London.[8] The method depends on having longitudinal data about a group of children in a number of schools. There has to be a measure of attainment (say a reading test score) for each child at one time, then another measure (say another reading test score, or a set of examination results) for each child at a later time. There must be information about the family background of each child. A mathematical model is set up to predict the later measure of attainment, for each individual child, from the combined information about the earlier measure of attainment and family background factors. The model assumes that the later measure of attainment may vary according to the school the child belongs to, and that the various relationships (for example, between early and later attainment) may vary between schools.

Because attainment at an earlier time is one of the factors used to predict later attainment, this procedure is roughly equivalent to analysing the differences between schools in the *progress* achieved by children with similar initial attainment and other characteristics. It turns out that family background factors explain a relatively small proportion of the variance in *progress* between individual children (whereas, as Jencks pointed out, they explain a relatively large proportion of the variance in attainment at any one time). Within the terms of this kind of model, school differences are at least as important as family background factors, but earlier attainment is much more important than either. Thus, if we discount the very strong tendency for the level of attainment to be stable over time for the same child, school differences are seen to be highly important compared to other factors. This is another way of saying that children with a given level of initial attainment achieve markedly different rates of progress depending on which school they go to. It remains true that these school differences are small compared to the large differences in initial (and final) attainment between individual children. Nevertheless, these differences are large in terms of the standard of education that the schools are delivering.

A feature of these procedures is that they allow for regression analysis (as described above) with multi-level data. In the case of the present project, there are just two levels: the child and the school. In the ILEA junior school project, there are three levels: the child, the class and the school. Information at the school level can be used in the analysis, as well as information at the child level. This means that we can show how much of the difference in progress between schools is associated with some characteristic of the school.

For the first time, these methods provide a framework for analysing school effectiveness in a rigorous way. The methods are much more advanced than those available for studying the effectiveness of most other kinds of organisation. This is because some, at least, of the objectives of schooling are very well defined, and because of the achievements of the mental testing movement, which has provided some of the necessary instruments. Nevertheless, there are still substantial difficulties in trying to understand the processes underlying school effectiveness. The rest of this chapter is an attempt to explain why.

RESEARCH DESIGN AND THE SIZE OF SCHOOL EFFECTS

The method just described allows us to make valid comparisons between the outcomes achieved by schools having different intakes, in terms of attainment, family background and so on. Another approach to the problem of making valid comparisons is to find two schools that are 'matched' or closely similar in terms of the attainment and family background of the children entering them, then compare the test scores or examination results of children in these schools at a later age. This method was used in a number of earlier American studies. There are great difficulties in finding matched pairs of schools, and it is not possible to match on more than a couple of characteristics, so the intakes of any 'matched' pair of schools will usually differ significantly with respect to characteristics that were not brought into the matching process. In principle, multi-level multiple regression procedures allow us to overcome these problems, by providing a method of validly comparing unmatched schools.

Nevertheless, there remain some problems of research design. It is important to recognise that the apparent size of the school effects will depend on the way the sample of schools is selected. If they are relatively homogeneous, or falling within a restricted range, then this will tend to reduce the size of the observed school effects. In practice, none of the main studies has covered the full range of schools. *Fifteen Thousand Hours* covered 12 local authority comprehensives in an inner city area, probably the most homogeneous sample of the four main studies. *School Matters* covered a representative sample of ILEA primary schools. This sample is considerably more inclusive than the one in *Fifteen Thousand Hours*, first because it covers the whole of inner London (as opposed to one borough) and second because it covers the full range of local authority primary schools in inner London (whereas there were selective secondary schools in the public sector not covered by *Fifteen Thousand Hours*). The Thomas Coram project covered 33 infant schools in multi-racial areas of inner London. As explained in the next chapter, in our own study we deliberately set out to select a heterogeneous set of comprehensives, and we covered four local education authorities, so of these four studies, ours was probably the one with the most heterogeneous sample of schools. At the same time, all four studies exclude the private sector of education, and none of them covers selective schools of any kind.

We have already argued that the size of school differences is not a direct indicator of the total effect of schooling. It should further be recognised that the existing studies cover only a restricted range of schools. It woud probably be possible to demonstrate larger differences in school effects if a single study could encompass schools of all types.

However, there are penalties as well as advantages connected with having a heterogeneous sample of schools. The more unalike the schools are, the more of a strain this puts on the statistical procedures used to compare like with like. Some of the schools will have unusual characteristics, or combinations of characteristics, which make it difficult to generalise from their results. They are all different, but not in a systematic way, so various possible types are not represented at all (for example, in our own study, there is no school with a high proportion of Sikhs, and no school with a high proportion of Bangladeshi boys).

These are the limitations of general purpose, descriptive studies, which aim to cover a fairly broad range of schools, and do not explicitly set out to test a theory or explanation of school differences. They are something of an uneasy compromise. They do not measure the full extent of school differences (because of the important exclusion of selective schools and the private sector). They are intended to be capable of testing many sorts of explanations of school differences, but there are many particular explanations that they cannot test, because this would require the selection of schools representing particular types which would serve as a test of the theory.

TESTING THEORIES

Both *Fifteen Thousand Hours* and *School Matters* are based on studies that collected an impressive array of information about schools and what happened in them. In *School Matters*, both school level and class level variables were examined for their relationships with school effectiveness. 'Given' variables at the school level were the building, resources, intake and stability of staff and pupils. 'Policy' variables at the school level were the Head's style of leadership, the type of organisation, the involvement of staff, the curriculum, the rewards and punishments used, parental involvement with the school, equal opportunities, the school atmosphere. 'Given' variables at the level of the class were number of pupils, the age, social class and ability composition of the class, the classroom, resources, curriculum guidelines, teacher characteristics, whether the teacher changed during the year. Finally, the 'policy' variables at the class level were the aims and planning of the teacher, the teacher's strategies and organisation of the curriculum, management of the classroom, including rewards and punishments, classroom atmosphere, the level and type of communication between teacher and pupils, parental involvement, and record keeping.

It should be mentioned, in passing, that most of these 'variables' are really complex structures or policies or processes that have been summarised in some way by the researchers. The analysis is in three parts. First, the authors describe the pattern of relationships between each of the school and class level variables and the measures of school effectiveness that have already been established. There are very many relationships of this kind. Next, the authors discuss the pattern of relationships between the school and class level variables themselves. This suggests theories about what is going on (say about how head teachers influence the way teachers plan their lessons) but the whole pattern of relationships is highly complex; many different theories could be put forward to explain it. Finally, the authors identify 'twelve key factors' that lead to an effective school. They say that this identification of twelve key factors is informed by the foregoing analysis, but not determined by it.

The main point to be made about this analysis is that it is alarming rather than helpful to find such a large number of relationships, unless there is a way of understanding how they all fit together. Without a theory of how schools work, contemplating this immensely complex pattern produces not enlightenment but a cognitive snowstorm. The authors of *School Matters* recognise this problem. When they come to identify the 'twelve key factors' they acknowledge that 'these factors are not purely statistical constructs. They have not been obtained purely by means of quantitative analyses. Rather, they are derived from a combination of careful examination and discussion of the statistical findings, and the use of educational and research judgement. They represent the interpretation of the research results by an inter-disciplinary team of researchers and teachers' (p. 248). This is equivalent to saying that they have used the results of the research to help them formulate a theory about how schools work (and what makes them work effectively), but that those results do not act as a test of the theory they have formulated.

One of the main reasons for this is that each of the school and class variables is related to many of the others, but at the same time to the measures of effectiveness. This means that it is often not clear which aspects of school policies and practices are the critical ones. The most interesting conclusions arise when there is no relationship between some school or class variable and effectiveness. For example, it was found that 'the amount of teacher time spent interacting with the class (rather than with individuals or groups) had a significant positive relationship with progress ... In contrast, where a very high proportion of the teachers' time was spent communicating with individual pupils, a negative impact was recorded ... Measures of the extent to which a whole class teaching approach was adopted were very weakly and not sig-nificantly related to progress ... It was the number of interactions *involving* the whole class, rather than any attempt to teach the whole class as one unit, that seems to be have been associated with beneficial effects.' (p. 228) Because some of the variables here were negatively or not significantly related with progress, the findings tend to support a specific theory (namely that the total amount of useful contact between teachers and pupils is the important factor). However, in many other cases, a whole set of policies are related to each other and individually to progress, so it is hard to know which ones are critical.

Certainly there are theories about how schools work and what makes them effective, which are associated with the recent research. Michael Rutter puts forward one general theory and a number of specific ones in his review article published in 1983. The general theory is that while individual teachers vary in their effectiveness, and while effects depend partly on the details of the curriculum, there is something called the 'school ethos', a set of schoolwide influences that make it more or less likely that teachers will conduct their lessons in an effective manner. An example of one of Rutter's more specific theories is that the way teachers manage the classroom is crucial to effectiveness; this he sees as essentially a matter of maximising the amount of time the pupils are engaging in useful learning or practice, and the teacher does this, for example, by engaging their attention, securing orderly behaviour and managing his or her own behaviour so as to maximise the amount of useful contact with each member of the class. He also points out that this theory has important policy implications, since teachers are given little instruction or training in classroom management, and are not helped to develop these skills on the job.

Evidence can, of course, be cited in support of both the general and the more specific theory mentioned above.[9] Nevertheless, these theories have certainly not been tested exhaustively, and in fact research has not been designed to test them in a rigorous manner, but rather to describe a vast web of relationships. Excellent techniques of research are now available, and some theories about school effectiveness have been quite clearly articulated. In the future, research should concentrate on testing clearly articulated theories in a more focused way.

STATIC VERSUS DYNAMIC CONCEPTIONS OF THE SCHOOL

The analytic model used for schools effectiveness research tends to be associated with a static conception of the school. Although the information about the schools is obtained over a considerable period of time, each measure is presented as though it described the school at one instant, and there is no attempt to describe any process of change. Instead, the apparently timeless characteristics of effective schools are compared and contrasted with those of less effective ones.

The limitations of this approach are most obvious when methods of management are under consideration. Both *Fifteen Thousand Hours* and *School Matters* show strong relationships between the style of management adopted by the head teacher and school effectiveness. This raises two related questions. One is about the direction of causation. It is not clear whether the head is able to adopt a given style of management (for example, ask teachers to provide records of children's work) because teachers are competent, relationships are good, and such requests can readily be met; or whether the standard of teaching and quality of relationships has been improved because the head has requested records of children's work. The second kind of explanation – that good management at the top makes all the difference – is of course irresistible to top managers like the heads of university departments who direct this kind of research: but it may be wrong.

The second related point is that schools, like other organisations, go through periods of relative stability followed by shortish periods of sudden change. The research will catch most schools in a period of relative stability. Let us suppose that the style of management by the head is, in fact, crucial in shaping the school. If the school is functioning badly there will be a style of management required to bring about a series of rapid changes, transforming the school into a good one. If the school is functioning well, there will be a style of management required to maintain stability. These two styles may well be entirely different. What research has tended to observe is the management styles associated with stable effective states. This says little about the styles required to transform a bad school into a good one, which would probably be entirely different. Assuming that what the head does is, in fact, critical in transforming a bad school, it is still quite possible that the head's style has little importance in maintaining an already good school, and that the causation in that case runs in the opposite direction.

This point can be summarised by making a distinction between the conditions existing in an effective school, and the actions that have to be taken to transform an ineffective school into an effective one, or to maintain the performance of an already effective one. These two sets of actions may not be the same.

Clearly, theories of how schools work need to be developed to take account of change and the maintenance of a stable state. These considerations suggest the need for a different kind of research, that studies schools as they change, and perhaps research that observes the results of taking specific actions.

NOTES

1 See Prais and Wagner (1985).
2 See Coleman *et al.* (1966).
3 See Jencks *et al.* (1972), p. 109.
4 See Rutter (1983), p. 1.
5 See Purkey and Smith (1983); Rutter (1983).
6 Rutter (1983), p. 2.
7 For a variety of reasons, however, Jencks et al. produced a very low estimate of the effects of school differences, even within the terms of their own argument. For example, they considered the difference in results achieved by different *categories* of schools, classified in various ways (for example, according to expenditure). The differences between the results achieved by individual schools might have been much greater; and the classification of the schools was not based on an understanding of the factors that actually influence effectiveness. It would not be surprising to find little difference between the categories of schools if the effective ones were fairly evenly divided between these categories.
8 See Aitkin and Longford (1986), and Goldstein (1987).

9 There is much evidence that the amounts of time spent in class and in useful learning ('on task') vary substantially between schools, and some evidence that they are related to achievement. For a review of the relevant research, see Bennett (1978).

REFERENCES

Aitkin, M. and Longford, N. T. (1986) Statistical modelling issues in school effectiveness studies, *Journal of the Royal Statistical Society*, A 149, pp. 1–43.

Bennett, S. N. (1978) Recent research on teaching: a dream, a belief and a model, *British Journal of Educational Psychology*, 48, pp. 127–147.

Colman, J. S. *et al.* (1966) *Equality of Educational Opportunity*, Washington: National Centre for Educational Statistics.

Goldstein, H. (1987) *Multiple Models in Educational and Social Research*, Oxford: Clarendon Press.

Jencks, C. S. *et al.* (1972) *Inequality: A Reassessment of the Effect of Family and Schooling in America*, New York: Basic Books.

Prais, S. J. and Wagner, K. (1985) Schooling Standards in England and Germany: some summary comparisons bearing on economic performance, *National Institute Economic Review*, 112, pp. 53–76.

Purkey, S. C. and Smith, M. S. (1983) Effective Schools: a Review, *Elementary School Journal*, 83, 4, pp. 427–452.

Rutter, M. (1983) School Effects on Pupil Progress: Research Findings and Policy Implications, *Journal of Child Development*, 54, pp. 1–29.

Index

Note: page references in italics indicate tables and figures.

access, for research 153
accountability 33, 43, 116, 143
advisers, role 117–18, 119, 121, 150; and staff appraisal 126, 131; and testing 37, 41–2
Aitken, M. & Longford, N. 155, 157, 175
Anderson, J. G. 28 n. 12
APU (Assessment of Performance Unit) 37, 38–40, 41–2, 52, 54–5, 59
art department, review 78–91
Ash, Maurice, *Who are the Progressives Now?* 12
assessment, *see* evaluation; performance; testing
ATO (Approved Training Organisation) 120
attainment, and class 25–6, 73, 157, 171, 174; factors 172, 174–6, 179; in mathematics vii-viii; targets 33, 43–5, 59
attendance rates 154, 156
authoritarianism 11, 22

Baker, Kenneth 33, 44
Ball, S. J. 153
Bantock, Prof. 11
Barnes, D. *et al.* 104
Beeby, P. 118–19
benchmarks, *see* attainment, targets
Bernstein, B. 165
Better Schools (White Paper) 140
Black Papers vi-vii, 18–24; effects 16–17, 36; first 5, 9; second vii, 3–17, 19, 21

Blakey, L. & Heath, A. 156
Bollen, R. & Hopkins, D. 166
Bolton, Eric 44
Bourdieu, P. & Passeron, J. C. 153
Bowden, Lord 13
Bowie, Janetta 20
Bowles, S. & Gintis, H. 153
boys, *see* gender
Boyson, Rhodes 7–8, 9, 23–4, 29 n.24
Brighouse, Tim 139, 140–51
Brimer, A. *et al.* 155
Bruner, Jerome 4, 10
Bullock Report 32, 36
Burgess, R. G. 153
Burn, Elizabeth 63, 64, 95–8
Burt, Sir Cyril 3, 25, 26, 76
Business and Information Studies, and learning styles 103–4, 106–12; and role of teacher 104–6; and student-centred evaluation 103; and TVEI dissemination 102; vocabulary 103–4

Cabot, Isabel 14
calculators, classroom use 56–7
Callaghan, James vi
choice, parental 8, 15
class, and attainment 25–6, 73, 157, 171, 174
classroom management 178, 180
Clegg, Sir Alec 3–4
Clift, Philip 63, 64, 78–91
Cockroft Report, 1982 32, 42, 59

coercion 159–61

Coleman, James 154, 171

colleges of education, and teacher standards 5

comparison, international vii, 47–9, 51–5, 56–7, 170; and monitoring 36–40

competition, advantages 8, 15, 23

comprehensive education, advantages 7–8, 25–6; and class 158; criticised 6–9, 12, 18, 21; and examinations 27; role of research 73

consensus, on education 16–17, 116

consumerism, and education 33

control, of learning 106–7

Cox, C. & Marks, J. 164

Cox, C. B. & Dyson, A. E. vii, 3–17, 19, 21

Cresswell, M. & Gubb, M. vii, 51–5

crisis, existence queried 23–6

Crisis in the Classroom (Gardner) 3, 4, 9, 11, 23

Cross Commission 24

Crowther Report, 1959 31 n.45

Croydon, testing 43

CSE (Certificate of Secondary Education) 27, 31 n.45, 33, 52

curriculum, effects of testing 41–2, 43, 45; evaluation 89, 166; mathematics 49, 52, 53–4, 57; national 33, 44, 45, 57, 129, 140; process 104; reform 20–1, 42, 90, 98, 112, 144

Cuttance, P. 155, 157

delinquency rates 152, 154, 156, 157, 159

deputy head, role 160

DES, *Developments in the Appraisal of Teachers* 64, 124–32; School Leavers Survey 33, 38; *Ten Good Schools* 141, 144

development, pupil 170; *see also* teachers, development

direct grant schools 6, 15

discovery, learning by 5, 10–11

Douglas, J. W. B. 7

economic crisis, and confidence in education 21–3, 25, 27

Edinburgh Reading Tests 41

Edmonds, Ron 166

education, infant 11; nursery 92–4; primary, effectiveness 161–2, 164;

progressive methods 12; and testing 43, 44, 45; private 15; secondary 5, progressive methods 12–13; tertiary 9, *see also* comprehensive schools; direct grant schools; grammar schools; public schools; secondary modern schools

Education Act, 1870 24, 27

Education Act, 1902 27

Education Act, 1918 24, 27

Education Act, 1944 27, 118, 150

Education Act, 1980 38

Education Act, 1986 149–50

Education (No. 2) Act, 1986 134

Education Reform Act, 1989 63, 117, 121, 129, 132

Educational Priority Areas 171

effectiveness, academic 157–9; characteristics 157–63; consistency 156; and government policy 149; and improvement 165–7; indicators 148–9; and LEA 149; measurement 33, 139, 140–51, 170–81; new model 175–6; and pupil background 157, 174–5; recognition 141–2; research 152–3; design 177–80; future 163–7 and restructuring 139; and school organisation 147–8, 157–62, 164–5, 166, 178; social 156, 157–59; and testing 150; *see also* leadership

egalitarianism vi, 16

Ellis, Terry 28 n.5

Elvin, Lionel 11

English, decline in standards 6; testing *35*

ethos, school 100, 101–2, 103, 113–14, 130, 159–2, 165, 178, 179–80

evaluation, aims & objectives 80–1; art department 78–91; autocratic 74, 75; bureaucratic 74; and change 64; democratic 74, 75, 76; external 119, 130; in learning 107–8; methods 64, 65–76, 91, 118–19, 121–2, multiple 69–72; selection 66–9, time-sampling 92–3, *see also* interview; observation; pupils 80, 129, 147; self evaluation 64, 124, 128, 130, 142–3, 146, 165; studies 63–4, 78–91; whole school 128, 134, *see also* curriculum; syllabus; teachers

examinations 13, 89, 140; abolition proposed 12–13, 30 n.43; increased success in 6, 18, 27; norm/criterion-referenced 38, 40, 41; school effects on results 155; standardised vii, 32

expectations, by pupil 148; by teacher 147, 150, 160, 162; of education 25–7

family background, and attainment 155, 157, 164, 171, 174, 175–6

Faulkner, Robert 69–71

Fifteen Thousand Hours, see Rutter, M. *et al.*

Ford Teaching Project 67, 71

Foss, Brian 11

France, mathematics teaching 56–7

Froome, S. H. 3, 21

Galton, M. & Simon, B. 144

Gardner, Keith, *Crisis in the Classroom* 3, 4, 11

Gath, D. 154

GCSE (General Certificate of Secondary Education) 33, 38, 112

gender, and language 98; and mathematics performance 39; and outdoor play 92–4; and use of Lego in play 95–8

Germany, West, comparison with 48–9, 50 n.1, 56–7, 171

Gipps, Caroline vii, 32–45

girls, *see* gender

Goldstein, H. 153, 175

government, central, and school development 139, 149–50

governors, and evaluation 64, 134–5

grammar schools 6, 7, 8, 9, 15, 21, 25, 27

Gray, J. 154

Gray, J. & Jesson, D. 156

Gray, J., Jesson, D. & Jones, B. 155, 157

Gray, J., McPherson, A. & Raffe, D. 155, 156

Great Debate 36

Green, Nancy W. 4

GRIDS project 101, 126, 166

GRIST strategy 102

Gurney-Dixon Report 21

Hargreaves, D., *Improving Secondary Schools* 166

Hargreaves, D. H. 153

Harris, Ralph 7, 8

Hartog, P. J. 30 n.43

head teacher, leadership 139, 143–6, 147, 160, 164–5, 167, 178–9; management style 180–1; role in appraisal 127, 128, 135; and testing 42

HMIs, *see* inspectorate

homework, policy 86, 90, 149, 158

Hudson, Geoffrey 16

Hudson, Liam 14

Husen, Prof. 14

Husen, T. 50 n.1

IEA (International Association for the Evaluation of Educational Achievements) vii, 47–9, 56

Importance of illiteracy, The 25, 29 n.26

improvement, school 165–7

incorporation 159–60

industry, and curriculum 23; and educational standards 40; and staff appraisal 126

inequality, social, and education 170–1, 174–5

inspectorate, and evaluation 41, 44, 63, 116–22, 126, 175; methodology 121–2; review 121; and standards 5; and testing 37, 43; Training Standards Inspectors (TSIs) 117–18, 120

International Schools Improvement Project 166

interview 69–70; teacher appraisal 80, 82–7, 89

IQ, *see* reasoning

Isaac, John 139–40

Japan, mathematics teaching vii, 47–9, 56–8

Jencks, Christopher 23, 171, 176

Jencks, Christopher *et al.* 154, 174

Joseph, Sir Keith 26, 33, 133–4

Labour Party, policies 6, 7

Lacey, C. 153

Laing, R. D. 71

Lakatos, Imre 16

Lawton, D. 44

LEA responsibility 139, 149

leadership, development 80; and effectiveness 138, 143–6, 147, 158, 160, 162, 164–5, 178–9; inadequate 145; and perceptive professional developers 144–5; qualities 146; and system maintainers 145

learning, as shared contract 148
learning styles, active 101, 102, 104, 106–
    12; collaborative 109–10, 110–11, 112;
    evaluative 107–8, 110–11, 112;
    integrative 108–9, 110–11, 112;
    responsible 106–7, 110–11, 112
LEATGS (Local Education Authority
    Training Grants Scheme) 126, 127, 128
Lewis, M. M., *The Importance of Illiteracy*
    25, 29 n.26
literacy levels 25, 40
Livingstone, Sir Richard 30 n.43
local management of schools 139
London, Inner, problems 28 nn.1, 4
Lyness, R. C., *Trends in Education* 5
Lynn, Professor 6, 9

MacDonald, Barry 72, 74–5
McGill, Linda 63, 64, 92–4
Maclure, Stuart 14
McMahon, A. *et al.* 166
McPherson, A. & Willms, D. 157
Mason, Stuart 12–13
mathematics, decline in standards 3, 25,
    56–7, 171; IEA report vii, 47–9, 56;
    improvement in standards 59;
    performance assessment 39, 42, 43, 47–
    9, 51–5, 56–9; school effect on 155; sex-
    differences 39; skills required 56–7, 58–
    9; teaching time 58; testing *35*, 51–5, 56–
    7; traditional approach vii
Maude, Angus 16
Mead, Margaret 76
media, and effectiveness 142; influence 18,
    24
methods, chold-centred 11–12, 102, 103–
    4, 110–12, 147; of evaluation, *see*
    evaluation; formal, in reading 4;
    progressive, criticised 4, 5, 8, 10–13, 16,
    18, and falling standards vi, 3, 18–28, in
    mathematics 5, 20–1, research support
    criticised 13–14
monitoring 36–7, *37*, 41, 63, *see also* APU;
    inspectorate
Morris, Joyce 4, 11–12
Mortimore, P. *et al.* 154–7, 163–5, 171,
    177–9, 180
Moyle, Donald, *The Teaching of Reading*
    11–12

MSC (Manpower Services Commission),
    and inspectorate 117
Murphy, R. 45
Murphy, R. & Torrance, H. 119
Musgrove, F. 153

National Child Development Study 19
National Children's Bureau 155, 156
National Conference of Head Teachers 5
National Council of Educational Standards
    41
National Curriculum working party, and
    mathematics teaching vii–viii, 56–9
Netherlands, mathematics standards 57
'new maths' 5, 20–1
Newbolt Report on the Teaching of
    English 24
Newcastle Commission 24
Newsom Report, 1963 21, 25
NFER (National Foundation for
    Educational Research) 51–5, 57
NFER/IMTEC review 126
Norwood Committee 25

observation, non-participant 79, 81–2, 89,
    91; participant 69–70, 72–4; and teacher
    appraisal 130–1
opportunity, equality of 16, 27, 33; to learn
    52–3
organisation, school 147–8, 152, 153–4,
    164–5, 166, 178; characteristics 157–
    63
Ouston, J. & Maughan, B. 68
Oxford Certificate of Educational
    Achievement (OCEA) 148

parents, and effectiveness 148, 159–60, 162;
    and evaluation 64, 133–5; and standards
    19, *see also* choice
payment by results 24
Pearce, J. 121
Pedley, R. R. 9
performance, assessment 43–4, 133–5,
    158–9; and student-centred learning
    102, 103, 112; teacher, *see* teacher
    appraisal, *see also* attainment
Perspectives on Plowdon 10–11
Peters, Prof., *Perspectives on Plowdon* 10–
    11
Pidgeon, Douglas 12
Pines, Maya, *Revolution in Learning* 10

Play, outdoor 92–4; and use of toys 95–8
Plowdon Report, 1967 3–4, 10–11, 153
politics, and pressure for testing 36
Pollard, Prof. 6
Power, M. J. *et al.* 154
Power, Michael 152
Powney, Janet 63–4
Prais, Sig vii, 47–9
public schools 6, 8, 15
punishment 23, 159, 160, 162, 180
pupils, background and school
   effectiveness 154, 157; effects of school
   organisation 153–6; and incorporative
   school 159–60
Purkey, S. C. & Smith, M. S. 171

Quality in Schools: Evaluation and
   Appraisal 124

Rasch technique 39
Rayner Committee, 1982 117
reading, decline in standards 4, 24, 28 n.5,
   36; improved standards 3, 27; readiness
   for 11; school effect on 155, 156; teaching
   4, 11, 21; testing *35*, 36, 43
reasoning, testing 35, *35*, 43, 173–4
Reid, K., Hopkins, D. & Holly, P. 166
relevance 23, 110
research, action 72–4; design 177–80; 'false'
   13–14; methods 65, 66–76, 79, 139;
   paucity 152–3; and researcher's
   viewpoint 72, 99–100, 113–14; selection
   of topics 73; teacher 76, 98
review, HMI 121
review, departmental 78–91; aims &
   objectives 80–1, 90; evaluation 88–91;
   retrospective views 87–8
'Revised Code', 1862 24, 150
Reynolds, D. 139, 152–67
Reynolds, D. *et al.* 155, 156
Rhodes, G. 117–18
Root, Betty 4
Rutter, M. 158, 171–2, 174–5, 179–80
Rutter, M. *et al.* 140, 153–4, 156–8, 163,
   164, 166–7, 171, 175, 177–8, 180

Sallis, Joan 64, 133–5
School Matters, see Mortimore, P. *et al.*
schools, classification 140; open-plan 4;
   static/dynamic models 180–1

Scottish Education Data Archive 155
screening, extent 35–6, 37
secondary modern schools, and
   examinations 27
selection 6–7, 73, 171
Senior Management Team 78–80, 81–91
Short, Edward 3, 7–9
Simons, H. 119
sixth form colleges 9
sixth forms, in comprehensive schools 9
skills, constructional 95–7
skills, physical, girls' 92–4
Smith, D. J. & Tomlinson, S. 140, 150,
   176–81
Smith, Nick 67–9
society, and educational standards 23–4,
   27–8
special needs 35, 36, 140, 150
spelling, testing *35*
Spens Report, 1931 25, 29 n.21
standards, changes vii, 18–19; decline vi–
   vii, 3, 9, 11, 18–19, 23–4; defined 32–4;
   enforcement 24; external 33–4;
   improvements 6, 18, 33–4, 59; post-war
   3, 4, 25; pre-war 21–2, 24–5; and rising
   expectations 25–7, *see also* mathematics;
   reading; testing
Steel, James 30 n.43
Stenhouse, Lawrence 76
stereotyping, sexual 87, 98
Stillman, A.B. 121
streaming 12, 149; abolition 20
Stronach, Ian 63, 64, 99–114
styles, learning 103–4, 106–12; teaching 20,
   103, 104–6, 110–12. 144, 179–80
Svenson, Nils 14
Sweden, comprehensive education 14
syllabus, evaluation 80, 89
Szamuely, Tibor 7, 8

tables controversy 5
teacher appraisal 64, 80, 81, 82–7, 89–90,
   118, 133–5; costs 128, 131–2; DES
   survey 124–32; growth & administration
   126–7; methods 127–8; national scheme
   129–32; pilot schemes 124–5, 126, 134;
   purposes 128, 129, 130; training for 128,
   130, 131
teacher training 4; in-service 128, 129, 131,
   146, 167

teachers, in curriculum planning 160;
development 80–1, 82–6, 89–90, 102,
126–8, 129, 148; international
comparisons 58; shortage 8, 28 n.4; and
sixth form teaching 9; turnover levels
164; women 98, *see also* styles, teaching
Teaching of Reading, The 11–12
team teaching 102
technical colleges 9
technology, girls' achievement 87
technology, new, and mathematics 57
Ten Good Schools 140, 143
testing, at 7/8 *34*, 35–6, 43, 45, 140, 150; at
11 *34*, 35, 43, 52, 55, 140, 150; at 13/14
34, 35, 52, 56–9, 140, 150; effect on
curriculum 41–2, 43; effects on children
44; extent 34–6, *34, 35*; and
measurement of standards 35–40, 41;
mental 173–5, 176; Multiple-choice 54;
norm/criterion referenced 38, 40, 41,
147, 163; and raising of standards 32–4,
40, 41, 45; and setting of standards 40,
41–2; and teaching to test 41, 42, 45;
time 52–3, 54, 57; uses 36–7, *37*
Thatcher, Margaret vi, 150
Thomas Coram infant school project 175,
177
Training Standards Inspectors (TSIs)
117–18, 120
triangulation 71
TSAS (Training Standards Advisory
Service) 63, 117–18, 120–1
TVEI, in Business and information Studies

102–4; dissemination 101, 102; and
evaluation 103, 112; Extension Project
101; learning styles 103–4, 106–12;
student-centred learning 102, 110–12;
teaching styles 104–6
Tyler, R. 119

USA, comprehensive education 8–9;
effectiveness research 139, 152, 162, 166;
external evaluation 119; international
comparisons 58; standardised
examinations vii, 32, 151; teaching of
reading 4

values, shared 139, 142–3, 146
Van Der Eyken, Willem 10

Walker, Rob 63, 64, 65–76
Warnock Report 36
Webb, E. *et al.* 71
Who are the Progressives Now? (Ash) 12,
13–14
Wilcox, Brian 63, 116–22
William Tyndale Junior School 28 n.5, 36
Willis, R. 73
Willms, J. D. 155
Willms, J. D. & Cuttance, P. 157
Wolf, R. M. 119
working class, able child 7, 8, 157
Wright, Nigel vii, 18–28

YTS (Youth Training Scheme), evaluation
117, 120–1